Praise for the Total Workday Control system

"Outstanding!"

"This system is outstanding! I had no idea the power Outlook has,when used smartly, to get my tasks under control. And Michael's system of converting e-mails to tasks makes it much easier for me to use e-mail productively. I can really make sense of my Inbox now."

Mark Christopulos, Owner, Red Skye Winery

"With only 45 minutes of training from Michael Linenberger, I had a tremendous boost in my ability to accomplish more each day. This system is simple to learn and really works."

Michael J. Atkinson, Project Manager for Wells Fargo

"Total Workday Control presents the simplest, most comprehensive means to control, prioritize and complete the multitude of tasks that beset today's workers. Using straightforward and practical principles and widely available tools, Michael demonstrates how to get even the most diverse and extreme workload under control, how to stay on top of it, and most importantly, how to find time to create a successful balance between work and home life. As a professional project management consultant, I'd recommend this book and the practices it describes, to anyone."

Andrew Hartnett, Senior VP, Pcubed

"Michael's process helps me to translate an in-box full of information into focused tasks."

Devon Johnson, Portfolio Manager, CSAA

"Michael Linenberger's email/Outlook management allowed me to stay on top of my hectic schedule... I highly recommend his technique to anyone who's interested in doing more with less effort in one's working environment. It is that good!"

James Chou, Financial Analyst, BEA Systems

"This course provides an intuitive and logical system for task/email management that even the most organized individuals may be lacking!"

Sarah Clark, Business Analyst

Praise from readers of Michael Linenberger's Previous Book: Seize the Work Day

"I thought I was organized before, but after reading your book, I am now more organized than I have ever been!"

"Your book "Seize the Workday" is fantastic!! Thanks for putting so much of your energy into making it a very useful project."

"A very well written and easy read which gives good insight on making your work day easier and even more fun!"

"Outstanding"

"Thanks for writing a great book!! It was just what I needed at just the right time!!!!"

"I purchased and read your entire book Seize the Work Day. I love it! It is excellent!"

"Your book is the most practical, easy to understand book on the subject that I have read. I hope you write many more."

"I recommend this to anyone…"

"It sets a milestone - by providing a wealth of practical tips and tricks on applying hardware & software *available* technologies to your advantage and help stay organized through a busy day/week/month"

"No need to look any further, this is the book you've been waiting for… a valuable book like this that is bound to be referred to again and again"

"Seize the Work Day is the most helpful and practical technology book I have ever read!"

"Efficiency increases with the proper tools. Seize the Work Day and a Tablet PC are a perfect match."

"Linenberger does an excellent job laying out a simple set of techniques... The book is cleanly written and easy to read. You can read it from cover to cover, but it's also easy to use as a reference work, allowing you to flip back to areas you find of particular use."

"You should DEFINTELY read this book"

"This book sits right on the fence between a computer book and a personal productivity book, and excels at both. By far the most interesting computer book I've read in the last 5 years."

"I just got my copy yesterday. Excellent book. I have already read almost half of it. Just couldn't put it down."

Total Workday Control
Using Microsoft® Outlook

The Eight Best Practices of
Task and E-Mail Management

By Michael Linenberger

New Academy Publishers
San Ramon, California

Second printing 2006

ISBN-13: 978-0-9749304-1-1
ISBN-10: 0-9749304-1-5

Library of Congress Control Number: 2005926451

Visit the book web site at www.workdaycontrol.com for additional information.

The following trademarks appear throughout this book: Microsoft, Windows, Windows XP, Microsoft Windows XP Tablet PC Edition, Microsoft Office, Microsoft Office Outlook 2003, Microsoft Outlook 2002, FranklinCovey, FranklinCovey PlanPlus for Microsoft Outlook, Tablet Enhancements for Outlook, Getting Things Done Add-In for Outlook.

To Hong

Acknowledgments

Deep thanks go to the following individuals for their assistance in the preparation of this book:

Marc Orchant, Rob Tidrow, Jim Boyce, Ruth Flaxman, Linda Raliegh, Marc Linenberger and Chuck Linenberger, Mark Christopulos.

Contents at a Glance

Contents

Chapter 2: The Best Practices of Task and E-Mail Management   23

Appendix A: Understanding Outlook Folders   233

Appendix B: Using Outlook AutoArchive   253

Foreword

By Marc Orchant

Like a lot of people, I "live" in Microsoft Outlook. It is the first application I launch when I begin my workday and the last one I shut down. I often refer to Outlook as a "dashboard" for my day because like the dashboard in my car, it provides a wealth of critical information about my travels. When Michael Linenberger told me he was developing a new book outlining an approach to task management using Outlook, I got very excited. His first book, *Seize the Workday: Using the Tablet PC to Take Total Control of Your Work and Meeting Day*, has become one of my most frequently recommended guides to personal productivity.

I am a Tablet PC user and a passionate advocate for the platform. But, like Michael, I recognize that broad adoption of Tablet PCs is proceeding slowly and it will be a long time before they are common in most workplaces. Outlook, by contrast, has become a corporate standard used by millions of knowledge workers around the world. And it is a unique application, combining a powerful e-mail client with all of the personal information management tools busy professionals need to manage their workday.

I write two weblogs that regularly address the topic of personal productivity. I'm a long-time practitioner of David Allen's Getting Things Done system, a productivity discipline that Michael has borrowed some key concepts from in crafting his Total Workday Control system. As I've reviewed the drafts of this book, I've adopted Michael's techniques for task and e-mail management and found that they have the quality I have learned is most important—flexibility. I've been able to take his ideas and map them to the kind of work I do without having to scrap every good habit I've already developed.

Total Workday Control addresses all of the things I believe are critical to achieving a high level of stress-free productivity including the following:

- Emptying your Inbox on a regular basis.

- Extracting what is actionable from every e-mail, memo, and document you receive (electronic or paper).

- Creating a task list that puts the most important actions you must take to succeed at your fingertips.

- Organizing your dashboard so you can see your calendar and tasks in context.

- Labeling every e-mail and task so it can be found quickly.

Total Workday Control will show you how to accomplish all of these goals. This is not a technology book—no programming or deep technical knowledge is required. This is a book about process, discipline, and rewards. The ultimate payoff I've gotten from following Michael's advice, and one I'm confident you too will enjoy, is that I feel much more in control. I know what I need to do, when I need to do it, and why I'm doing it. I go home every evening, at a reasonable hour, and feel good about what I've accomplished that day. I rarely bring work home with me. I rarely stay at work after hours. When a coworker asks me for information, I can find it in a matter of minutes.

Michael has taken the best lessons he's learned in his many years of consulting and counseling knowledge workers—people who work with information every day—and constructed a system that addresses many of the most common mistakes many of us make, such as:

- Using our Inbox as a task list or filing cabinet.

- Failing to create a list of strategic next actions that keep our important projects moving forward.

- Accepting the default setup Outlook provides "out of the box" which denies us the ability to use this immensely powerful application to its fullest advantage.

- Getting so lost in the mire of our day that we lose the ability to keep the "big picture" in mind and fall into the all-too-easy trap of making tactical, rather than strategic, decisions.

Total Workday Control defines a set of eight best practices for time and task management. What I think you'll discover as each is described in this book is that it's actually a lot easier to get control over your work and your life than you may have thought. And, once you develop the right "muscles" by practicing these techniques and exercising your new productivity strengths, you'll find you're expending less effort to get more done in less time.

As an example of this, let's talk about the art of delegation. Like a lot of overachievers, I was guilty of falling into the trap of telling myself, "By the time I explain what I need done, I might just as well do it myself." Have you had this conversation with yourself at one time or another? If you're the kind of person who's motivated enough to pick up a book like this in search of a way to be more effective and productive, chances are you have.

What *Total Workday Control* reinforced for me was that when delegation is practiced properly, everyone wins. The benefit to me as a manager is that I set a good example for my staff by showing them that I have a solid grasp on the big picture and know how to make sound decisions about how I can best invest my time. I also demonstrate my confidence in them by delegating important, often critical tasks to them. And, by using the tracking and reporting techniques Michael has taught me, I show them that even when I hand off a task to them, I remain engaged, interested, and ready to provide whatever support or assistance they might need to get the task completed properly and on time.

You're about to venture into new territory. It's a journey I've enjoyed taking with Michael as my knowledgeable, patient, and understanding guide. To be sure, there are a few twists and turns along the way and I found myself having to let go of some habits I'd developed over many years. But every time I rounded one of these curves and saw a new perspective, I got more excited about what lay ahead.

As I've shared what I've learned from *Total Workday Control* with my coworkers, I've seen them experience that same kind of excitement. We've discussed Michael's ideas and techniques and found new ways to map them to the kind of work we do. This is another hallmark of a truly excellent system—that it is capable of generating authentic enthusiasm and enhancing teamwork.

Microsoft has developed a unique and powerful tool called Outlook. But like many tools, the way it is used has everything to do with the quality of the work you can produce with it. After reading *Total Workday Control*, learning the best practices of time and task management it teaches, and implementing the techniques it describes, I can honestly say that I have raised the bar on my own sense of mastery over my workday. I have a rich new set of tools and techniques for using them to build results I can be proud of.

Dive right in and prepare yourself for a thought-provoking and energizing experience. If your experience in learning, implementing, and using the tools and techniques Michael has developed is anything like mine, you're about to rise to a new level of productivity, focus, and satisfaction. It's a great ride— enjoy it!

Marc Orchant
Albuquerque, New Mexico
April 2005

Total Workday Control Using Microsoft® Outlook

The Eight Best Practices of Task and E-Mail Management

Introduction

It's All About Task and E-Mail Management... and Microsoft Outlook

A Common Symptom

If you feel your workday is out of control, you are not alone. A large percentage of the workforce feels they are overworked. The common complaint among white collar workers is having to work late into the evening to get everything done. We all base our increased prosperity more and more on increased hours at work. The workday never seems to stop.

In addition to having too many tasks, our other complaint is out-of-control e-mail. Reading e-mail is not optional, and yet the volume seems to increase exponentially. The inbox doesn't empty itself; buried in those months of old e-mails are important communications you know you cannot afford to throw away. The inbox just keeps getting bigger and bigger.

Two Simple Problems

An out-of-control workday usually stems from two problems:

- Not having an effective system to manage tasks and time to work tasks, and...

- Not having an effective way to manage actionable incoming communications, like e-mails.

Solve these two problems and in most cases you have your workday under control. This book is about how to do that using Microsoft Outlook.

One Solution: Best Practices in Microsoft Outlook

Assuming you are in a busy work or management role you probably have hundreds of tasks assigned to you each month, either by others or by yourself. And you probably receive thousands of e-mails per month, e-mails that you are having trouble processing in a timely manner.

If so, managing tasks effectively is the most important skill you can improve on as a work manager. It's a skill that can help you leave work earlier each night. It's a skill that will increase your sense of accomplishment. A skill that will help you get your e-mail under control. You achieve this skill by learning and applying best practices to task and e-mail management.

Applying best practices to tasks and e-mail is key to effective use of your time, key to the perception by your superiors that you have your responsibilities under control, and if you have staff, it is key to effective delegation and follow-up of work to those staff. Good task management is necessary for managing projects. My productivity and effectiveness rose dramatically when years ago, I finally developed an effective and efficient personal task-management system, based on the best task and e-mail management practices available.

Microsoft Outlook is an excellent tool within which to implement best practices for task and e-mail management. It is powerful, it's ubiquitous, it is easy to use, and it has everything you need. And you are probably already using it at your office. However, Outlook does need a little custom configuration and application of new workflows to make these best practices practical. You need to learn these best practices and the specific ways to implement them. That is what this book is all about.

In the pages ahead, I will help you learn the very best practices for effective task management. I will describe how to use Microsoft Outlook to implement those practices effectively. And I will show you how to use your e-mail system to help in that effort, using underutilized but simple features of Microsoft Outlook. I will show you approaches that I and others have found successful in active management roles.

Side Note: *This book is about Microsoft Outlook (specifically Outlook 2002 or Outlook 2003). Do not confuse this with Outlook Express, a piece of software that is delivered free with all Windows computers. I also assume you are using the desktop or laptop version of Outlook rather than accessing Outlook through your web browser. The task-management features of the web browser version of Outlook (called Outlook Web Access) are not quite powerful enough to implement the teachings in this book. More on this at the end of this introduction.*

You Currently Use Outlook, But Not for Tasks

Most likely, you already use Microsoft Outlook at the office. Most workers do; it is the e-mail system of choice of over 60 percent of all companies. And you probably use Outlook to make appointments in your day. You may have tried Outlook's TaskPad or Tasks folder, yet you have probably found that by itself it really does not help you get your tasks under control.

Most People Use Only a Small Percentage of Outlook

This is understandable because most people use only a small percentage of Outlook's power. Sure, you can list tasks in Outlook and even prioritize them. However you have probably found that those lists quickly become unusable. And furthermore, most people do not receive training on high quality task-management approaches.

However, there are ways of using Outlook that will help you get your tasks under control and your e-mail organized. These methods are simple to learn and use, yet relatively few Outlook users are aware of them.

What you need to learn is easy — and dramatically effective. And there are only a few new things to learn in Outlook. Following the 80/20 rule — 20 percent of the features of Outlook will give you 80 percent of its possible power — I focus on that most powerful 20 percent.

Unlike other techniques, these approaches are not boring nor do they require great discipline. In fact, they are relatively fun. However, in spite of their simplicity, these approaches represent the very best practices for task management and e-mail management available anywhere.

A Summary of Benefits to Reading This Book

Truly Getting Your Workday Under Control

In this book, you will learn methods of task and e-mail management using Microsoft Outlook that will take your work-task control to new levels. Using these task-management techniques you should experience dramatic increases in productivity, including the following:

- How to use Microsoft Outlook effectively for task management.

- How to eliminate the "everything is a fire" mentality by learning how to identify which tasks to do immediately and which tasks can wait. You will learn how to determine when you can leave guilt-free at the end of the day.

- How to accomplish tasks more efficiently and get them done more quickly, freeing up time on your schedule.

- How to get your e-mail under control so that you do not drop action items and can respond in appropriate time frames.

- How to use PC–based methods of effective delegation and follow-up that really work, so that you can actually get tasks off your list.

You will learn techniques that will help you get your projects under control. Good task and e-mail management helps you manage projects more effectively. Whether these are large professionally managed projects, or the small more common projects we all encounter each day at work, learning effective methods of task management will help you succeed at both.

Gain an Executive Perspective

Imagine if all those improvements to your work life were available. You have seen people like this; people who truly seem to have an executive perspective at work. People who, in spite of their many responsibilities, not only get their work done, but also seem to retain a big-picture perspective of their jobs and the jobs of the people around them. They appear more capable, more alert, and more in control of themselves and others around them.

One reason such effective people appear this way is they are ahead of the curve on their workday. Having their day-to-day tasks neatly in control, they can then spend time to take a strategic look at their jobs and their roles in the company.

Being ahead of your day-to-day responsibilities allows you to do that. This is what learning effective task and e-mail management can help bring to you.

Who This Book Is For

Serious and Casual Readers

This book is directed primarily toward readers who feel their workday needs more control. It is for people who are prepared to invest in new work habits to dig themselves out from under the pile of disorganized tasks and e-mail they may be experiencing. The book gives you a step by step, chapter by chapter, set of learnings to make, and it will guide you successfully through those learnings. To get the full benefits of the system taught here, I recommend you work through them all, from beginning to end.

Casual readers will also get significant benefits from this book. Many of the techniques taught here can be used on their own. You can find new approaches to add to your current arsenal of workday organization skills.

By far though, the biggest bang will come to those who are prepared for full adoption.

You Probably Already Know Outlook Basics

One important note: while nothing in this book is technically difficult, this is not a beginner's guide to Outlook. Rather, I assume you are already successfully using Microsoft Outlook at your office for e-mail and appointments, at least in basic ways. If you are brand new to Outlook, and looking for a book on how to install and get started with Outlook, you probably want to start with another book, or use the Outlook tutorials first. This book is a guide that builds on the fundamental e-mail and appointment scheduling you probably already do with Outlook, and takes you well beyond. It is a guide to using Outlook in ways you have never used it before. It is a guide that will jump-start increased productivity and work satisfaction.

I have directed this book at a wide range of readers. I have purposely kept the technical level relatively simple so business users with little computer expertise can navigate easily through it. The main value of the book is not to convey technical concepts of Microsoft Outlook. Many books do that and do it relatively well. Rather the value of this book is to teach best practice business workflows and automate them in simple ways on Microsoft Outlook. So even if you *are* a technically oriented person, and already consider yourself pretty good at using Outlook, I am confident you are going to learn a lot.

As you go through this book, you'll need to make some modest configuration steps, but nothing more complicated than pulling down a few menus and making choices on the resulting configuration windows (and I describe these completely in the chapters ahead). But by far the bulk of your learning is about principles of task management and e-mail management, and how to apply these effectively within Outlook. In the process, you'll become a good Outlook user. Even the most experienced of you will learn new ways of using Outlook, primarily through new workflows. So as you can see, whether you are new to Outlook or are an "old pro," there is something here for everyone.

Versions of Microsoft Outlook Covered

As mentioned earlier, this book covers Microsoft Outlook 2002 (the version delivered with Office XP, and sometimes called Outlook XP) and Microsoft Outlook 2003 (the version delivered with Office 2003). The full and official name of the 2003 version is Microsoft© Office Outlook© 2003. For purposes of brevity, I will refer to this as Outlook 2003.

If you have a full copy of Outlook but are uncertain which version you are using, do this: from within Outlook go to the Help menu and choose the menu entry: About Microsoft Outlook (or it may read About Microsoft Office Outlook). Outlook will display the full version name at the very top of the window that opens.

Again, do not confuse Microsoft Outlook with Outlook Express, the software that Microsoft delivers free with all Windows computers. While it is a useful piece of software, Outlook Express lacks the feature depth needed to implement the techniques taught in this system, and so I do not support it in this book.

Outlook on the other hand is a full-featured e-mail, calendar, contacts, and task-management system. You will find it included as part of your purchase of Microsoft Office, Microsoft's productivity suite. You can also purchase it standalone (see page 21 for how to get a copy).

Versions of Outlook prior to Outlook 2002, such as Outlook 2000, are in many ways similar to Outlook 2002. If you are working from an earlier version, and that is all you have, you may find as you work through this book that many of the Outlook feature behaviors I describe are also present in your version. However, I make no assurances of this; you are essentially on your own.

One more caveat. I also assume you are mostly using the desktop or laptop version of Outlook rather than accessing Outlook through your web browser. The features of the web browser version of Outlook (called Outlook Web Access, or OWA for short) are powerful, but this version lacks a few features needed to fully implement the teachings in this book. This is even true of the Outlook 2003 version of Outlook Web Access; even though very powerful it still lacks a few of the necessary elements; you may need to adapt your usage from the book a bit to make it work. Certainly, the Outlook 2003 version of Outlook Web Access can be used periodically to supplement access to your main copy, when away from your desk.

Outlook 2002 and 2003 have very similar task functionality. Because of that, this book describes many features for which Outlook 2002 or 2003 could be used interchangeably as examples. In such cases, I favor Outlook 2003. I show screen shots of both versions only if not doing so will cause the reader confusion.

How This Book Is Organized

Overall Approach

This book takes the very best techniques of time and task management, condenses them down to a set of key principles, and incorporates them into simple yet effective Microsoft Outlook techniques for task and e-mail management.

These are principles and techniques that you can easily incorporate into your daily work life. They have been used by thousands of people with dramatic results. Everyone to whom I have taught these techniques has benefited greatly. With relatively little practice you can too.

The theme and approach of this book is simple. We are going to use a two-step system that is easy and effective. The two basic steps are these:

■ Learn the eight best practices of task and e-mail management.

■ Reconfigure Outlook and then implement those best practices in Outlook.

You need to do both of these to get the benefits of the book.

In the next chapter, I cover the basics; the chapters beyond teach you all you need to know to succeed.

Overview of the Chapters

■ The first chapter discusses the basics of gaining workday control.

■ Chapter 2 lists the eight best practices of task management and briefly explains them.

■ The third chapter shows you how to configure Outlook to implement the first five best practices; this lays the groundwork for your task-management system. At this point you will want to be working with the book at your computer.

■ Chapters 4 and 5 then show how to use those configurations and the first five best practices in Outlook to create a simple, but world-class, task-management system.

■ Chapters 6 and 7 cover important e-mail techniques that improve your task management and help get e-mail under control. Note that the e-mail management techniques build on the task-management techniques; do not try to skip ahead to the e-mail chapters first.

■ Chapter 8 is all about delegation techniques, which is the final best practice.

Side Note: *All these chapters assume that you have a basic knowledge of using Microsoft Outlook 2002 or 2003. For example, you should know how to send and receive e-mail and how to set an appointment on your calendar. Little more than that is required.*

■ The final chapter (chapter 9) builds on those basic and intermediate techniques and shows even more powerful solutions for task and e-mail management. It provides advanced techniques you may want to try after using the system for a while.

The Journey Begins

So welcome to a journey, a journey that begins with the recognition that you want to improve your workday success. A journey that leads you to the discovery of best practices in task and e-mail management, and concludes with your successful mastery of Microsoft Outlook to accomplish these goals.

I also encourage you to visit the book web site at www.workdaycontrol.com for training options, book updates, and tips on using this system with Outlook.

Chapter One
Gaining Workday Control

General Thoughts on a Disorganized Work Style

I have seen this many places I have consulted. Staff routinely complain of being overloaded with tasks. They complain of working long hours to try to fit in their tasks.

Managers complain that assigned tasks are not getting done. It's as if individual work assignments are deposited into a black hole, and the only way they get done is through repeated nagging by the task assigner.

And staff seem too busy to reply to or act on most of the e-mails they get. Important e-mails with requests for a reply are ignored. E-mails with clear requests for actions get buried in the recipient's Inbox.

In some cases the root cause of these problems is staff really are assigned too many tasks, that they are overloaded. But in most cases the problem is lack of good task and e-mail management skills. Tasks are never really incorporated into an effective system of getting tasks done. Teachings on the proper use of e-mail are completely absent.

Finding a Solution Is Important

Solving this problem, so that you can get the most important work done at a reasonable pace, is important. If struggling staff try to "do it all" by rushing through the day at 200 mph, they become even more inefficient. Dr. Edward M. Hallowell, in a January 2005 *Harvard Business Review* article, describes a near-clinical mental condition staff and managers can reach when they try to push through their out-of-control workday at a near-panic pace. When under this type of stress, the human brain functions differently, less effectively. The degraded functionality can grow worse, month after month.

Or staff can mentally "give up" and divest from work goals.

In either case, the results of all this can be devastating to productivity. As task and e-mail management gets out of hand, individual productivity plummets. Perhaps worse is that team productivity suffers. Team collaboration suffers because teammates cannot trust each other to complete tasks they have agreed to, or to reply to simple requests for assistance. When team members cease collaborating and team collaboration becomes ineffective, the goals of the organization suffer.

You Know the Symptoms

- You work late and feel you have far too much work to do.

- You have a sense that there is no time in the day to get things done.

- You leave important tasks uncompleted.

- You focus only on the work that is right in front of you, and rarely plan tasks in advance.

- You may have a number of loose task lists, but you have them spread around and they are generally out of control.

- Rather than controlling your e-mail, you find yourself just barely reacting to e-mail.

- You know that buried in your e-mail are many requests for action and you regret not getting to them quickly.

- If you are a manager, you find yourself practicing *reactive* management, acting only on the emergencies as they arise around you.

- You find yourself reacting to visitors, phone calls, and immediate needs, but rarely gain a sense of completion of important tasks.

- You have a sense of forgotten or misplaced tasks.

- People are often reminding you of things you promised that are not yet complete.

- You consistently leave work knowing something important is not finished.

Unmanaged Tasks and E-Mail Derail Work Effectiveness

While you may in fact have too many required tasks, it is more likely that your problems stem from *unmanaged* tasks. The fact is we all will always have too many tasks; the secret is in managing them. Unmanaged tasks can derail your work effectiveness because:

- You spend too much time on low priority tasks.

- You drop important tasks and actions in e-mails and they then become emergencies that require inefficient activity to fix.

- You do no planning of synergies; this leads to inefficient task completion.

- You are forced into too much wheel spinning, rehashing of tasks, and rereading of e-mails.

- You have a sense of being out of control, which leads to a poor attitude; you really do not expect to get to assigned tasks, to get to all your e-mail.

Ambiguity Is the Main Problem

Ambiguity is the main problem with casual task and e-mail management approaches:

- We are not sure where tasks lists are and which are up to date.

- We are unsure how to plan and prioritize action on tasks.

- We are vague about what to do with items like e-mails that have tasks implied in them.

Effective Task and E-Mail Management Is the Solution

Removing Ambiguity

Getting tasks organized goes a long way. Having your tasks clearly organized and prioritized helps you work on the most important tasks first. When properly organized, tasks that you postpone or drop due to lack of time are usually the least important tasks. Having a way to translate tasks embedded either explicitly or implicitly in e-mails into your task system will bring your e-mail under control.

Having your tasks and e-mail organized and under control makes you more efficient at accomplishing them; you actually spend less time finishing more activities. Why? Because when all your important tasks are clearly in front of you, you can multitask in meetings. You can take advantage of chance encounters with people and places. You can, during unexpected free slots of time, see and pounce on your most important tasks and get many of them done during "the holes in the day." And you can organize your day to attack tasks in optimum order.

An Improved Attitude

But perhaps just as important is this: having your tasks and e-mail under control changes your attitude. If you are like me, you probably tend to carry uncompleted tasks with you in your subconscious throughout the day (and sometimes night!). Uncontrolled tasks tend to nag us. We carry a subtle sense of being behind the game, of being on the wrong side of the curve. A sense of something that we should do, something we have been remiss about. This is often what drives us to work late nights with the thought: "If I work more hours I'll get this all done and this feeling will go away." However, usually it is exhaustion that finally quenches the feeling instead, along with the thought: "I have worked far more hours than is reasonably expected; surely I can go home now." Unfortunately, without good task management, fate will curse us to stay late night after night. Eventually, many workers just do not expect to complete their tasks, even important ones.

Once you get your tasks controlled, you lift this burden. It is such a relief to know you have identified and organized everything on your plate. It is a relief to clearly identify what is most important (and work on it first) and to know what can wait and how to defer it with appropriate follow-up. It is such a relief to be able to say to yourself: "That's all of it; I've got it all under control." Achieving this organized state enables you to know when you can leave the office guilt-free at the end of the workday. Your mind is free and clear to enjoy the evening at home or the weekend out and about.

When your mind is free from the subconscious message "I am out of control," you can more effectively execute activities. You can plan to get at tasks before they become emergencies. When you accomplish tasks in nonemergency mode, they fall into place more cleanly and easily and with less expenditure of energy.

Tasks or Goals: Which Come First?

Nearly all teachings on time and task management start with a discussion of goals. The general line of thought is this: how can you work on any tasks unless you know what your own goals are? The message is usually that you should not focus on tasks unless you have first mapped out your personal vision and goals and have ensured that your tasks link to those goals through planning.

This is sage advice. However, my experience is this: most people cannot get even their minimal daily tasks off their plate effectively enough to have time to focus on visualizing and planning their goals. They have no system for doing so. In the heat of the business day, inspired goals are usually the first things that they abandon as they scramble to stay ahead of the freight train of work. There is nothing more frustrating then seeing your favorite goals crash upon the rocks of an out-of-control workday.

In my opinion, you should first perfect your system of tracking and working tasks, because tasks are at the top of the action stack (see figure 1.1). And you should practice this with the tasks you have currently at hand. You need to get very good at working your daily tasks; your system should be nearly second nature. Once it is (and this system will enable that), you can then work on ways to inject your goals into your task stream.

Figure 1.1
Action stack:
tasks are at
the top.

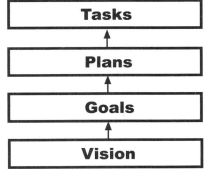

In the best of worlds, your goals and your work tasks will overlap. Many sales positions base their incentive system on that. However, unless you are in sales, or self-employed, or at a very senior level in your organization, it is unlikely that all or even most of your daily tasks will map to your own goals. If you work in a hierarchical organization, your boss is much more interested that you spend the majority of your time on tasks that map to the goals of the organization and to his or her department. If you work in a team environment, most of your tasks will be to support team activities. You need to add personal goal–inspired tasks on top of these.

In order to do that, you need to be able to tackle your work assignments so efficiently that you can get the most important and visible ones done and with time to spare. Only then can you know with confidence that your own goal-driven tasks will fit appropriately into your workday. I cover how to work your own goals into your task stream in chapter 9.

Tasks versus Appointments versus Projects versus Operations

Before attacking your tasks let's get some definitions in place. A task is a reasonably small unit of work that you can accomplish in one or two sittings and usually by yourself. A task is something that you may or may not assign a due date to. A task is the sort of thing that you write on your to-do list. Note, however, if a task is so time-specific that it actually needs a clock time assigned to it on a given day, it would be better to define the activity as an appointment and enter it on your calendar; don't put it on your task list.

Projects we will define here as work units that require multiple associated tasks, tasks that may individually end up on your to-do list. Projects that are large enough to warrant their own set of planning and follow-up meetings (separately managed projects) are best managed using formal project management techniques, not just a to-do list.

Similarly, operational environments that have daily repeated tasks and work steps are best managed by dedicated workflow systems, either manual or automated. If you process one hundred invoices a day, you would not put them on a to-do list; rather, other systems are better suited for that kind of work.

However, even in the midst of a well-managed and systematic project management or operational organization, myriads of loose-end tasks arise that do not fit smoothly into the formal systems. These are the sorts of tasks that tend to fall through the cracks because they often lie outside of the daily operational flow, and they usually have fewer defined processes and timeframes. All organizations and staff have such tasks. Organizations that are still defining operational procedures, or that are growing or changing rapidly, have lots of them.

And regardless of project and operational excellence, at the senior management level of organizations few predefined processes exist, nor should they. Senior managers usually define their activities at the time of each new initiative or crisis.

Tasks with this wide range of ad hoc origins are best managed individually, each on its own merit and time frame. These are the tasks that the typical out-of-control to-do list tries but fails to rein in. And fewer managers have assistants to handle these loose-end tasks; so it is up to the manager to handle them all. These are the tasks that the system in this book gets under control so well.

Background Projects

As a manager it is likely that you will have "background projects," things you need to do and complete but which are not your entire focus. Background projects tend to be start and stop projects that you work on a few hours a day and then return to several days later. These projects tend to have many loose ends hanging about. They have indistinct delegations to a variety of staff, loosely defined deliverables, and often loosely defined schedules. Because they are lightly planned and probably incompletely scoped, they are not amenable to formal project management techniques. These projects are perfect for a task-management system and will be one of the targets of the Outlook-based system that I will describe.

Time Management versus Task Management

It is also important to point out the distinction between time management and task management. In my opinion, there is little operative distinction; if you get task management under control then you will solve your time management issues. They work hand in hand. That said, much of what has been written about getting organized is more about time management, with relatively little focus on task management. Such writing gives much coverage to some basic work principles related to time usage, such as avoiding interruptions, finding the most productive work times in the day, remembering to delegate tasks, managing meetings, and so on. You can find many good books that cover these topics. Chapters 5 and 9 will focus on some time management best practices to help optimize your ability to get your tasks done. However by far the most important skills for you to learn are task-management skills, and that is the primary focus of this book.

Processes versus Tools

Some time ago a company I worked for adopted Microsoft Outlook as its e-mail system, so it was natural at that time for me to try out Outlook's task-management system. This was not the first time I had tried to manage tasks with an automated to-do list like the one in Outlook. I'd attempted this with many other automated packages, including Palm handheld software synchronized with the desktop version of the Palm software. I have also tried software on the Pocket PC synchronized with Outlook.

However, in the past, and again this time, I found that within a few weeks the automated to-do list quickly got out of hand, and invariably I stopped using it. What happened was that a large list of tasks built up. These were tasks that I intended to get to but that I was vague about when I needed to complete. Not wanting to lose sight of these tasks I did not delete them from the task list, and the task list grew to a size that I found either psychologically overwhelming to look at or just impossible to scan through. Of course, I tried assigning priorities to tasks, but then I ended up with a large number of high priority tasks, most of which were important but not important for any given day. Therefore, while they remained sorted high on the task list I constantly skipped them as I used the list, and the list became weak and useless. Outlook did not seem to solve the problem for me.

The moral of this story is that while the tool was in place, the usable *processes* were not. What changed all this and allowed me to finally implement an effective automated task-management system was adopting a few key task-management best practices as a set of management processes, and *then* using Outlook software to automate those processes. This kicked my task-management results into high gear.

Sources of Best Practices

A number of systems out there claim to have the task-management processes optimized. I have used many of them. The two systems that I have used the most are the FranklinCovey system and David Allen's Getting Things Done system.

Over the years I have studied nearly every system there is on time and task management. I have borrowed from various systems and have developed my own approaches. It is all these experiences that have led to the best-practice system you find in this book.

Why Automated Systems Are Nearly Always Better

All systems can be implemented using paper. You may have once used a paper-based planner system and I am sure you have seen many others using them. These planners often contain ten or more template-style forms for implementing system functionality. Paper systems have worked for years and many people continue to use them.

However, a software-based system is almost always better.

How Software Helps

There are several advantages to using a software-based task-management system. Perhaps the main advantage is the automatic forwarding of incomplete tasks to the next business day. If you use a daily task system without a computer you need to manually copy any uncompleted tasks to a new day's list. If you forget to do this and start on a fresh day's list with only its own originally assigned tasks, you will lose track of many important tasks.

It is just less work to let the computer do the forwarding for you. Since many if not most of your medium or low priority tasks will be forwarded from day to day, automatic forwarding is a big value here. This advantage is present with software used on both computer systems and personal digital assistants (PDAs).

Task Management on Your Work Computer

There are even greater advantages to automating your task-management system *on your primary work computer* system:

- Integration with e-mail and other desktop systems: Many of your tasks will arrive by e-mail so the ability to easily copy or convert them into a task is convenient. Similarly, you have the ability to copy task information into e-mails to notify others.

- Integration of your task management with your calendar: Many of the tasks you create will lead to creation of appointments, either specific appointments to meet with individuals or blocks of time set aside to work on tasks. Being able to view both your appointments for the day and your tasks for the day on one single system provides a control panel–like view of your day that is invaluable.

■ Single point of work focus: More and more of what you do at work you do on your computer, and so it only makes sense to include your tasks system there as well.

■ Flexible views: The ability to view your tasks and e-mail from various perspectives leads to optimal task and e-mail processing.

■ Powerful sorting and searching: The ability to search for all tasks you have assigned to a given individual is useful and easy in a software-based system. You will also see optional techniques for classifying and sorting on classified tasks. Being able to sort on task priority is critically important as well.

As you'll see, Outlook offers the best of all these solutions.

Going Mobile

Using a PDA Device

If using task management with Outlook on your main work computer is the best approach, what if you already use a PDA-like device? Palms, Pocket PCs, Smartphones, Blackberrys (see figure 1.2) — they all have Outlook-like capabilities. My recommendation is this: if you like the PDA form factor, then use your PDA in combination with Outlook on a computer, using the solutions in this book. PDAs are a reasonable way to go mobile with your tasks.

I do not, however, recommend using a PDA by itself instead of using Outlook on the PC. The reason is primarily the form factor and functionality.

Figure 1.2
One way to attain mobility is to synchronize your desktop copy of Outlook with a mobile equivalent of Outlook.

The screen on a Palm Pilot or Pocket PC is just too small to easily implement the techniques taught in this book. And techniques like converting e-mails to tasks depend on functionalities of the desktop version of Outlook which are not present in PDA-based task-management systems.

Rather, use your desktop copy of Outlook as your primary command post, and then synchronize your desktop-based Outlook with your PDA to bring your tasks on the road. That is what I did for many years.

Tablet PC: Best Solution

After years of experience with various approaches I have now come to prefer using a Tablet PC (see figure 1.3); it is by far my favorite solution. It has the full power and screen size of a laptop, and the quickness of a PDA. You can use it in most of the office situations where you would use a PDA but with far greater functionality. Being able to plug in and out of the corporate networks is ideal because it can be your main computer while at your desk, and then when you run to a meeting you have everything you have been working on with you. Your full copy of Outlook is available for inputting tasks as you get them in meetings. And the form factor and pen input is far superior to a laptop for use in meetings.

The Tablet PC in a work environment is the topic of my book *Seize the Work Day: Using the Tablet PC to Take Total Control of Your Work and Meeting Day.*

Figure 1.3
A Tablet PC is your best mobile solution, especially when also used as your primary work computer with Outlook.

The best solution is making the Tablet PC your primary work computer. Unfortunately, the Tablet PC is not yet widely used nor widely accepted in the corporate world, and so is not allowed on the networks of many companies. The next best solution is synchronizing your tablet with your work computer; this is nowhere as handy, but still usable.

Printed Paper Schedule

When I cannot use my Tablet PC, my next favorite approach is simply printing out my schedule and task list for use while on the move during the day. While a printed copy of a schedule and task list is not the perfect solution, it is easy, and the functionality is sufficient for most people's needs.

There are times I miss a handheld PDA, particularly when away from my desk and looking up someone's phone number or address. However, a good cell phone address book works nearly as well. That and a printed copy of my schedule and task list offer me enough mobility during my daily meetings.

Side Note: *If your place of work has Exchange 2003 set up for Outlook Web Access (OWA), and you own a Windows Mobile smartphone, you can use the OWA protocol and ActiveSync to synchronize your phone with contacts and appointments on your work system, over the air. With this, even a printed schedule is unneeded.*

See chapter 4, pages 80-82, for an expanded discussion of mobile solutions.

Why Use Outlook as Your Central Command Post

Outlook Is Ubiquitous and Has All the Right Tools

In summary, Microsoft Outlook on a desktop, laptop, or Tablet PC is your best command post. Why? Because it has all the right tools and it is ubiquitous. It has an e-mail system as good as or better than any of the competition. It has become the corporate standard e-mail client for over 60 percent of America's companies. Its integration of calendaring with e-mail is unsurpassed; if using with Exchange Server, the ability to check colleagues' schedules, schedule meetings, and send meeting notices all in one step is polished and highly effective. Also, if using with Exchange, its web-based e-mail integration for mobile workers is unsurpassed. And its integration of task management into all the other components of Outlook, especially e-mail, is the best available.

Outlook Task Management Is Integrated with E-Mail

Let's talk a bit about this integration of task management with the e-mail system. You will find that many if not the majority of your daily tasks actually arrive by e-mail. At first this may not seem true, but as you work through the system in this book you'll see that many of the e-mails that you leave in your Inbox (only to be lost later) actually represent tasks you've implicitly assigned yourself.

Since so many tasks arrive by e-mail, the fact that Outlook has a phenomenal capability to convert e-mails to tasks (which we will cover in some detail in chapter 6) is important. You'll be making extensive use of that.

You will also find that e-mail is an excellent task follow-up mechanism. As you delegate tasks to others, one of the principles of delegation that I teach (in chapter 8) is to provide consistent reminders to your staff. Ease of converting tasks to e-mail makes this simple.

Outlook Is Easy to Use

The design of Outlook is quite intuitive. Microsoft has put considerable effort into user interface design and it shows. They have had years to get it right, and millions of users to advise them. I have rarely met anyone who's had trouble simply checking e-mail or placing appointments on the calendar. And you'll have lots of people to give you help with it: coworkers, help desk staff, online guides.

Outlook Has Powerful Optional Features

In addition to being easy to use, Outlook also has significant feature depth. Integration with other Microsoft applications is probably one of the first advanced features users pursue.

More recent releases of Outlook provide the unique ability for mobile users to plug in and out of the network with smooth reconnection and synchronization capabilities. The grab-and-go capabilities of the Tablet PC combined with the new Cached Exchange Mode feature of Outlook and Exchange 2003 are examples.

Cached Exchange Mode

The new Cached Exchange Mode feature of Outlook and Exchange 2003 enables Exchange users to disconnect their mobile PC from the network without disrupting use of Outlook. All server-based messages and data are cached locally and synchronized automatically upon reconnection to the network. Previous versions of Outlook required a restart of Outlook to do this, and had limitations. With the new Cached Exchange Mode feature of Outlook and Exchange 2003, users can now easily grab their laptop or Tablet PC and run to a meeting with no interruption in their Outlook work.

Outlook Has Many Add-In Tools Available

Because Outlook is such a ubiquitous and popular tool it has been the target of much add-in software. There are scores of software packages that extend the power of Outlook. It is good to know that if Outlook's functionality does not meet your needs you can probably find a vendor who has written an extension to Outlook that does what you want.

Many of these add-in software packages have nothing to do with time management best practices but are still useful. For example, some excellent packages extend and improve the search capability of Outlook, making e-mail filing by topic less critical.

A few add-in packages are in fact designed to improve the use of Outlook for task and time management. I mention these in chapter 9. However, all the best practices I recommend in this book can be implemented in Outlook directly, without the need for add-on software.

Obtaining a Copy of Outlook

If you do not currently own a copy of Outlook you may wonder, how do you get a copy? Outlook is a standard component of the Microsoft Office product suite, which includes Word, Excel, and other Microsoft productivity titles. A few years ago it was not unusual to find Outlook preinstalled on new Windows computers either with or without the Office suite; but those days are gone. These days, Microsoft Office is usually a pricey add on to new computers. So if the company where you work doesn't already issue copies of Outlook or the Office suite, plan on either buying Outlook by itself, or if you don't already own Word and Excel, buying the entire Microsoft Office suite. Also, check the Microsoft website as downloadable trial copies are often available. You can also obtain a copy of Outlook in conjunction with a MSN account on Microsoft Outlook Live (see the Resources section, Appendix C, at the end of this book).

Outlook 2002 and Outlook 2003 Implement Tasks in Essentially the Same Way

The differences between Outlook 2002 and Outlook 2003 are remarkably minor with regard to the methodologies taught in this book. This is a good thing since many corporations are slow to upgrade their distributed copy of Outlook. The functionalities — e-mail, calendaring, and task management — are very similar. There is a notably better user interface in the newer version (Outlook 2003). Outlook 2003 also has a far better personal folders file structure which virtually eliminates the off-server mail storage limits of earlier versions (this critical feature alone makes a good case for upgrading). Outlook 2003 also has some added tools, such as Search Folders, which I find useful. And if you are using a Tablet PC, or tend to work with your laptop disconnected from your office network often, some invaluable architectural improvements in Outlook 2003 will make your disconnected use of Outlook much easier.

But no matter which of these two versions you are using, this book will clearly explain the differences and allow you to succeed with both.

Next: The Two Steps to Effective Task Management

So what comes next? In the chapters ahead, we will step through the two steps to effective task management:

- Learn best practices.

- Implement them in Outlook.

Chapter Two
The Best Practices of Task and E-Mail Management

Best Practices

You may recall the two simple steps to effective task and e-mail management:

- Learn best practices.

- Implement them in Outlook.

This chapter focuses on the first of those. Before plunging in and learning about Outlook, you should study the task and e-mail management best practices themselves. This chapter explains those processes and workflows that will form the basis for your success with Outlook.

Best Practices Defined

The term "best practices" is commonly used in the consulting and business world. It refers to identification of work practices that over the years have proven themselves most effective in their category.

As you know, there are often tens or hundreds of ways to accomplish the same goals in any given work discipline. But as common business processes tend to be repeated throughout an industry, tried and true approaches rise above the others. These are processes that prove to be most practical and most beneficial for an organization working in that industry, that work the best and produce measurably better results. They are commonly referred to as best practices.

Best Practices in Task and E-Mail Management

Similarly, in the field of task and e-mail management, some practices rise above others as being most useful, most effective, and most efficient. Time management books and teachings have existed for years. With them, authors and experts have developed many different theories on how to do time management. Some of these theories have withstood the test of time. And some of those have even excelled in their results. These include techniques that work and that you can easily implement. The best of the techniques you'll see repeated by many different authors.

So as in other management and business techniques, best practices have emerged that yield the most consistent results. And over the years of using Outlook, I have extended those and developed my own best practices to optimize Outlook's features. I combine all of these in this book.

Eight Best Practices

I have chosen eight best practices that will lead you to total workday control:

1   Tracking all tasks in Outlook Tasks System

2   Using a master tasks list kept separate from your daily tasks list

3   Using a simple prioritization system that emphasizes must-do-today tasks

4   Writing only next actions on your daily list

5   Doing daily and weekly planning to keep your task lists up to date

6   Converting e-mails to tasks

7   Filing e-mails using Outlook Categories

8   Delegating tasks in an effective manner

Best Practice 1: Tracking All Tasks in Outlook Tasks System

Collecting Your Lists

The very first and most important thing you can do to get your tasks organized is to track all tasks in ONE location. And it will come as no surprise that my recommended location to track your tasks is within the tasks tools of your Outlook system. What you should *not* do is try to use Outlook task tools in combination with other formal or informal task tracking systems. This applies to obvious external task systems such as paper to-do lists, yellow stickies on your computer monitor, journals, and so on.

This can also lead to rather subtle distinctions. For instance, something we all tend to do is leave important e-mails in our e-mail Inbox with the intention of returning to them later to act upon them. By doing this, however, you have created a second home for storing your to-dos. Similarly, we all tend to leave important voice mails in our voice mailbox with the intention of following up later on them as well.

So one subtle but important discipline is to get into the habit of immediately transferring both explicit and *implied* tasks into your task management system as soon as you receive them. Later in this book, I will show you easy ways of implementing this goal.

Keeping Tasks Out of Your Head

One more place you should not store tasks: your head! All good task management experts recommend getting out of the habit of trying to rely on your memory for tracking to-dos. This was a personal epiphany for me, when I finally accepted this lesson years ago. You may think you have a good memory, and you might have, but that is not the point. The point is that until you spread your task list out in front of you visually, it is impossible to properly prioritize, filter, defer, and dismiss tasks that are bouncing around in your mind all day. You should use your valuable brain cycles for strategic thinking, planning, analysis, appreciating life, and so on, not for constantly tracking and revisiting responsibilities. And if you are currently experiencing any anxiety about the number of tasks you seem to have on your plate, storing them only in your mind will exacerbate the anxiety.

It's the tasks that you cannot remember but you know are there that have the most destructive effect. That nagging feeling that you are ignoring important responsibilities has a negative effect on your attitude, your sense of well being, and your self-esteem. For some, it can be hard to relax in the evening after work or on the weekend when they sense that they have much work left undone.

What a tremendous relief my clients report when they finally get all of their to-dos out of their head and into one visible location. One of my clients, after taking my course, approached me with visible elation: "Michael, I cannot tell you how much control I now have of my work. This is amazing!"

And if you maintain that approach—recording to-dos immediately in one location as they come up rather than holding them in your head—you will be amazed at the sense of freedom this continues to provide.

In Summary

- Do not store tasks on paper even at your desk: not slips of paper, not note pads, not notebooks.

- Do not try to track to-dos in e-mails or voice mails.

- Do not try to track and work tasks from meeting notes and journals (although you certainly can initially record them there).

- Do not try to track tasks in your head.

- Rather, transfer all tasks from e-mail, voice-mail, paper memos, paper slips, meeting notes, journals, and your mind into Outlook's task management feature.

Getting Tasks Out of Physical Piles

One of the common sources of tasks is stacks of paper on your physical desktop, bookshelf, cabinet, or in a desk drawer. A primary benefit of implementing an effective task management system is no longer feeling haunted by piles of paper that you know contain things you need to work on. If you find you are overwhelmed by an out-of-control pile of materials on your desk or an overflowing physical in-basket, David Allen, in his book *Getting Things Done*, has some great techniques to get you past that. He describes a system that will get rid of your piles and create very simply organized and highly usable file cabinets. Following with the best practice of tracking all tasks in one place, you need to get those tasks out of your piles and into your task system within Outlook. Nonactionable items should be stored neatly away within files.

Best Practice 2: Distinguishing Between Master and Daily Tasks

Next to tracking all tasks in one location, the most effective practice you can do to get your tasks list under control is to create a lower priority list called the master tasks list. This one step is probably the most common task management technique across all the successful task management systems. FranklinCovey is the most recent system to do this. Alec Mackenzie in his book *The Time Trap* wrote about the same concept, using the same name, back in 1972. David Allen's concept of "someday maybe" tasks is very similar.

Master Tasks

Master tasks, as I define them, do not need to be done right away and have no specific due date assigned to them, but they may need to be done at some point in the future. The master tasks list then becomes a running task list of tasks of lower time-based importance. These are tasks that you do not put on the list that you look at every day (your daily tasks list). Rather you keep them out of sight on most days. The idea is that periodically, at least once a week, you visually scan this master tasks list to identify whether, through time and changing circumstances, any tasks there have become more urgent. If so, at that point you put the task on your list that you look at every day, your daily tasks list.

Daily Tasks

In contrast, the daily tasks list is what most people think of as a task list. It's the list you work off during the day as you get tasks done and look for additional high priority tasks to do that day. It is your daily to-do list, your list of items of immediate importance. Do not confuse this with your appointment calendar where you actually assign times to meetings and activities, which is a separate tool.

Removing Clutter

This approach of separating your master tasks from your daily tasks greatly unclutters your most important to-do list: today's. And it leaves you a structured and organized way to access lower priority and future tasks so they are not lost

This two-list concept, a daily tasks list and a separate master tasks list, freed me from the endlessly long single task list that I described in chapter 1 that eventually became too unwieldy for daily use.

Roles of Daily and Master List

Daily List

Therefore, in this scenario, your daily list becomes the list you work from every day. This is where you put tasks that you need to do today or in the next few days (again, these are *tasks* not *appointments*: they do *not* have a specific time assigned to them). There are some subtleties in deciding what tasks to put on this list that we will discuss more in the chapters ahead.

However, for now think of the daily list as the list of tasks that you want to work on today, or want to *consider* working on today. In practice, you'll probably find that the daily list will come to represent tasks you want to work on today or sometime this week. Anything you do not intend to work on this week you will probably put on your master list.

Master List

Your master list will hold items that you think you might get to next week, or some weeks out. The master list (see figure 2.1) is also good for items that are "nice to do" — they sound like great ideas, but you know you may not get to them for some time. It is good to get them recorded quickly within your master list so you do not lose those ideas. They may eventually mature into actionable plans.

Figure 2.1
Sample master tasks list containing a combination of nice-to-do ideas and postponed daily tasks.

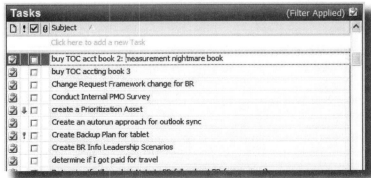

The power of this list is very important because it gives you a place to park items that you sense are important but that you are not ready to schedule into your workday. It gets the item out of your mind and onto your list and frees you from that nagging feeling that you need to do something about it. Without using the master list, you might be tempted to do the item today or this week just to make sure you don't forget it. That may rob time from more important tasks.

You will also use the master list as a place to move daily tasks that are not fitting into a busy week and that you can put off for some time.

With the master list you have a place to safely store ideas, long-term intentions, future projects, important but not now items, and anything really that just doesn't make sense to do right away. It is satisfying to be able to capture these types of ideas and tasks. And it is valuable because many of them really do become fruitful activities later.

You'll see later that the master list is also where you should store your current projects list and weekly planning perspectives. We'll cover that in much more detail in a future chapter.

So again, in summary, the value of the master list is:

- It provides a place to park ideas, future projects, and lower-importance tasks.

- It keeps your daily list clear and of a more manageable size.

- It stores your list of active projects.

- It stores your list of planning perspectives.

We will go over how to configure Outlook to enable using master tasks in the next chapter.

What about Appointments?

You may be wondering, how do appointments fit in with this task system? Remember the distinction between tasks and appointments: you can do *tasks* pretty much any time during the day, whereas you need to attend an appointment at a particular time in the day. Think of tasks and appointments as two separate sets of commitments, both of which you need to keep in a day.

Outlook has an excellent calendar system that automates most of the things you need to worry about when setting and announcing appointments. Unlike working with tasks, few subtleties are involved. This book will not go into those features because other authors cover them well in standard Outlook books.

There *are* a few best practices you can apply to appointments. In the pages ahead, you will see recommendations to create general task time appointments on your calendar within which you should work your tasks. And you'll see that in some cases I recommend that you make a specific appointment for a specific task.

However, other than those suggestions, treat your calendar appointments separately from your tasks, and honor each type equally as you work through your day. This is one reason I like the TaskPad layout within Outlook (described on pages 46-48) where you see both the appointment calendar and your task list at once. They both are equally important.

Best Practice 3: Using a Simple Prioritization System That Emphasizes Must-Do-Today Tasks

Background

You need to use a simple prioritization system in your daily list that emphasizes must-do-today tasks.

If you have ever managed any sort of task list at all you probably have gotten used to prioritizing. It is the one step that nearly all task management disciplines teach, particularly the simplistic ones. And intuitively it is something that we feel we ought to do; we know we have a limited amount of time and so it makes sense to identify those tasks that are most important to accomplish first.

The easiest approach, and one we probably do every day, is to apply a simple numbering system to our task list (1, 2, 3, 4, and so on). However, keep in mind that creating a basic numbered list of tasks will not prevent the runaway task problem I described earlier.

More sophisticated systems identify tasks in a way that implicitly prioritizes them. For instance, our classification of tasks between daily and master tasks is an implicit prioritization: daily tasks are more important to do now, and master tasks are less important.

And for prioritizing within the daily list, experience shows it is better to clump tasks into a few general categories of priority, rather than using an unlimited numbered list. The reason is that determining the fine level of distinction between individual tasks requires more energy than it is worth. Not to mention that inserting tasks in between consecutive numbers becomes difficult. Rather, most systems find that clumping tasks into three levels of priority: high, medium, and low, provides enough resolution without getting out of hand.

FranklinCovey uses an A, B, C nomenclature to identify those three categories. Microsoft Outlook uses High, Normal, and Low categories. What is important is not what you call the categories, but what they *mean* to you.

Within the simplest systems, these categories are merely relative rankings for tasks. High is more important than Medium which is more important than Low.

Unfortunately, this basic, importance-only approach will not get you very far. It lends itself to ambiguous interpretation of timing, context, and assignment. The better systems define clearly what each of the three categories mean, and that is what we do in the Total Workday Control system, starting with the High priority. In our system, High means *must do today*.

Must Do Today

The most important single element of establishing an effective prioritization system is to clearly assign a *must-do-today* designation to those tasks that really need it.

When I first started using a system that firmly enforced this rule, I was amazed at the sense of relief and freedom from guilt that I would feel when I could look at my list at a reasonable hour and confidently state, "All really important tasks for the day are complete, and I can now go home."

The Working Late Syndrome

This point is worthy of more discussion. Unfortunately, many of us get in the habit of working late every night. If you are in this situation, I suspect your first reaction to this comment is to state proudly: "I am an important and busy person and as a result I have too many things to do. This is the cost of being such an important person, a cost that I must accept, now that I am making the big bucks." Stephen Covey has written several books that talk very clearly about this issue. As many of the Covey books point out, this mental dialog is usually an incorrect one that you can and should revise.

The idea in the Covey books is that over time, people lose perspective of the real importance of things, and in that blur they perceive all things at work as urgent. Without correction, every day one becomes trapped in a never-ending stream of urgent work tasks that end only when exhaustion kicks in or when higher levels of urgency call from home. Many of us are in this situation now and leaving work at a reasonable hour is difficult if not impossible.

What makes this situation hard to correct is that in the late hours of a workday people are often too tired to judge accurately which tasks they really can postpone.

Or worse, because of endless meetings or poor prioritization throughout the day, they have delayed the really important tasks to the end of the day and these tasks really must be done before leaving.

So a system of classifying a short list of tasks that you absolutely must do on a given day allows you to, at the end of the workday, clearly decide whether you need to stay late or not. You simply check to see if your must-do-today list is done or not. If you have not completed it you stay knowing you must.

If you have completed it and you have worked a reasonably full day, you can leave without guilt.

In Outlook you implement this by using the High category within the prioritization column in the task views (I will show how to add that column, a little bit later). You then focus energy through the day to ensure that you complete those tasks as early as possible. This truly and accurately represents the right meaning of a high priority task.

Easily Abused

Note however that using this best practice is not a slam-dunk. The trouble is that you can easily abuse it. It is tempting to assign a high priority to things you just happen to feel strongly about at the time you write them down. The problem with this is that you can often end up with eight or ten highest priority items on your daily to-do list, which presumably all must be done today. And assuming these items are reasonably complex, it is likely you will not complete them that day. This has two problems: it forces you to reevaluate your list continually to identify the *real* must-do-today items, and it causes you to lose respect for the category.

So using this category accurately takes a little practice. The best way to accurately assign a high priority to a task is to ask yourself this: "Is it absolutely necessary that I complete this task today; if needed, would I work late tonight to make sure this task is completed?" If the answer is no then do not assign a high priority to it.

My goal is to have no more than three to five high priority tasks in a given day. On most days, I have two or three, and on many days I have none. If I start my day with more than three to five then I know I may need to start contacting stakeholders to negotiate extensions.

Medium and Lowest Priority

So what about the other priorities? What I have found over years of perfecting my system is that nearly all my tasks on the daily list are medium priority (the Normal priority in Outlook, or the B priority in FranklinCovey).

The reason for this is that I find the master tasks list is the best tool to use to handle low priority tasks (or when working in Outlook, assigning it to a date in a later week; more on that later). If a task just really is not very important you might as well get it off today's daily list, where it will only clutter your thinking, by calling it a master task. Remember, if you are using master tasks correctly then you are revisiting your master list at least once a week, so you can reevaluate this task again later.

So if you are about to assign a task on your daily list to the low priority category ask yourself this: "Do I really need to complete the task this week?" If the answer is no, and your daily list is relatively large, it is probably best to move that task out to a later week or to the master tasks list. And certainly if the task is low priority and has no discernible deadline—in other words it's a nice-to-have task—move it to the master list without hesitation.

As a result, the low priority designation on my Outlook daily list is usually used by me as a *medium* low classification, and assigned to tasks that are timely today or this week but that are less important than other tasks for the week.

Best Practice 4: Writing Only Next Actions on Your Daily List

The next most important best practice to implement is using the concept of *next actions* in your daily tasks list (figure 2.2). This is a best practice I highly recommend because it helps ensure that your tasks actually get done. There is nothing worse than a task list full of items that sit there without completion; using this technique helps avoid that.

I first saw this concept in the book *To Do… Doing… Done*, by G. Lynn Snead and Joyce Wycoff. Lynn describes a system of top-down task creation where a small project is planned out as a whole, and then periodically the next action for each project is "time activated" and moved out to the daily tasks list or appointment calendar.

I have adopted David Allen's particular next action approach in my Outlook-based system. In contrast to the top-down approach described above, David takes a very powerful bottoms-up perspective. He challenges users to examine tasks they have on their daily list and to ask themselves, "What is the very next physical action I need to do to accomplish this task?" The goal is to identify the most discrete and significant next action possible, and write that down on the task list. This stimulates action more effectively and unsticks tasks that tend to remain uncompleted. David's application of the concept goes further and states that you should write *only* next actions on the list you work from daily, nothing else. And once again, proving that most good task management practices have been around for a while, David attributes the idea to one of his mentors from twenty years back: Dean Acheson.

Figure 2.2
Sample daily tasks list containing tasks written only as next actions.

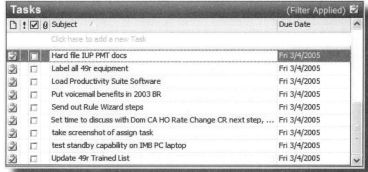

Let's explore this concept in some detail because it is a centerpiece of the Total Workday Control system. David Allen feels that the concept of a daily to-do list is overemphasized in most time management systems. Instead, what should be focused on is the concept of a *next action list.* This is a list of next actions for projects and priorities that you have on your plate that need to be done as soon as possible but that aren't usually assigned to any given day. So they don't appropriately sit on a low priority list like your master tasks list because they *do* need to be done as soon as possible, but they aren't urgently assigned to any given date either.

One reason many important tasks may hang around on your to-do list without completion is not because the priority is in fact low, but rather because you may not have described the task in action language. David recommends that all tasks be written in language that describes a discrete physical action, such as "Call Fred and ask for new meeting date," "E-mail James about proposal," or "Review Ted's summary notes." They should not be generally stated tasks such as "James's proposal," or "Ted's notes," because these descriptions leave you, on cursory review, uncertain of what to do. It may take a minute or two of thought to decide what the action really is, and in the heat of the busy business day that delay can prevent you from acting on the task. A better approach is to state them clearly as actions at the time you write them down on the list.

Very Next Action

More importantly, you should write the task in words that describe the very next discrete and significant physical action that you need to do to move the task forward. David Allen spends chapters on this point in his book and it is worthy of further discussion here.

Stuck Tasks

Most stuck tasks get stuck because you really haven't thought through and identified the very next action needed on the task. Rather you often end up writing midstream outcomes that in reality require further dependent actions before you can get to them. Or you write higher level goals with no indications of next steps needed to get there. And so in the midst of a busy day, when you see the item, you get stuck; the task description does not ring true as something that you can do immediately. So it is essential that you clearly think through what this very next action is to achieve a task, and write only that down on your daily tasks list. This keeps your tasks list action-oriented and focused on the immediate.

Therefore, in my system I recommend this: make sure what you write on your daily tasks list is *always* a very next action, with no exceptions. As you write down tasks, take a few moments to think this through. Ask yourself several times, "Is there anything else I need to do first before this?" If you find something, write only that down.

Side Note: *Clearly, if you are on the run and don't have time to think this through, get the task recorded as best you can. Then redefine it later, as described in Loosening Stuck Tasks, below.*

For example, I had received a request to assist the planning department in my company with a project proposal they were developing. I started to write down Assist Planning Dept. with Project, but then I thought, "No, there's something ahead of that." So then I thought "Of course, I need to call up the planning specialist to discuss the project." However then I imagined myself doing that and realized "I know nothing about this project and if I get questions during that call, the call is going to be counterproductive." I knew we had some material on their planned project somewhere, so really the first thing to do was to review the project material. I started to write that down but thought, "Where is the material?" I thought this through and remembered that Tom last worked on the project and had the file on it. So what I finally wrote down was this: Call Tom and Get Planning Dept. Project File.

Loosening Stuck Tasks

This process is not only useful when first writing down tasks, but it is also useful if tasks seem to float on your list for several weeks without completion. If a task seems to be stuck on your daily list, ask yourself again if it is written in action language and ensure that it represents the very next action needed to complete the underlying task.

This can sometimes get rather subtle. For example, I had a task on my daily list that sat for several weeks: "Make doctor's appointment." It was for a routine physical, I had no psychological stress associated with it, and it was written in action language, but it just wasn't getting done. I was wondering why I was not moving on it. So finally during the next weekly planning session I stopped and considered the task and the problem. Then I realized this: subconsciously I knew that making a trip to the doctor required at least a half day off from work; the doctor was in a different town, and so with travel time it was more than a simple one-hour appointment. In my busy schedule, finding that large a block of time was not an easy thing to do and so I always hesitated before calling for the appointment. Every time I looked at the task I sensed it was going to be a difficult thing without really understanding why. And, in the heat of the busy day, due to that hesitation, I consistently skipped it and moved on to other tasks. The real next action was this: examine my calendar in the weeks ahead and either find a day with a half day open, or cancel some appointments to make it possible. I wrote that down on my daily list as "Find half day available for doctor's appointment." That's what broke it free: the next time I was at my calendar and making calls, that task was easily accomplished, and I moved right on to making the appointment call.

So that is the power of the very next action process. If you write all your tasks on your daily list in this very next action manner you will find that your goals get accomplished much more quickly and easily. This approach tends to get your tasks moving and helps you get much more done during the day.

However, there is more to this. This thought process sometimes leads to the creation of what I am calling miniprojects.

Identifying Miniprojects

In identifying a next action for a particular task, you will probably find that more than one action step is required to accomplish the goal of that task; that is what happened in the examples above. Sometimes the multiple steps naturally follow from each other and by writing down and then starting on the first one you naturally and easily conclude the rest in one sitting. Other times, the multiple steps imply a series of time-separated actions, each of which you have to come back to later. In these cases, if all you do is write down the first step, you may not remember to come back to the rest of the actions. So when multiple, time-separated actions are needed to achieve a goal and you want to keep these actions alive, it is useful to reclassify the original task as a *miniproject*.

For instance let's say after further analysis we determine that the task called Write Quarterly Plan will take at least five discrete actions to complete, probably with several days between each one. If so, identify this as a miniproject and then, as described above, ask yourself "What is the very next action I need to take to move this project forward?" Place only the very next action item for the project on your next action list: Call Jim and Ask Him to Send Last Quarter's Plan. Then place the miniproject (Write Quarterly Plan) on your master list so that you are sure to revisit it weekly to identify any subsequent next actions, in case the momentum stalls out. I put a "P-" in front of the miniproject name on the master list (P-Write Quarterly Plan) to remind myself that it is a project; this also allows me to sort and view all my miniprojects at once within the master list.

Side Note: *This notation a just one possible notation. I also use "P:" to mark these miniprojects. And if I have "subprojects" or master tasks associated with miniprojects, I might write "P:Website: Home page design" where Website is the miniproject name. Feel free to explore various uses of this notation. Just be consistent so when you sort alphabetically the associated items sort together.*

Background Projects

One thing we will go into more detail about in chapter 5 is the concept of a background project, which is essentially the same as a miniproject but arrived at top down rather than bottoms up. A few words about it here are useful.

I come from a career of managing large projects, requiring large full-time teams and dedicated full-time management efforts. These projects require high levels of project management discipline, methodology, and attention in order to succeed.

In contrast to this are the kinds of projects that most managers encounter in most companies. These managers have multiple responsibilities and operational duties, and added to these duties are occasional projectlike assignments, which require on and off again attention to complete. These are what I call background projects. They are presented as a project, usually with management interest in the outcome. However they have no full-time staff assigned to them, they have tasks that may be shared amongst other staff in their spare time, and they have deadlines that are often vague or flexible. Work on deliverables assigned to staff from these projects often disappears for a while as operational duties take precedence, and resurfaces with or without completion at the next check-in point. These background projects are essentially managed on the side, in one's spare time.

In many ways, these are some of the most difficult projects to accomplish. Why? Because there is no continuous attention paid to them, and keeping track of the various handoffs and tasks that you are waiting for can become daunting. It is very easy to let the project drop off the radar, to fall through the cracks, without action for weeks or months.

Traditional project management approaches do not really work because of the on-and-off-again nature of the assignments; there is no way to assign predictable staff attention to the component tasks. And in many cases the projects are too small to be worthy of traditional project management approaches. It's these projects that the concept of the very next action is especially useful for.

I have found that, as long as projects do not have any full-time staff associated with them, managing these background projects in a manner similar to miniprojects works very well. In other words, place an entry for this background project on your master tasks list, and then feed tasks from that item to your daily tasks list as needed. Use the delegation techniques in chapter 8.

Why Next Actions Works So Well, and What Is the Cost?

The beauty of using the next action concept is that in your short moments of available time throughout a day, it is much easier to act on a task you have described as a physical, next action step. When you see only next actions during those "what can I do next" holes in your day, you avoid those hand-wringing moments when you stare at your task list and just can't move on important tasks. Often this inertia stems from no actual simple action jumping out at you from your list. With all tasks written as next actions, you are able to complete more tasks throughout the day, and you need to stay late less often.

This efficiency does not come entirely free, though. There is a cost. To make this really work you need to transfer your "hand-wringing" time to dedicated time set aside for planning your tasks. This is discussed next.

Best Practice 5: Daily and Weekly Planning

The next best practice is planning. Common to nearly all task management systems is the requirement to set aside time to do task planning. For task management to be successful you can't just drop tasks on your task list and do them, at least not for long. Rather you periodically need time to stop and reflect on the tasks that are on your list and think through changes in priorities, schedules, and next actions.

This is particularly true with your daily list because you will find that it very quickly gets too long to handle. You need to do some quick daily planning to get your list in usable shape each day. It is a good habit to plan your day and to rethink which tasks really are must-do tasks for today, and which medium level tasks you are going to pursue.

This is also true when you start maintaining a master tasks list. You should set aside time every week on your calendar to review that list and decide if any of the items have matured enough to advance to your daily tasks list. And you should examine the projects on that list to see if any new next actions are ready to be moved out to your daily list.

The time spent on these planning exercises is an investment with very high returns. It enables the rest of the system to work smoothly and to gain the valuable benefits of implementing a successful task management system. We will go into great detail on the steps you should take in your daily and weekly planning in chapter 5.

Best Practice 6: Converting E-Mails to Tasks

Many if not most of your daily tasks arrive by e-mail; I know they do in my office. So it is not surprising that most if not all the problems users have with work e-mail stem from poor management of explicit or implicit tasks that are embedded in work e-mail. Your Outlook Inbox is not an appropriate place to manage tasks, yet most Outlook users unconsciously attempt to use it that way; this leads to a multitude of e-mail problems.

If your primary complaint before reading this book was that your e-mail was out of control, then from one point of view, everything you learn about task management in best practices 1 through 5 enables you to manage tasks that arrive by e-mail. Once you know how to manage your Outlook task list effectively, then this next skill, learning to convert task-laden e-mails into Outlook tasks, can be the final added skill needed to get a grip on your e-mail.

If your primary complaint was that you had way too many tasks to do, then, while better e-mail processing is not a task management topic per se, it will greatly impact your ability to get tasks done. Setting up an effective e-mail processing workflow is an essential step toward increasing your effectiveness with your tasks. Making a near empty Inbox one goal of this processing goes a long way toward helping you know that you can finally focus on important but not urgent activities (like strategic thinking or going home on time). And converting e-mails to tasks will be the center point of your e-mail workflow.

Therefore you need to take advantage of simple but powerful methods to convert e-mails into tasks within Outlook. And once under control, e-mail is an effective tool to follow up on tasks that you are waiting on others for. Using e-mail effectively will go a long way toward getting your tasks under control.

I cover e-mail thoroughly in chapters 6 and 7. Chapter 6 focuses on converting e-mails to tasks and on e-mail workflows. Chapter 7 focuses on the next best practice: filing e-mails.

Best Practice 7: Filing E-Mails Using Outlook Categories

Compared to best practice 6, converting e-mails to Outlook tasks, best practice 7 is much less important. Once you have extracted explicit or implicit tasks from incoming e-mail, what you do with e-mail after that is by comparison immaterial. That said, I consistently refer to my old e-mails as I work through my day. So I appreciate having a good filing system in place to facilitate finding stored e-mail.

Most sources on Outlook e-mail management recommend creating multiple custom folders and filing e-mails in those folders by topic. This is one place I diverge from typical recommendations; I have found using multiple custom folders to be cumbersome and almost unusable. Rather, I recommend assigning Outlook Categories to your e-mails, and filing all of your e-mail into one folder. Then display folderlike views of your filed mail, using Outlook Show in Groups or an Outlook 2003 feature called Search Folders.

Chapter 7 explores this in detail and shows you how to implement it.

Best Practice 8: Delegating Tasks Effectively

New and even experienced managers often have trouble delegating tasks effectively. You need to work into your task management system a delegation procedure. You need to find a way to indicate clearly (1) which tasks have been delegated, (2) what due dates have been agreed upon, and, most importantly, (3) when and how to follow up on delegated tasks.

Nearly all good task and time management systems provide techniques for assigning and tracking delegated items. For example, FranklinCovey uses a special symbol that you place next to a task that has been delegated. David Allen uses a category called "waiting for" that he recommends you check periodically to follow up on delegated items. Outlook also comes with a task assignment system.

In practice, I have found none of these systems really meets my needs, and I have developed a better approach that optimizes tools built into Outlook (but that avoids use of its assign task methodology which is often not suitable for your coworkers). The system in this book provides clear and unambiguous steps to accomplish all these requirements. I will cover those steps in chapter 8.

Summary

In summary, the system used in this book applies a collection of best practices drawn from the very best task management approaches on the market and from the author's many years of experience. It adapts and adds to those systems in order to optimize them for use with Outlook. New practices for task management are incorporated and explained, practices that advance the science of task management well beyond the existing systems and books on the market. If you use Outlook, this system is the very best to get your workday under control.

In review, here again are the eight best practices of applying task and e-mail management to Outlook.

The Eight Best Practices

1 Tracking all tasks in Outlook Tasks System

2 Using a master tasks list kept separate from your daily tasks list

3 Using a simple prioritization system that emphasizes must-do-today tasks

4 Writing only next actions on your daily list

5 Doing daily and weekly planning to keep your task lists up to date

6 Converting e-mails to tasks

7 Filing e-mails using Outlook Categories

8 Delegating tasks in an effective manner

Chapter Three
Configuring Outlook for Task Management

Best Practices 1 through 5 are all about establishing a strong task management system. To use them, you need to make some simple custom configurations in Outlook. They are not very difficult to do and should take you only about 30 or 40 minutes. Helping you make those configurations is the goal of this chapter. Also go to www.workdaycontrol.com for other options.

In addition, I will take you through some basic Outlook usage lessons to get you familiar with fundamental Outlook features you will need when using this system. But first, a little background on task management capabilities in Outlook.

Why Most Users Are Unsuccessful with Outlook Task Management

The vast majority of Outlook users either do not use the task management portion of Outlook at all, or use it ineffectively. In fact, recognizing this limited use, Microsoft removed display of the TaskPad from the default configuration in Outlook 2003 (we will add it back in).

Ineffective Initial Configuration

The underlying problem with the way Outlook is configured and used out of the box for task management is ambiguity. When using tasks in an unmodified Outlook, the difference between importance and timing of tasks is ambiguous. The difference between actions and goals for tasks is ambiguous. Because of this, it is impossible to define a clear strategy for attacking the task list. Long-term tasks get wrongly mixed with those of shorter term. Broadly defined tasks get mixed with sharply defined ones. As a result, tasks jotted into a non-custom-configured Outlook system are hard to complete or properly "file," and they quickly build up in volume until they are overwhelming and unmanageable.

This is not a criticism of Microsoft. Given that most users lack task management best practice teachings, the out-of-box configuration of Outlook for tasks is set up appropriately. However, once you learn best practices you'll see that new configurations are needed.

Specific examples of out-of-box configurations that will prevent you from being successful once best practices are learned include:

- No distinction between daily tasks and master tasks

- No separate Master Tasks view

- No separate All Daily Tasks view

- No date information displayed in the TaskPad

- No priority information displayed in the TaskPad

- All tasks shown in TaskPad no matter what the assigned date

- Automatic reminders set by default for newly created tasks

- Default configurations inappropriate for repeated tasks

- And many more

Most if not all of these task management configuration issues can be solved by reconfiguring Outlook yourself to incorporate the needed changes.

In this chapter I go over how you can make the configuration changes to Outlook yourself.

Some Outlook Task Basics

Outlook 2002 and 2003 Have Nearly Identical Task Capabilities

Outlook 2002 and 2003 are very similar, and both programs provide everything we need to implement the eight task and e-mail management best practices. Outlook 2003 does have a few advantages. If you are using a laptop or a Tablet PC and tend to disconnect from your office network often and work offline, Outlook 2003 and Exchange 2003 have much better facilities for handling this. Outlook 2003 also has some nice e-mail filing features that we will discuss in chapter 7. However, regarding tasks, the features are nearly identical.

That said, some of the menus and control windows for task management operate a little differently between the two versions when using identical functions, so throughout this book you will often see separate menu instructions and screen figures to ensure you will succeed with either version. If the screens are nearly identical, Outlook 2003 will be favored.

Side Note: *See page 5 of the Introduction, if you are uncertain which version of Outlook you are using.*

Navigating Through Outlook

Folders and Views

Folders

Outlook folders are simply specific organizations of Outlook data. If you currently use Outlook as your primary e-mail system, then you are using Outlook folders. Every time you view your calendar, your e-mail, or your contacts, you are choosing to open a specific Outlook folder.

Three Primary Folders

Most people use these three folders: Inbox, Calendar, and Contacts. Of these three, we'll use the first two in this book (see figures 3.1 and 3.2), and also add use of the Tasks folder. Additional standard folders exist such as Journal, Notes, and so on, that are not pertinent to the system in this book. And beyond the standard Outlook folders are personal folders you can create. A detailed look at Outlook folders, including personal folders, is provided in Appendix A; the basics are provided here and in chapter 7.

Side Note: *From this point on, I recommend you maximize your Outlook window to get the best view of all the Outlook features.*

Figure 3.1
Inbox folder.

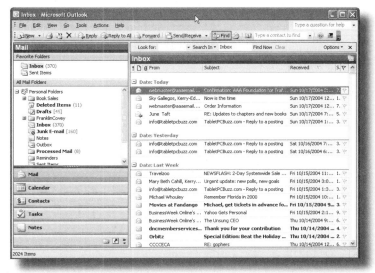

2024 Items

Figure 3.2
Calendar folder
(Day/Week/
Month view
shown).

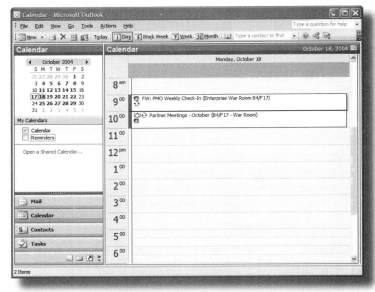

Views

Most users do not realize that accessible within each of these main folders are various optional *views* that allow them to look at a given folder's data formatted and filtered in different ways. There is a main default view for each folder that opens the first time you use Outlook. Beyond this, there are a large number of optional Outlook views that you probably do not even know exist; they are usually variations on the main default views. More importantly, for implementing task and e-mail best practices, you can create and save your own custom views for each of these folders. We will be doing that later.

Side Note: *Within a single Outlook window, you can display the contents of only one folder at a time and only one view at a time; a discussion of using multiple Outlook windows is ahead on page 53.*

Choosing Between the Major Folders

In case you are new to Outlook, let's go over how to select and display each of the major folders. Choosing between the Inbox folder and the Calendar folder varies between 2002 and 2003, and varies if you have changed the default configuration of Outlook by adding the folder list pane (see figure 3.3).

Side Note: *I discuss how to add the folder list pane in chapter 7 (pages 153-155); I will assume for now that you have not yet added that pane.*

To see the contents of the Inbox folder in Outlook 2002, merely click the Inbox shortcut button on the Outlook Bar on the left side of the screen as shown in figure 3.4.

Figure 3.3
The Outlook 2002 Inbox folder with both the Outlook Bar (far left) and folder list pane (mid-left) shown.

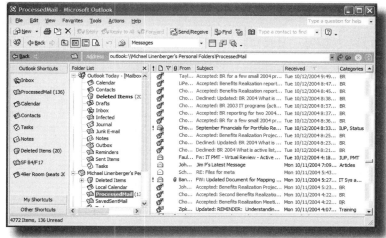

Figure 3.4
To display the Inbox folder contents in Outlook 2002, use the Inbox shortcut on the Outlook Bar.

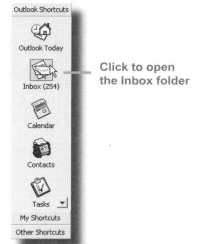

Click to open
the Inbox folder

Choosing Folders in Outlook 2003

In Outlook 2003, the left side of all windows is dominated by a large navigation structure called the Navigation Pane. To view the Inbox folder contents, first click on the Mail banner button in the bottom portion of the Navigation Pane, and then if needed click on the Inbox folder in the folder list that appears (see figure 3.5). To view the Calendar folder, click on the Calendar banner button in the Navigation Pane.

If the Outlook 2003 Navigation Pane shown in figure 3.5 is not visible on your screen, then open the View menu, and click Navigation Pane to activate that portion of the Outlook window (see figure 3.6).

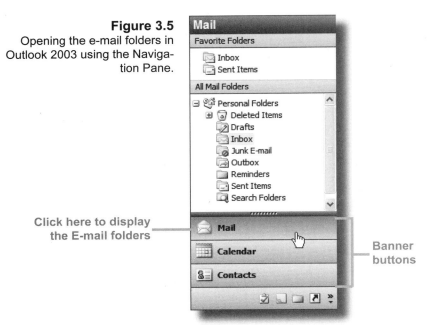

Figure 3.5
Opening the e-mail folders in Outlook 2003 using the Navigation Pane.

Click here to display
the E-mail folders

Banner
buttons

Side Note: *If the Navigation Pane menu choice is not visible within the View menu as is figure 3.6 (facing page), you may need to click the Expand button (shown below) found at the bottom of the menu list to show all optional menu choices.*

In Outlook 2003 you can also use the Go menu to switch between the major folders.

Viewing the TaskPad

The Calendar folder is where you are able to see the TaskPad, which is an abbreviated depiction of tasks. Out of the box, the TaskPad shows simpler columns of task information than views within the Tasks folder (described ahead), making it a good quick-review location for tasks. And we will further configure the TaskPad to show only the most important daily tasks. This TaskPad will become your primary task input and review facility (see lower right corner of figure 3.7).

Adding the TaskPad in Outlook 2003

If you do not see the TaskPad within your default Calendar folder view as in figure 3.7, then open the View menu at the

Figure 3.6
Adding the
Navigation
Pane in
Outlook 2003.

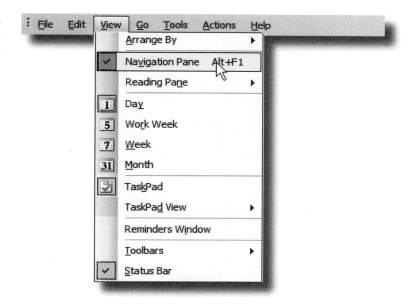

Figure 3.7
The TaskPad
occupies the
lower right
corner of the
default Calen-
dar folder view.

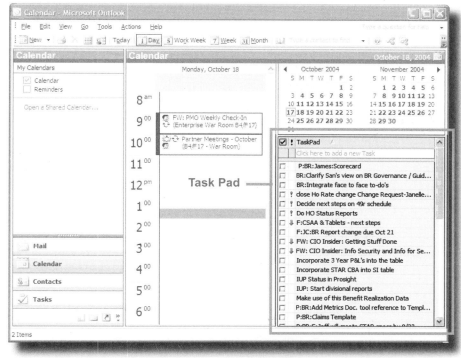

Side Note: *The default Outlook 2003 Calendar folder view does not show the TaskPad out of the*
box; you need to specifically add it following the instructions at left.

top of your Outlook window and choose TaskPad from that menu to insert the TaskPad into your Calendar folder view (see figure 3.8).

Figure 3.8
Showing the
TaskPad in
Outlook 2003.

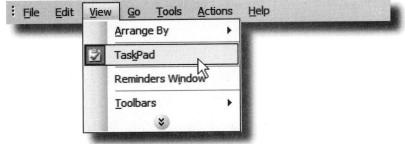

Beyond Outlook Basics

Tasks Folder

We will also be using the Tasks folder. It amazes me how few Outlook users have ever used the Tasks folder. Let's remove any confusion. While the TaskPad is an abbreviated table listing your tasks, the Tasks folder is a full window depiction of the same tasks list. Outlook, out of the box, shows the same tasks through both of these options. The main initial difference is that the standard views in the Tasks folder include a few additional columns of information about each task.

What you can do, which is significant, is configure and save various additional *filtered* views within the Tasks folder so that it *does* show different tasks than the TaskPad. These custom views you can then select from a menu when you need to use them. These configurable views will be very useful to us, and I will cover how to create them later in this chapter.

Opening the Tasks Folder

Opening the Tasks Folder in Outlook 2002

In Outlook 2002, you open the Tasks folder by clicking on the Tasks shortcut button on the Outlook Bar on the left edge of the Outlook window (see figure 3.9).

Opening the Tasks Folder in Outlook 2003

In Outlook 2003, you open the Tasks folder by clicking on the Tasks banner button near the bottom of the Navigation Pane on the left side of the Outlook window (see figure 3.10).

Note that depending on the size of your window and the options settings in Outlook, that Tasks banner button may not be visible as shown in figure 3.10.

Figure 3.9
In Outlook 2002 the Tasks
folder is opened by clicking
the Tasks shortcut button on
the Outlook Bar.

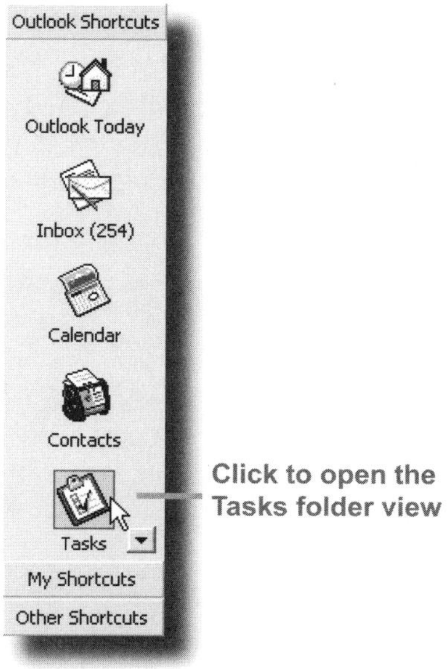

Figure 3.10
Tasks ban-
ner button in
Outlook 2003.

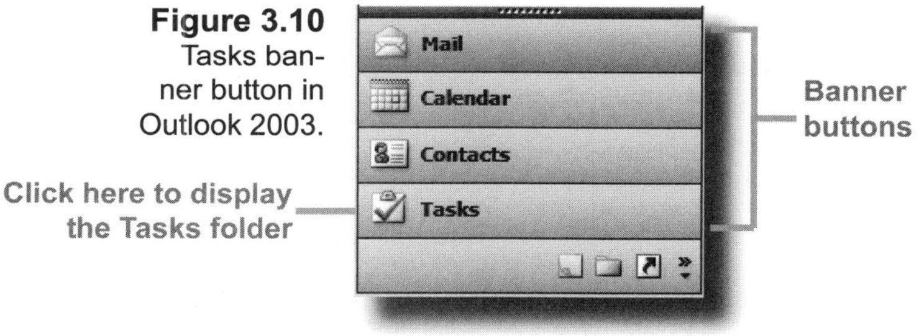

Click here to display
the Tasks folder

If not, look for the Tasks folder icon at the very bottom of the Navigation Pane (see figure 3.11). Clicking that also opens the Tasks folder.

Since you will be opening the Tasks folder quite a bit, if the Tasks folder banner button is replaced with the small icon, I suggest you change the Outlook settings to make it visible as a full-sized banner button. You have two ways to do this.

You can enlarge the banner button area by clicking and dragging the boundary at the top of the banner button area. As you do this, Outlook will convert the small icons at the bottom of the banner button area into full-sized banner buttons, one at a time (see figure 3.12).

Alternatively, you can click the small Configure Buttons icon in the very bottom right corner of the Navigation Pane, also shown in figure 3.12. This will open a popup menu that allows you to show more or fewer banner buttons in the Navigation Pane. Click the Show More Buttons menu choice (see figure 3.13).

Again, as you repeatedly click this menu item, you will sequentially convert the small icons from the very bottom row to banner buttons. Click the Show More Buttons menu choice as many times as needed to convert the Tasks icon into a Tasks banner button.

Figure 3.11
Depending on settings, in Outlook 2003 the Tasks folder banner button may be reduced to a small icon at the bottom of the Navigation Pane.

Task folder icon

Figure 3.12
There are two ways to show more banner buttons in the Navigation Pane.

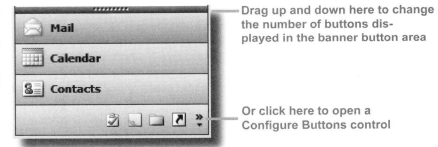

Drag up and down here to change the number of buttons displayed in the banner button area

Or click here to open a Configure Buttons control

Figure 3.13
You can use the Configure Buttons menu to show more banner buttons.

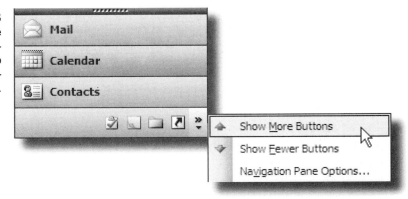

Tasks Folder Views

Outlook, out of the box, ships with a default Tasks folder view called Simple List. It is basically a list of all tasks in the system with only the task subject name and the due date displayed. It is this view that opens when you click on the Tasks folder button the first time. See figure 3.14.

Note that Outlook displays completed tasks (designated with a strike through dimmed font) in this Simple List view.

Figure 3.14
Simple List
view, in the
Tasks folder.

You can display a number of other optional Tasks folder views. For example, Outlook 2003 ships with ten Tasks folder views you might want to use. Think of these views as filtered or selected subsets of your entire task list. Let's say you want to see a list of your tasks without viewing the completed tasks. To do that you would choose the view labeled Active Tasks. The views also vary by showing different task information columns.

Choosing Between Optional Task Views

Outlook 2002

In Outlook 2002, you can select views from the View menu. Open the View menu, choose Current View, and all available views for the currently selected folder are displayed at the top of the submenu, ready for you to choose from.

However, if you wish to be able to see at a glance which view is open, there is a better method of selection. It requires that you add another toolbar allowing you to see and change folder views; here is how you do that. Go to the View menu and click Toolbars; then choose Advanced on the submenu. This adds a new toolbar to the top of your Outlook window (see figure 3.15).

Figure 3.15
The Current
View selec-
tor on the
Advanced
toolbar (Outlook
2002).

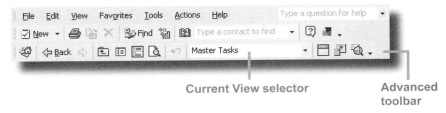

Current View selector   Advanced
toolbar

In that toolbar you will see a box that lists names of task views, with most likely the view named Simple List shown by default (in figure 3.15 Master Tasks is the view name displayed). This is the Current View selector. You use this tool to select other views that may be available for the currently selected folder. For instance, click now on the down arrow at the right edge of that list and choose Detailed List. Note that the task view now changes to a new view (one very similar to Simple List but containing a few more columns). Select Simple List again from that box to return to the default view.

Figure 3.15 shows the Advanced toolbar in Outlook 2002. A similar toolbar exists in Outlook 2003, and is added the same way (View menu, Toolbars submenu). Again, the advantage of using this control over the View menu for choosing views is that it allows Outlook to display the current view name at the top of the window. This is an important feature for users of this system.

Selecting Views in Outlook 2003

You can select these custom views in Outlook 2003 by adding and using the same Advanced toolbar described above for Outlook 2002. There are other means to choose views, but I prefer using the Advanced toolbar because, as with 2002, when in use, it allows me to more easily see which view is open.

Another Current View Selector in 2003

For completeness, however, note that Outlook 2003 has an additional way to select views right on the Navigation Pane. You can select views by choosing from the Current View selector on the left side of the screen (see figure 3.16); it should display after you click on the Tasks banner button. If this Current View selector control is not visible, activate it on the current folder as follows. From the View menu choose Arrange By, and from the Arrange By submenu select Show Views in Navigation Pane. This applies to current folder only.

Always Choose the Folder First

One important lesson to learn about choosing views is this: you always need to choose the folder your view applies to first, before trying to choose the

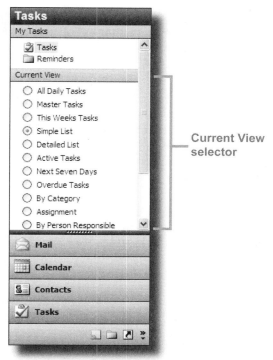

Figure 3.16
Another Current View selector in Outlook 2003.

view from the view list. So if you are trying to open one of the task views, make sure you first click the Tasks folder. Only then will the list in the Current View selector open what you want.

You Are Going to Add New Custom Views

Other than the Simple List view (the default Tasks folder view), I do not advocate that you use any of the other task views that ship with Outlook. The names of the views at first appear to be useful but in fact they really don't fit with the system I'm teaching you. They do not implement the views in just the right ways that I have found work best.

Instead, I am going to show you how to add custom views to the Tasks folder that are more appropriate for use with the eight best practices. You will be accessing those custom views using the same techniques above, however, so become familiar with how to choose these views.

Using Multiple Windows

Something even many experienced users of Outlook do not realize is that you can open multiple windows within Outlook showing different views in each one. This makes it possible, for example, to keep your calendar with TaskPad open in one window and your e-mail open in another. To do this, right-click the icon or banner button for the view that you want to open in the second window, and choose from the shortcut menu: Open in New Window. If you have a very large monitor, then you can display both windows in different parts of your screen. If you have a smaller monitor and the windows overlap, you may wish to use the keyboard shortcut, Alt + Tab, to move between the windows.

If you use multiple windows like this, and you want to have the same windows reopen automatically the next time you open Outlook, be sure to use the File menu Exit command to quit, rather than using the close box on the windows. The latter only closes the current window when multiple windows are open. Using Exit reopens the multiple windows on next use of Outlook.

Outlook Remembers View and Window States

One thing to keep in mind is that any specialized task views you select are retained by Outlook. That means if you select a specialized Tasks folder view and then navigate to one of the other major functionalities like mail or calendar, when you return to the Tasks folder, the previous specialized tasks view that you selected will be what Outlook displays again. This can sometimes be confusing if you have been experimenting with different task views and forget that you left one of the unusual views in place. You need to make a point of reselecting the view you want to come back to later.

Another important point: if you customize a view that is in place, like adding the Task-Pad to the calendar page, Outlook will retain those customizations in that view, even if you quit and reopen Outlook. So if you are experimenting with some of Outlook's many view-formatting options, be sure you know how to undo whatever changes you make; the current named view that is open at the time you make the changes will be forever changed until you manually change it back. In Outlook 2003, you can reset any default view fairly easily; see section entitled Manually Resetting a Default View in Outlook 2003 on page 169 of chapter 7 for details.

Similarly, whatever customizations you make to a window, the next time you open Outlook, it will re-display those customizations. This includes things like the size, dimensions, or number of windows and the position of the windows on the screen.

More about the TaskPad

The TaskPad will be your primary view for inputting and reviewing tasks. Again, you view it by displaying the Calendar folder in Outlook (see figure 3.17).

Side Note: *If you do not see the TaskPad on your Calendar folder as in figure 3.17, you'll need to add it following the instructions on page 46 above.*

While you could work solely from the Tasks folder views described above, using the TaskPad is more convenient than the Tasks folder views because of the TaskPad's location next to the appointments view on the calendar screen. It is important to be able to view both your appointments and your important

Figure 3.17
The TaskPad
is the most
convenient way
to manage your
daily tasks.

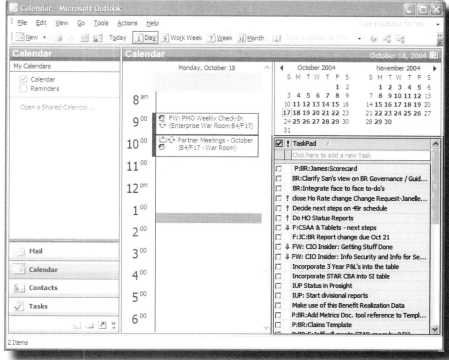

tasks at the same time, and the TaskPad enables this. The TaskPad is just too convenient not to use.

Summary of TaskPad versus Tasks Folder

Let's summarize the similarities and differences between the TaskPad and the Tasks folder views and when we will use each.

■ The TaskPad and the Tasks folder both display different views of the same database of tasks, with the TaskPad usually showing fewer columns of information.

■ The Tasks folder allows a larger window to view your tasks in; the Task-Pad is more limited in size.

■ The TaskPad is conveniently located within the Calendar folder views; in contrast, the Tasks folder opens a separate view that you need to choose from Outlook navigation controls.

■ The TaskPad's custom configurations are saved with the current Calendar folder view; Tasks folders can be customized independently.

■ We will be using the TaskPad for nearly all of our task input and review; we will use the Tasks folder for accessing specialized task views that we will customize.

Ignore the TaskPad View Submenu

Both Outlook 2002 and 2003 have a number of specialized TaskPad views that you can choose from the View menu, under the TaskPad View submenu (see figure below). However, other than starting with the default view called Today's Tasks (which we will modify), none of these specialized views are useful to us once we start using this system. The reason is once you customize the TaskPad view in any manner, the choices in this TaskPad views submenu become void: choosing any of them displays your same modified TaskPad view the way you currently customized it. So, essentially, you should ignore the TaskPad View submenu.

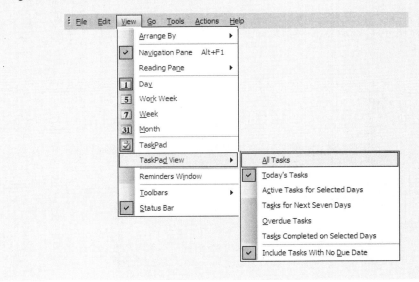

Entering Tasks

Two Methods of Task Entry

There are two methods of entering tasks and they both work whether you are working from the TaskPad or from one of the Tasks folder views. You can use either method according to your preferences and the needs of the moment. The two are the quick entry method and the full entry method. You will access both methods by clicking in the New Item Row, which is located at the very top of the TaskPad and Tasks folder. Note the blank line labeled Click Here to Add a New Task; that's it. (See figure 3.18.)

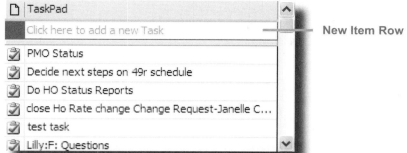

Figure 3.18
Task entry point
in the TaskPad
is the New Item
Row labeled
"Click here
to add a new
Task."

Showing the New Item Row

If the New Item Row is not visible in your TaskPad or Tasks folder, do this:

1   Right-click the column heading of the TaskPad, or the Tasks folder view, and choose Customize Current View... from the shortcut menu as in figure 3.19.

Figure 3.19
Configuring the
TaskPad.

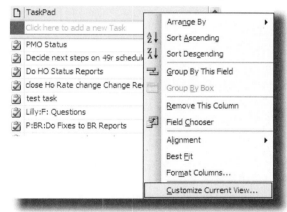

2   A dialog box will open labeled Customize Views. In that dialog box, click the Other Settings button on the middle left.

3   A dialog box labeled Other Settings will open (see figure 3.20). In that dialog box select the Allow In-Cell Editing check box near the top right of the screen, and then select the Show "New Item" Row check box just below it as shown in figure 3.20.

4   Click OK and then OK again to exit the configuration dialog boxes.

The second check box is necessary so that you can edit your tasks in place within the TaskPad.

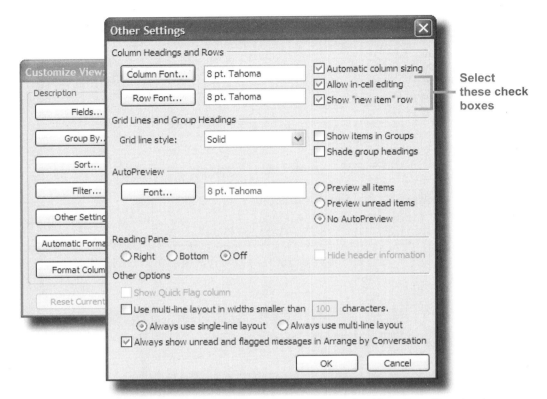

Figure 3.20. Configuring Outlook 2003 to ensure the New Item Row is visible and that tasks can be edited in place. The Outlook 2002 dialog is similar.

Once you are sure the New Item Row is configured to be visible, you can start using either method of task entry.

Quick Entry Method

To use the quick entry method simply single-click anywhere on the New Item Row and that line will become editable. I prefer to click in the Subject box, the wide box in the middle, because it then is selected for editing, and this is normally the first piece of information you will be entering in a new task. I then type in the name of my task. Press Enter on your keyboard or just click off the task line, and your entry will be saved.

Full Entry Method of Creating Tasks

To use the full entry method, instead of single-clicking on the New Item Row, you should double-click that row. This brings up the standard Outlook Task dialog box. (See figure 3.21.)

Figure 3.21
Outlook Task
dialog box.

Side Note: You can also double-click on a blank row below the bottom task to open a new task. This double-click method of opening the Task dialog box also works on existing tasks, if you want to edit them.

Side Note: You can also open a Task dialog box for a new task by using the New command on the toolbar (in the upper left corner of your Outlook screen). Just click on the down arrow next to the New button and choose Task.

Note that the Task dialog box has two tabs near the top of the dialog. The only important tab (to users of this system) is the Task tab, which opens by default and is illustrated in figure 3.21. The most important boxes on that tab are the Subject box, the Due Date box, and the Priority box. I will go over the use of these boxes in a moment.

In general, in this system of task management you can ignore the second tab called Details; you will not be using it.

When to Use Each Method

So which method of creating new tasks do I use? I nearly always use the quick method from within the TaskPad. It is just quicker and easier. However, if you have any text to enter along with the task, you will need to use the full entry method.

Practice Entering Tasks Now

If this is your first time using Outlook for task management, you might want to practice entering some tasks now. Try using the different entry procedures explained above. If you have some task lists on paper, collect them and enter them into Outlook. This is the first step of the first best practice of task management: track all tasks in one location. You may as well start now.

Enter just the Subject box now; ignore the date boxes and all other boxes. We will go over proper use of those boxes later in this chapter.

Editing Tasks

Note that, assuming you made the settings in figure 3.20, you can also edit task information right in the task row; for example, you can change the text in the subject line by clicking on the subject text and typing.

Side Note: *If you're accustomed to double-clicking a word to select it for editing you'll find that operation on a task item opens the Task dialog box instead. This can be a little disturbing at first, but it is not of concern because you can then double-click the subject text from within the Task dialog box to accomplish your editing. Alternatively, click once and then use drag-select on the task item word rather than double-clicking it.*

Marking Tasks Complete

Later, once you complete working on the task and no more effort on that task is required, you should mark the task complete. This changes the task's status and, depending on the view, either removes it from the list or changes its appearance. In the TaskPad, you mark a task complete by checking the box in the Completed column at the left edge of the task (see figure 3.22). Doing this actually changes the value of the Status box of the task to Completed. You can also make this change from within the Task dialog box by editing the Status box.

Completed column

Figure 3.22
Checking the box in the Completed column for a task changes the status of the task to Completed.

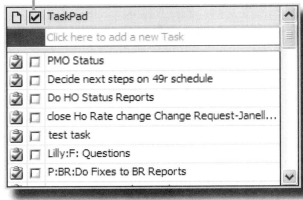

Configuring Outlook for the First Five Best Practices

Now that you have learned how to enter tasks, and you understand the basic use of task views in Outlook, it is time to configure your task views to work with our best practices. You may already have made a few custom configurations in the pages above to expose the New Item Row. A few more configurations are now required.

For this first part of the book there are three configurations you will need to make.

1   Within the Tasks folder, you will create a new custom view to display only master tasks.

2   You will need to reconfigure the TaskPad to represent a daily tasks list. That means we will be applying a custom filter to the list to show only daily tasks (and filter out master tasks). We will also be adding some columns to the TaskPad.

3   And within the Tasks folder, you will create a new custom view called All Daily Tasks. You will see the importance of this view later.

In chapter 9, Advanced Topics, you will be optionally creating additional views; but these three are enough for now.

Creating the Master Tasks Custom View in Outlook 2002 and 2003

If you do nothing else recommended in this book, you should at least implement the master tasks list approach. Doing so will take you further than anything else you might do in Outlook to get control of your tasks.

To start using master tasks in Outlook, you will need a view that displays only master tasks. Let's implement this now in Outlook. It is a relatively simple configuration change to enable.

Key Differentiator: No Dates

First, let's discuss how you're going to distinguish a master task from a daily one in Outlook. The key differentiator between master tasks and daily tasks in this system is that master tasks have no dates assigned them. In contrast, daily tasks *do* have dates assigned: either a due date or a start date. This is a very simple concept to remember: if you want to create a master task in Outlook just create a task without any dates assigned.

For this view then, you are simply going to create a new Tasks folder view, which filters out all tasks except those with no start or end date. You are also going to filter out completed tasks. And you will make some specific selections for which columns of task information to show, and what order to sort the list of tasks on.

A Creating the New View

1 In both versions, you should first make one of the Tasks folder views active. To do this, click the Tasks folder in the Shortcut Bar (in 2002), or click the Tasks banner button on the Navigation Pane (in 2003). This step is required because custom views are usually associated with the currently open folder.

2 Open the View menu.

3 When defining new views, the only significant difference between Outlook 2002 and 2003 is the menu choices you use to get to the Current View window.

In Outlook 2002, choose Current View.

In Outlook 2003 choose Arrange By, and at the bottom of its submenu choose Current View.

From here on the steps for Outlook 2003 and Outlook 2002 are nearly identical; only minor differences in dialog box layout and names exist.

4 Select "Define Views..." from the Current View submenu. The Custom View Organizer dialog box opens (called Define Views in Outlook 2002).

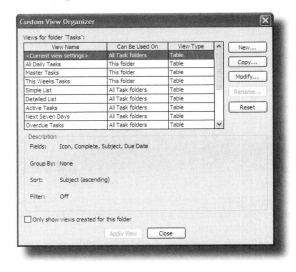

5 Then click New... in the upper right corner.

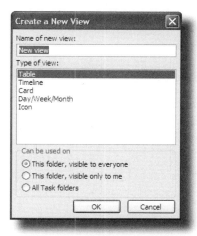

6   Over-type the phrase "New View" with "Master Tasks." Leave the other default settings. Click OK and the dialog box titled Customize View: Master Tasks opens as shown below (in Outlook 2002 this dialog box is titled View Summary).

B   Adding Some Fields

By "fields" we mean the columns of information that are displayed in the new view.

1   Continue by clicking Fields..., which opens the Show Fields dialog box (figure 3.23; this dialog box looks slightly different in Outlook 2002, but all the controls we need to use are the same in both versions).

Figure 3.23
Show Fields
dialog box.

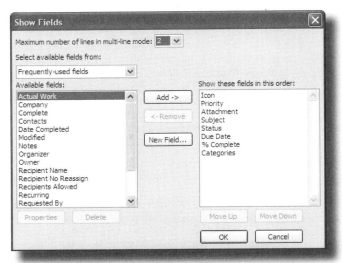

2   The field list in the right side of figure 3.23 may be what you initially
see, but you will need to change it. Use the Add and Remove buttons to
create the following field list on the right side: Icon, Complete, Priority,
Attachment, Subject.

To do this: if you want add a field, first find the field on the list of available fields in the left side of the dialog box, select it, then click Add. If
you want to remove fields from the right side of the dialog box, click the
name on the right first then click Remove.

Note, you must match these names exactly. For example the Complete
field is not the same as the %Complete field.

If you have any trouble finding any of the field names above in the list
on the left, try a different choice in the selection box titled: Select Available Fields From:. Specifically, try the All Task Fields selection in that
box, and then look again at the scrolling field list on the left. That should
display the fields you need.

3   Note that the top to bottom order of fields in this righthand list is the
order that they are displayed left to right in the new view. Adding new
fields to this list will usually put them at the bottom of the list, which
means it will be displayed at the far right of the view. We want these
fields displayed left to right in the following order:

Icon, Complete, Priority, Attachment, Subject

If your order of fields does not match this, then the next step is to use the
Move Up and Move Down buttons below the right side of the dialog box

to adjust the positions of the fields; or simply click the field name and drag it to the desired position.

4 Once the field list is correct and in order, click OK, which returns you to the dialog box shown in Step 6 of Section A.

C Setting the Filter

A filter is a logical statement, or test, that limits the task items that Outlook displays in the new Tasks folder view.

1 On the dialog box that is now open, click Filter… The Filter dialog box opens.

2 Click the Advanced tab. You are going to use this dialog box to build a query-like filter to show only certain kinds of tasks.

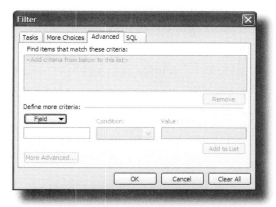

3 Start by clicking Field in the middle left of this dialog box.

4 From the Field list, choose Date/Time fields, and from its submenu choose Due Date (you might have to look under the All Tasks category to find this field).

5 Choose Does Not Exist in the Condition box.

6 Then click Add to List to place this condition in the criteria list at top middle of the dialog box.

7 Leave this dialog box open (do not click OK).

8 Repeat steps C 3 through 6 for Start Date (also set Condition to Does Not Exist). Your dialog box should now look like the next figure.

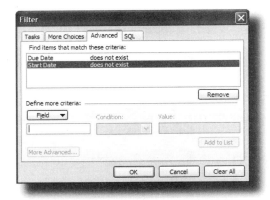

D   Filtering Out Completed Tasks

We do not want to display completed tasks in this view because they will clutter up the task list (and there are other views you can navigate to, to see them).

1   Click Field, and from the Info/Status Fields category choose Status.

2   From the Condition list choose Not Equal To, and from the Value list at right, choose a value of Completed.

3   Then click Add to List to place this condition in the criteria list at the top middle of the dialog box; you should now have three rows of filter criteria.

4   Click OK to close the Filter dialog box, and then click OK again to get out of the Customize view dialog box (View Summary in 2002).

5   Confirm that the new Master Tasks view has been added to your list of views in the Custom View Organizer dialog box (called Define Views in Outlook 2002), then click Apply View to view it.

Your new Master Tasks view looks like figure 3.24 (you may not yet have any tasks in there).

You can now use the Advanced toolbar Current View selector control (added on pages 51 and 52) to pick this view within the Tasks folder whenever you want. And in Outlook 2003 you can choose this view from the Navigation Pane (again, from within the Tasks folder). In fact, note that the only way to determine that the view is present is by referring to this Current View selector; the window retains the folder name Tasks even after configuration.

In the next chapter, we will cover how to use this view effectively. Before that, we need to configure the TaskPad, and one more Tasks folder view.

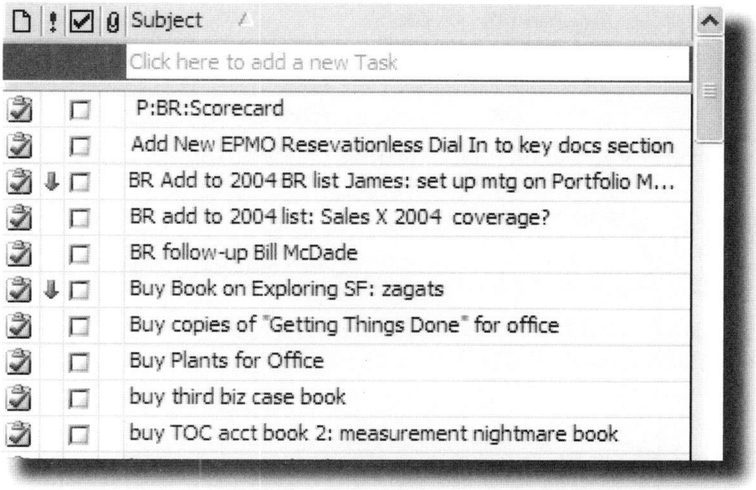

Figure 3.24
The new Master
Tasks view.

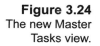

🗋	!	☑	𝕀	Subject ╱	^
				Click here to add a new Task	
📝		☐		P:BR:Scorecard	
📝		☐		Add New EPMO Resevationless Dial In to key docs section	
📝	⬇	☐		BR Add to 2004 BR list James: set up mtg on Portfolio M...	
📝		☐		BR add to 2004 list: Sales X 2004 coverage?	
📝		☐		BR follow-up Bill McDade	
📝	⬇	☐		Buy Book on Exploring SF: zagats	
📝		☐		Buy copies of "Getting Things Done" for office	
📝		☐		Buy Plants for Office	
📝		☐		buy third biz case book	
📝		☐		buy TOC acct book 2: measurement nightmare book	

Configure the TaskPad

Sitting adjacent to your appointment calendar, the TaskPad will be the primary command post for your daily tasks. However, out of the box, the TaskPad in Outlook is not configured correctly for use with this system. You want to get it just right so it works smoothly into your new daily routine and takes advantage of the best practices. To do this, you need to customize the TaskPad so that it will:

- Show only today's daily tasks.

- Filter out completed tasks.

- Show a few additional task columns.

- Sort on priority and due date.

- Display some custom formatting.

First, remember that with the TaskPad there is no way to define a saved TaskPad view like we did for the Tasks folder; rather you need to edit the current view in place. All TaskPad customizations are then saved with the current Calendar folder view. This is not a problem since, once edited, we will be using only one TaskPad configuration. Your configuration will then stay in place indefinitely (unless for some reason you make other configurations to the TaskPad, or select a different Calendar folder view).

Side Note: *Throughout this book and system, we will be working with only one Calendar folder view (the default view called Day/Week/Month). If you decide for some reason to work with or create multiple Calendar Day/Week/Month style views, you will need to add the custom TaskPad configurations to each of them.*

A Configuring the New View

1 Right-click anywhere on the TaskPad heading bar (the bar with the word TaskPad on it).

2 Choose Customize Current View… from the shortcut menu. The following dialog box will opens. You are going to set a few of the view attributes in this dialog box.

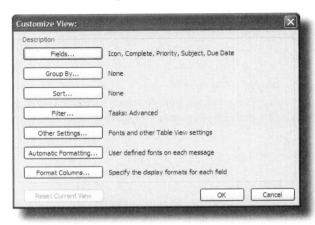

B Adding Some Fields

1 Start by clicking Fields…, which opens the following Show Fields dialog box.

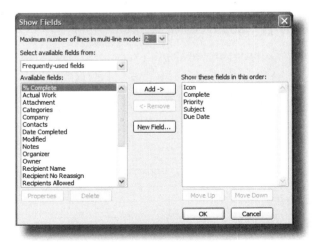

2   Use the Add and Remove buttons to create this list in the right side of that dialog box:

Icon, Complete, Priority, Subject, Due Date.

Use the Move Up and Move Down buttons to place them in the right order; or simply click the field name and drag it to the desired position.

Note again, you must match these names exactly. If you have any trouble finding any of the field names above in the list on the left, try selecting All Task Fields in the selection box titled Select Available Fields From:, and then look again at the scrolling field list. That should display the fields you need.

C   Showing Only Daily Tasks

Once you have all the fields and they are in the correct order in the right side of the dialog box, click OK and return to the Customize View (View Summary) dialog box shown on the previous page.

1   On that dialog box, click Filter....

2   The Filter dialog box opens; click the Advanced tab.

3   Start by clicking Field in the middle left of this dialog box.

4   From the Field list, choose Date/Time fields, and from its submenu choose Due Date.

5   From the Condition list choose On or Before.

6   Type the word Today in the Value box; there is no Today list choice.

7   Then click Add to List to place this condition in the criteria list at top middle of the dialog box.

8   Leave this dialog box open (do not click OK); you are going to create a second query.

9   Click Field in the middle left of the dialog box.

10   From the Field list, choose Info/Status fields, and from its submenu choose Status.

11   From the Condition list, choose Not Equal To.

12   In the Value box select Completed.

13   Then click Add to List to add this condition to the criteria list in the middle of the dialog box, as shown in figure 3.25, and click OK.

Figure 3.25
Setting the
TaskPad filter
condition.

Side Note: *If you happen to look at your TaskPad after doing this configuration, you may notice that some tasks may have disappeared from the TaskPad. Do not worry, this is normal. Think about what you have just done. You have filtered out any tasks that do not have a due date assigned. So if any of your tasks meet that criteria they will be filtered out of the TaskPad view. You have not lost the tasks; rather they will be visible either in your Master tasks view that you created earlier, or in the Simple List view. Later you will go through all your tasks and verify whether they should be master tasks or daily tasks.*

D **Setting the TaskPad Sort Order**

We want high priority tasks to sort to the top of the TaskPad. It is also useful to have medium priority tasks with newer due dates sort to the top of the medium group of tasks. To enable this:

1 From the Customize View (View Summary) dialog box click Sort...; you will see the dialog box in figure 3.26.

2 Set the values of the first and second boxes to what you see in figure 3.26. Then click OK.

Figure 3.26
Setting the
TaskPad sort
order.

E   Disabling the Overdue Tasks Rule, and Formatting Tasks Due Today

The above configurations represent the primary changes needed to the Task-Pad. Now for some final formatting.

1   From the Customize View (View Summary) dialog box click Automatic Formatting, and you will see the next dialog box.

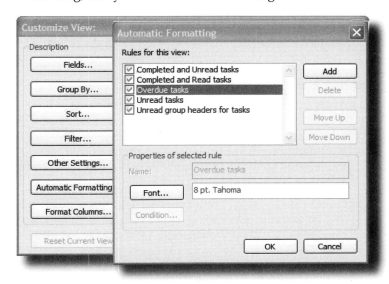

2   Clear the check box next to the Overdue Tasks rule in the middle of the dialog box.

3 Click Add to create a new rule and call it Due Date Today.

4 With the new rule selected, click Font…, and on the Font dialog box select the Underline check box, then click OK.

5 Click Condition… on the left side of the dialog box, and define a filter, as shown below.

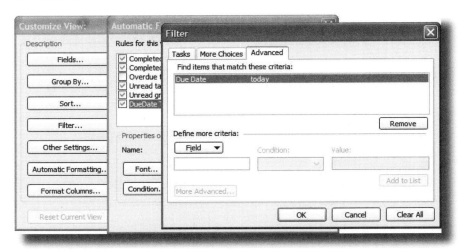

6 Then click Add to List, and then click OK. Click OK again, and then again, to exit all configuration windows.

That's it for the initial setup of the TaskPad Custom View. Chapter 4 discusses how to use this view. First, one more view.

Creating the All Daily Tasks View

In configuring the TaskPad to show daily tasks, what we have really done is configured it to show daily tasks that we are ready to work on now. In other words, we are showing tasks that *we have not deferred to start work on later*. When working from the TaskPad we only want to see tasks that we might want to work on today; this configuration accomplishes that. Let me elaborate.

One common task management technique we will teach ahead is that if you decide that it is better to start a particular daily task later, rather than today, then you should set the date to a later date. What this does is remove the task from the current daily tasks list that you see in your TaskPad. This removes clutter from your current daily view and allows you to focus better on the tasks at hand. The deferred task will appear in the TaskPad when its day comes.

What this leads to, however, is the need to have an additional view that allows you to look at those daily tasks you have deferred. For example, let's say today is Monday and you have deferred a task to start appearing on your task list on Thursday. You may need to refer to that task today, either to change it or to see details of it. You cannot do that from the TaskPad the way it is configured.

So to view that task, you could go into the Simple List view in the Tasks folder; all tasks are displayed there, and it will be visible there. However, that view mixes all tasks together, daily and master, as well as all completed tasks; it can get busy. Better is to create a view that shows only daily tasks, both current and deferred. That is what the All Daily Tasks view provides. We will create it as another view in the Tasks folder.

A   Creating the New View

Recall that when defining new views, the only significant difference between Outlook 2002 and 2003 is the menu choice you use to get to the Current View window.

1   In both versions you should first click on the Tasks folder in the Folder List (in 2002), or on the Tasks banner button on the Navigation Pane (in 2003), to make one of the Tasks folder views active. This step is required because Outlook creates all custom views within the currently open folder.

2   Open the View menu.

3   In Outlook 2002, select Current View.

In Outlook 2003 choose Arrange By, and at the bottom of its submenu choose Current View.

From here on the steps for Outlook 2003 and Outlook 2002 are essentially identical.

4   Choose "Define Views..." from the Current View submenu. The Custom View Organizer dialog box opens (called Define Views in Outlook 2002).

5 Then click New… in the upper right corner.

6 Over-type the phrase "New View" with "All Daily Tasks." Leave all other default settings unchanged. Click OK and the dialog box called Customize View: All Daily Tasks opens (in Outlook 2002 this dialog box is called View Summary).

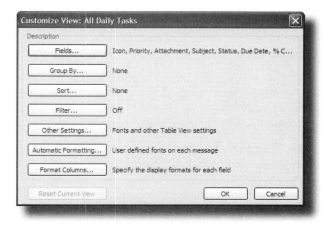

B   Adding Some Fields

Again, by "fields" we mean the columns of information displayed in the Tasks folder views.

1   Continue by clicking Fields…, which opens the following Show Fields dialog box (this dialog box looks slightly different in Outlook 2002, but all the controls we need to use are the same in both versions).

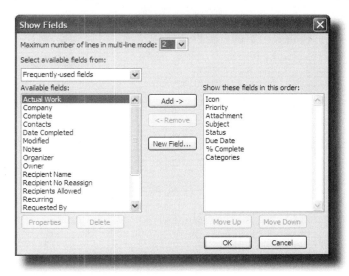

2   Use the Add and Remove buttons to create this list in the right side of that dialog box: Icon, Complete, Priority, Attachment, Subject, Due Date.

Use the Move Up and Move Down buttons to place them in the right order (or simply click the field name and drag it to the desired position).

And again note, you must match these names exactly. For example the Complete field is not the same as the %Complete field.

If you have any trouble finding any of the field names above in the list on the left, try selecting All Task Fields in the selection box titled Select Available Fields From:, and then look again at the scrolling field list. That should display the fields you need.

3 Click OK... which returns you to the Customize View: All Daily Tasks dialog box (in Outlook 2002 it's called View Summary).

C Setting the Filter

Showing Only Tasks with Dates

1 On the dialog box that is now open, click Filter..., and the Filter dialog box opens.

2 Click the Advanced tab. You are going to use this next dialog box (figure 3.27) to build a query-like filter, to show only tasks with dates assigned.

3 Start by clicking Field in the middle left of figure 3.27.

Figure 3.27
The Advanced tab on the Filter dialog box.

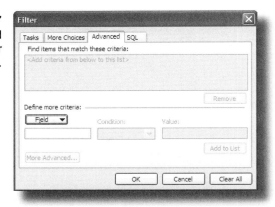

4 From the Field list, choose Date/Time fields, and from its submenu choose Due Date (you might have to look under the All Tasks category to find this field).

5 Then, from the Condition list in the middle of the screen, choose Exists.

6 Then click Add to List to place this condition in the criteria list at top middle of screen.

7 Leave this window open (do not click OK).

D Filtering Out Completed Tasks

1   Click Field, and under the Info/Status category, choose Status (you might have to look under the All Task Fields category to find this Statue field).

2   Choose a Condition of Not Equal To, and from the Value list at right, choose a value of Completed.

3   Then click Add to List to place this condition in the criteria list at top middle of screen.

4   Click OK to close the Filter dialog box.

E Making Some Formatting Settings

1   Back at the Customize View (View Summary in 2002) dialog box click Automatic Formatting.

2   Clear the Overdue tasks check box. This prevents tasks whose due date is older than today from being colored red, which is something not needed in our system.

3   Click OK to close the Automatic Formatting dialog box.

4   Click OK to close the Customize View dialog box (View Summary in 2002).

Now confirm that the new All Daily Tasks view has been added to your list of views in the Custom View Organizer dialog box (called Define Views in Outlook 2002), then click Apply View to view it. Your new All Daily Tasks view looks like Figure 3.28.

Figure 3.28
The new All Daily Tasks view, within the Tasks folder.

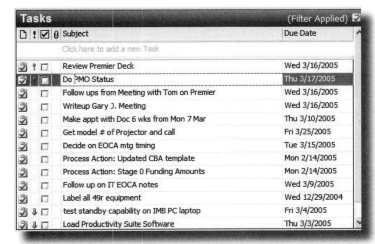

You can now use the Advanced toolbar Current View selection control (added on pages 51 and 52) to pick this view within the Tasks folder whenever you want. And in Outlook 2003 you can choose this view from the Navigation Pane (again, from within the Tasks folder).

Summary

By now you understand the basic use of task views in Outlook, and you have applied the custom configurations described above. These configurations will allow you to use your task views to work with our eight best practices.

Note this: if by chance you found the above step-by-step instructions cumbersome and did not complete them, visit www.workdaycontrol.com for other configuration and training options. There we will try to get you fully ready for gaining the benefits of this system in the chapters ahead.

In the next chapter, I cover how to use these new views and configurations effectively.

Chapter Four

Applying Task Management Best Practices in Outlook

The first four of the eight productivity-enhancing best practices incorporated into the Total Workday Control system represent the core task management set. They are:

1 Tracking all tasks in Outlook Tasks System

2 Using a master tasks list kept separate from your daily tasks list

3 Using a simple prioritization system that emphasizes must-do-today tasks

4 Writing only next actions on your daily list

The material here takes the configurations made in chapter 3 for these four best practices and shows you how to use them. Implementing the fifth best practice, daily and weekly planning, is the topic of chapter 5. Effective e-mail management is covered in chapters 6 and 7, and the final best practice, delegation, is the subject of chapter 8.

1. Tracking All Tasks in Outlook Tasks System

Why Track Tasks in One Location?

Keeping Things Simple

You need to track all your tasks in one location, and that's Outlook's tasks management system. Period. Why?

Because the time and confusion associated with tracking tasks listed in multiple locations will preclude you from taking your tasks lists seriously. It will preclude you from prioritizing across all tasks effectively.

You need to be able to look at one daily tasks list and know that it holds everything of concern for the day. You need to be able to prioritize and plan within one system. Multiple systems become confusing and unreliable. One system keeps things simple. Outlook is your best single system within which to do this. Refer to chapter 2, page 24, for further discussion of this topic, if needed.

What This Means in Practice

This means if you are sitting at your computer you should never enter a task anywhere but directly into the TaskPad within Outlook. So no more sticky notes on your computer screen, no more slips of paper with today's list, and you should even avoid using a journal to collect to-dos while sitting at your computer. Rather, as soon as the need to record a new to-do becomes apparent, type it right into Outlook. This might take some getting used to, but before long it will become second nature.

It also means copying the action items in voice mail into your system as soon as you listen to it. It means having an effective means of dealing with tasks you get when away from your desk.

Mobile Strategies: Meetings

I briefly addressed the topic of mobile solutions in chapter 1 (page 17); let's cover it more here.

The challenge with having all your tasks on your desktop Outlook is how to update and review tasks easily while you are in a meeting away from your desktop computer. Certainly, writing down tasks on paper in a meeting is expected. When you do this, however, as soon as possible enter them in Outlook when you get back to your desk.

PDAs (or Smartphones and Blackberrys) may also appeal to you. As discussed in chapter 1, I previously used a Palm handheld extensively and later a Pocket PC. After that I moved to a Tablet PC and found that platform by far the most useful; I found that for use in meetings, the small screen size on the Palm and Pocket PC was pretty limiting compared to the full-sized screen and full-powered software of the Tablet PC; I have been spoiled. So using a Tablet PC is my current recommendation for meetings, and even much preferable to using a laptop. This is the topic of my first book, *Seize the Work Day: Using the Tablet PC to Take Total Control of Your Work and Meeting Day*. But by all means, if you are happy using your PDA in meetings then continue to do so.

Using Paper versus a PDA

I have also recently worked in an office environment with just a desktop computer. In that environment, the extent of my travel was from my desk to a meeting room and back. I, for the first time in a while, had no Tablet PC and no PDA. The Tablet PC was out, because it was a nonstandard device and not allowed on the network in that organization. The PDA I gave up on because I found I was using only a small portion of it: only the to-do list and a little of the calendar. And given that's all I was using, I found I had more success with merely printing out my desktop-based Outlook task and appointment list for the day on one page and taking that to meetings (figure 4.1).

Figure 4.1
How a printed Outlook schedule (Day View) looks; this is probably your simplest mobile solution.

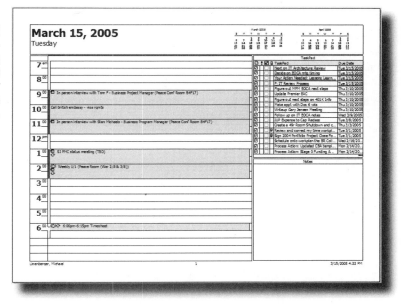

I found using a full-sized piece of paper preferable to navigating through the tiny screens on a Palm or Pocket PC during a meeting. Because of the small screen and the need to scroll and change views often to see what I wanted to see, using a PDA in a meeting was distracting. I disliked having to click carefully the tiny on-screen buttons to scroll through and find the information I needed. I often had to study the small PDA screen closely to update it correctly, and that tended to break the flow and interactions of the meeting. In particular, trying to enter a new task into a PDA during a meeting was difficult. So I ended up writing down my new tasks on paper anyway, which defeated the advantage of having a mobile device.

Compared to a PDA, I like having a full sheet of paper to see the complete view of my day and tasks at a glance while in a meeting. I like having lots of room to add thoughts about newly added tasks. It fits better into the flow and

dynamics of a meeting. In other words, there is a certain favorable convey-
ance to a full-sized paper task list that the small screen of a PDA lacks. I need
to ensure of course that whatever changes I make on the paper I then enter
into Outlook when I return to my desktop computer, but that becomes a part
of my task review process. You can do quite well with a simple desktop computer and a networked printer, and that's the assumed mobile configuration
we will use throughout this book.

Optional PDA Software

Both the Palm and Pocket PC PDAs ship with calendar, task, and synchronization software. There are third party synchronization and organizer software packages available
that often do better than the default packages, particularly in their ability to imitate and
synchronize with Outlook functionality. For Palm these include Intellisync by Intellisync
Corp, KeySuite by Chapura Software, Beyond Contacts by DataViz, and Agendus by
Iambic. Many of these enable synchronizing an unlimited number of Outlook categories, which later you'll see can be important.

For the Pocket PC, the default package Pocket Outlook is hard to beat. But also look at
Pocket Informant and Agenda Fusion.

Paper over a PDA is just my preference; yours may be different. And if I were
in a more mobile environment, say traveling often by car or by plane, then I
suspect I would prefer a PDA or Smartphone.

If you do use a PDA, keep in mind that you will need to get in the habit of
synchronizing your PDA consistently (see inset next page). And you will not
be able to implement most of the views that I've described in Outlook within
your PDA. This latter point, not being able to implement the same views in
a PDA as you can in Outlook, is usually not a problem as long as you can
return to your desktop (or laptop, or tablet) for your serious task and e-mail
management.

The details of using and configuring a PDA are beyond the scope of this book;
I refer you to the following books for instructions: *How to Do Everything with
Your Palm Handheld,* and *How to Do Everything with Your Pocket PC.*

The Preferred Mobile Solution

One final plug for the Tablet PC: using the Tablet PC is still my preferred
solution, particularly when the mobile use is in meetings. The Tablet PC
has none of the shortcomings I have listed above. Its screen is large enough
and its handwriting recognition fast enough. And my full copy of Outlook
is available for inputting tasks as I get them in meetings, with all the custom
views defined in this book available.

Side Note: *As mentioned in chapter 1, I recommend using a Tablet PC for task and e-mail management primarily if you can plug your Tablet PC into the network at work; unfortunately, many companies will not allow that. If you cannot then try synchronizing; one useful tasks and calendar synchronization tool that does not require a network connection is OutlookSync by Curosoft.*

Tasks Received While on the Run

Once this system is in place you will find that there are a number of mobile scenarios that complicate things. They may require some thought to keep them worked into your system. Each of these represent common situations where you may receive tasks while in-between meetings or away from the office. The goal of the points below is to prevent you from falling back into the habit of trying to keep tasks in your head.

Hallway Conversations

If a colleague or supervisor stops you in the hall and dumps an unwanted to-do on you, put the onus back on them by stating: "Hey, could you send me an e-mail on that, otherwise I will forget this." The system taught here handles such e-mailed tasks extremely well.

Capturing Tasks

For other scenarios, and if the above approach is not practical for the hallway conversation situation, you need a way to capture tasks effectively and remember to transfer them later.

If you are proficient with entering text into your PDA and you have it with you, do that. Or you can carry a small pocket notepad. Alternatively, consider carrying a voice recorder; many cell phones have voice recorders built in.

Home Computer

If you are working at your home computer when a task is identified, you can send an e-mail to your work address whose title describes the next action. I do this a lot and it works great. Skills learned in the chapters ahead of converting e-mails to tasks will serve you well when you get back to the office. The reverse is also useful: if you are at work and you remember things you need to do when you get home, send an e-mail home.

Mobile Voice Mail

Often you receive and listen to a voice mail on your mobile phone that contains a to-do which you later forget is saved there. There are a couple ways to handle this. You can leave the message unsaved. On many phones, this leaves the message icon active; so when you see this fact at your desk, you can listen to messages again and record it in Outlook. Or instead, after listening to the message, you might call your voice mail at work and dictate to yourself a summary of the task.

Getting Started: Collecting Your Scattered Tasks

When you first start using this system you will probably have task lists hidden in many locations. So one of your first actions after you set up and configure Outlook correctly for task management is to find those task lists and transfer them into Outlook. They may be in the paper notebook you carry around with you. They may be implicit within stacks of paper on your desk. They may be buried in e-mails far down your Inbox list. They may be in your head.

Tasks inside Your Head

Let's start with tasks inside your head. After all, if you feel any anxiety at all about the large number of tasks you have to do, you probably have many of those tasks bouncing around inside your head right now. Get them out of there. Spend some time at your TaskPad and do a brain dump. Just write down whatever comes to mind that seems to be an action item. To do this right, you should use some of the task recording approaches described in the sections ahead; but if you are inspired, do it now. You can sort out the right way to classify these tasks later. Many people feel tremendous relief when they do this brain dump and then can keep up with new tasks in the days and months ahead.

Tasks inside E-Mails

One major source of tasks these days is your e-mail Inbox. It is remarkable how many actions are either explicitly requested or subtly implied in the text of the e-mails that you get. Many e-mails require a follow-up action beyond just a simple quick reply.

A common reason why we leave e-mail in our Inbox is that we know there is something more that we need to do as a result of a given e-mail. In other words, the e-mail contains a task. Since we often review mail in brief periods between meetings, there is often no time to act on e-mail immediately, and so we commonly leave important read e-mails in the Inbox intending to come back to them later to complete the required actions. Unfortunately, more often than not, it is usually some time before we finally go back through our old e-mails. On each new visit to the Inbox, we usually focus first on the new mail that has arrived since our last visit. And when (or if) we do finally find time to go through the *old* e-mails, we usually do not have enough time to get through *all* of them. As a result, a large number of explicit or implied tasks go unanswered. And some important task assignments can fall through the cracks. Sound familiar?

The solution is this: as soon as you read an e-mail that contains an implied task (other than a quick reply), immediately convert the e-mail to a task on the Outlook task list. This is a form of the age-old rule to identify whether an action item exists in incoming communications and to record it. In this case, the entire e-mail is converted and the title reset to match the implied next action. Very easy built-in Outlook techniques convert e-mails to tasks in seconds; we review those in detail in chapter 6.

Once you get in the habit of converting e-mails with tasks in them into Outlook tasks, it is remarkable how much relief you will feel. No longer will your e-mail Inbox cause your stomach to tighten every time you look at it. You will start to gain a reputation as someone who can be trusted with e-mail communications. People will find they do not need to interrupt you to give you simple requests. There is a dramatic change in team efficiency once an entire

Unified Messaging

Regarding work voice mail, one of the greatest recent inventions in voice mail technology is unified messaging. This is an intelligent link between your voice mail system and the Exchange e-mail server that places entries into Outlook for each voice mail you receive. From there you can convert them to tasks as needed. If your company does not have unified messaging and you receive many voice mail messages, encourage them to get it.

Unified messaging is available from a variety of vendors, and usually from your voice mail vendor. This is a major upgrade to a company's voice mail and e-mail system, so do not expect this to arrive overnight.

team adopts this habit. E-mail is an incredibly efficient tool if it is used correctly and not ignored; this technique alone allows that to happen.

Tasks inside Your Piles of Paper

If you are to be truly successful in clearing your psyche from a sense of being out of control, you also need to go through your paper stacks, find those hidden tasks, and transfer them to your task list. Once you do, and you have classified tasks according to the rules below, there is a remarkable sense of knowing where you stand. You will have defused your hidden time bombs. No longer will you have the nagging feeling that you have forgotten things. There is an increased sense of confidence in your ability to command your world.

Note however that going through your physical paper piles can be a daunting task. This is because each piece of paper often has a history of uncompleted actions associated with it. If the papers are important, your mind is likely to get swept up in a swirl of regret over uncompleted commitments and uncertainties on how to proceed. Most people do not get very far through their piles before they give up or get sidetracked on one of the identified activities and never come back to the rest. Because of the energy and time required, I suggest this is one of the last things you do in this attempt to get truly organized.

That said, David Allen in his book *Getting Things Done* has an excellent chapter on how to do this effectively. He is a master at this and I recommend you read this section of his book if you are preparing to dig out from an out-of-control collection of desktop piles. My interpretation of his message is this: clearly separate your pile-cleaning time from your task-processing time. If you discover things that need to be done on one of the papers you are cleaning out, don't do it immediately (unless it is to toss it out). Rather, write the to-do on a sticky, stick it on the paper item, put the paper in a "to be processed" pile, and keep going. Do not get sidetracked from your cleaning. Only after all your stacks are cleaned and you are left with one "to be processed" pile, only then come back and either work on the discovered tasks (if they can be done quickly) or copy them into your Outlook TaskPad. See the section below, Collecting versus Working Tasks, for more on this. To really do this well, though, get David's book and follow his instructions. He also has an excellent section on simple approaches to filing so you have a place to put all those things in your paper piles. His system is the first paper filing system that has really worked for me and I highly recommend it.

One of David's recommendations for dealing with paper that I want to emphasize here is this: once you get your piles cleaned up, create one physical Inbox to receive all new pieces of paper that come to your desk. Make yourself a promise that as new paper arrives (particularly if it may contain tasks) you place that paper in this physical Inbox. Then you should set time aside to process the contents of that Inbox. During that processing, as you find tasks in those papers, you should immediately write those tasks into your Outlook task list and then file the paper away. Again, you can find details in David's book.

Collecting versus Working Tasks

An important best practice when collecting your tasks is to separate the task *collection* time from the task *action* time. I can guarantee that you will be tempted to act on many of them as you find them. There are several problems with doing this. First is that until you see and prioritize all your tasks you really do not know which tasks you should be working on first.

Second, the act of getting all your tasks collected, and all of your hidden spots emptied, is a phenomenally liberating accomplishment. It's one you should achieve as quickly as possible. If you allow yourself to interrupt your collection process, you may find that you never get to the bottom of all your piles, and you will be left with a nagging feeling that you haven't gotten everything under control.

Third, the energy required for task collection is different from the energy required for task action. A different mindset is needed for scanning through large numbers of items as opposed to focusing and working on one. Once you are into the cleaning and task collection mode, take advantage of that energy while you have it and don't disrupt it while it's present. Working within one mode will keep you optimized for the goal; you will become much more effective if you stay in that mode. Spend as much quality time as you can collecting tasks and copying them into Outlook, and plan on working them later. Urgent items should be marked with a High Outlook priority so you get to them first when you do start working them.

That said, if you are in the collection and cleaning mode, say by going through your piles on your desk, going through old e-mails, or going through old voice mails, and you come across an important task that takes only a minute to complete, you might as well act on it at the time. Otherwise, the time it takes you to think about and write down a task will exceed the action time itself. Do not, however, fall into the trap of estimating one minute and actually taking ten to complete the task. Be attentive to this, and if you catch yourself doing this then immediately return to task collection mode.

2. Using a Master Tasks List Kept Separate from Your Daily Tasks List

As stated earlier, using a separate master tasks list is one of the most important best practices you can adopt for task management. It enables you to create a manageable daily list free from the clutter of lower importance tasks. And it gives you a safe place to store those lower priority tasks so you can revaluate them later to check for changes in their importance and timeliness. A long list of tasks becomes unmanageable; using the master tasks list helps prevent this from happening with your daily tasks list. See chapter 2, page 26, if you want to review our earlier discussion of this important best practice.

Implementing in Outlook

We have already created the master tasks list view in the configuration steps in chapter 3. So how do you use it? Interestingly, you can assign master tasks without ever opening the master tasks list view. I create most of my master tasks from within the TaskPad. So how does this work? The key is in the way we configured Outlook to differentiate between master tasks and daily tasks.

Distinguishing Between Daily and Master Tasks

Master Tasks Are Tasks Without Assigned Dates

This system rests on the convention that master tasks, by definition, have no dates entered for them in Outlook. The presence of a start or due date indicates a daily task. Any task without any assigned dates is treated as a master task.

This is why if you already had tasks in Outlook before you configured your TaskPad per the instructions in chapter 3, your tasks were automatically placed in either the master task view or the daily tasks view.

Converting Between Daily and Master Tasks

In fact, and this is key, you can convert a daily task to a master task merely by removing the date entries. You can convert a master task to a daily task by merely adding a date entry. This fact will become very important as you use this system.

If you had tasks in your Outlook task list before starting to use this system, you may want to stop at this point and go though both your daily and master list to true up the placement of those previous tasks. Add or remove dates as needed to move tasks to their correct lists.

Entering Tasks

Enter from Any Task View, but Usually from the TaskPad

We went over how to enter and edit tasks in Outlook in chapter 3, pages 56-60. As a reminder, you have two places from which you can enter tasks: from the TaskPad (figure 4.2) and from any one of the dedicated Tasks folder views. I tend to enter all my tasks within the TaskPad. This is primarily because I have meetings scheduled throughout the day and so I always

Figure 4.2
TaskPad.

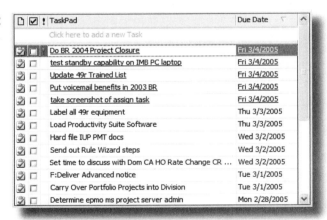

have my Calendar folder visible within Outlook to keep track of those meetings. Having the TaskPad right there, in sight, is quite convenient. Keep in mind that it is the daily tasks list that you'll be looking at throughout the day, and this is what the TaskPad, the way we have configured it, shows.

And as you recall you can enter tasks either directly into the new item row at the top of the task list, or by opening a new Task dialog box and entering there. Since I normally just enter the task subject, due date, and priority, and since all of those fields are visible on the TaskPad in our configuration, the in-row entry method is sufficient and what I usually use.

My Usual Entry Routine

My task entry process is usually this: as soon as I am aware of the need for a task to be recorded, I type in the subject, stop to consider whether this should be a master task, and if not, mouse over and enter a due date. I then stop and decide whether the due date is a hard due date, meaning I consider if this is an absolute delivery day or not. If not (more on this below), I usually leave the priority at normal, and then click off the new item entry row which enters the task. It is important to remember that as soon as you click your mouse off the new item row, Outlook saves the task and clears it from the row. So be sure you are done editing before clicking away from the row.

Disappearing Tasks

Make especially sure you have entered a due date in the Due Date field (if you intend to) before you click off the task; otherwise, the task will disappear from your TaskPad and move to the master tasks list. Remember, master tasks are defined by the absence of a date entry.

If you did not intend this task to be a master task, the disappearance can be a bit disconcerting. To recover you need to open the master task view, scroll through it and find the newly entered task, and then add your date information. Since the master task view does not normally display dates as columns in the view, you'll have to double-click the task to open it to be able to add a due date. You will accidentally create master tasks a number of times before you will get the hang of always entering date information for daily tasks.

Use of Date Fields

This brings up the subject of entering start and due dates. Some subtleties are involved.

The Due Date Is Your Start Date

For daily tasks, you may wonder when you enter task information in the task tab of the Task dialog box (figure 4.3) whether you should enter a date in the Start Date field or Due Date field or in both. In the system I teach here, I recommend you either leave the Start Date field blank or set it to be the same as the Due Date field. In other words, I generally ignore the Start Date field, and treat the Due Date field like a start date.

You could use either Outlook's Start Date field or the Due Date field and ignore the other. The reason I focus on the Due Date field and ignore the Start Date field is both due to technical limits of Outlook and principles of this system.

Outlook Technical Limits

Technically, if you are only going to use one field, the Due Date field is the only one that works in Outlook. Here's why. If within the task tab of an Outlook task you try to set only the Start Date field, Outlook will automatically

Figure 4.3
Task tab of the
Task dialog box.

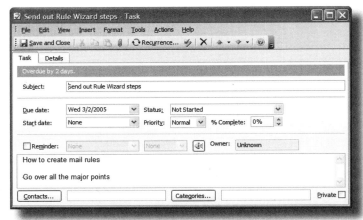

set the Due Date field to the same as the Start Date field. The reverse is different. If within the task tab of an Outlook task you try to set only the Due Date
field, Outlook will leave the Start Date field alone. So the Due Date field is the
one to use.

Key Principle: Your Due Date Is Your "Do" Date

This technical limit also fits with the way daily tasks are defined in this system. Remember, you will be writing all daily tasks as next actions, and next
actions are usually doable in one sitting. So the day you start a next action is
normally the day you complete it. Thus the due date is your start date. Think
of it this way: the due date is your "Do" date, your action date. Since the dates
are the same you really only need one date to work with.

And unless you mark a task as must do today, there is no problem letting a
task forward on past the date in the Due Date field. So the Due Date field acts
even more like a start date in that respect. We will use this behavior to our
advantage.

For example, all the views that we have configured in chapter 3 assume that
you will be using the due date this way, that is as your start date. So, for
instance, in the TaskPad, if you forward-date a task, it will first show up on
your TaskPad the date the due date arrives. If you choose not to work the task
that day, it will then continue to forward from day to day on your TaskPad
until you mark it completed.

Future Due Dates

If the due date is set to a date in the future, when you save the task it will
disappear from the TaskPad (and then reappear the day of that due date).
This feature keeps your daily tasks list uncluttered by not showing you tasks
until you need to work on them; remember we only want to see *active* tasks
on the TaskPad for any given day. If after the task disappears you think you

may have made an error in entering the task, then you can find the task by examining the All Daily Tasks view within the Tasks folder (we created that view in chapter 3).

By the way, you might think that if you select a future date on the Calendar folder view, that forward-dated tasks associated with that date will come into view in the TaskPad. This is not how the TaskPad operates. Rather it always displays the same list of tasks no matter which date you have visible in the calendar; the filter on the due date is always relative to today (as indicated by the clock date and time on your computer). This behavior makes sense since we are dealing with a next action list, and items in this list, once they appear, are normally to be completed as soon as possible. But if you do decide you need to view tasks scheduled to appear on future days then, again, just navigate to the All Daily Tasks view within the Tasks folder.

Future Hard Due Dates: Enter in Subject Line

You may wonder, though, if the Due Date field is used to indicate the task start date, and the task will forward on from day to day until you complete it, what if you actually have a hard due date for that task? What if the draft sales report really is due to your boss on Thursday October 12? How do you indicate that when you enter the task? How do you show that you should not let the task forward on, that you should really finish it that day?

First, note that next actions with hard due dates are relatively rare; next actions usually represent intermediate steps to larger goals. So most of the time you do not need to indicate a hard due date.

But sometimes indicating a hard due date *is* necessary and here's how you should handle that: write the due date into the subject line of the task. For example, enter in the subject line: "Write sales report draft, DUE: Oct. 12." That way, every time you look at the task you know that this task has a hard due date, and you know immediately what that date is. This is a great way to emphasize a hard due date and still make use of the Outlook Due Date field for tasks with softer actual due dates. See inset next page for discussion of how to do same with soft due dates.

Other Fields in the Task Dialog Box

Large Text Field

Perhaps 10 percent of the time, I enter text in the large text field at the bottom of the Task tab. This is a very good place to put task details and, most commonly, is where I will paste details of a task copied from the e-mail that generated the task (automatic ways of doing this are described in chapter 6). Or I may copy notes out of my notebook, notes that I collected when the task was assigned to me in a meeting.

Artificial Hard Due Dates

You may be tempted to assign hard due dates to tasks that are not really due but that you want to complete in a timely fashion. This is a common practice among the older task-management techniques; they usually state: "Assign a due date to all tasks or they will not get done."

There is some truth to this, but in practice this technique usually fails. Why? Because you are trying to trick yourself and your mind is not so easily tricked. If you write down an artificial due date, your mind knows it is artificial and will treat it differently from your other tasks. You then will get into the habit of letting these tasks with artificial due dates slip beyond the stated date. Then what happens? You start to lose respect for any recorded hard due date. You begin to waste time by asking yourself every time you see a hard due date: "Is this really due today or did I just set that artificially?" Energy is lost and important tasks are dropped in this second-guessing. Rather, reserve hard due dates for those tasks that really are due on a certain day.

An alternative technique for soft due dates is this: use an approach similar to above but write the word "GOAL:" instead of "DUE:" That way you avoid weakening true due dates but still have a way to indicate a preferred time frame.

There are also other means to drive medium priority tasks to completion. I discuss those in chapter 5, pages 111-113.

Status, Percent Complete, and Owner Fields

The other primary fields are shown in figure 4.4, and include Status, % Complete, and Owner fields. I ignore the % Complete field. Reason: since I am creating only next actions on my daily tasks list, these tasks should be relatively discrete and not subject to partial completion. I have found little value to marking such a task partially complete. That's also why I do not use the

Figure 4.4
Primary task fields in the Task dialog box.

various values available in the Status field such as In Progress, Deferred, and Waiting on Someone Else. While these status values are used extensively in the FranklinCovey system, Outlook has other ways that we will use to indicate these status values.

For example if you move a task to the master tasks list or set its start date in the daily list to a future date, that is the same as deferring the task, and it will disappear from your TaskPad view. There is no need to set the status to say the same. And the status In Progress makes little sense for discrete next action tasks that you normally complete in one sitting. The status Waiting on Someone Else is also not needed because we will use more effective tracking tools to indicate when tasks need follow-up (described in chapters 6, 7, and 8). I also ignore the Owner field. This and many of these other fields are more useful when integrating Outlook tasks with other Microsoft products such as Microsoft Project, or if using the formal Assign Task button described (but avoided) in chapter 8, Delegation.

Reminder Check Box

I leave the Reminder check box on the Task dialog box unchecked. And I reconfigured Outlook to by default leave that check box unchecked when creating new tasks. You do that reconfiguration by going to the Tools menu, Options, Preferences tab, click on the Task Options button, and clear the bottom choice: Set Reminders on Tasks with Due Dates. (See figure 4.5.)

Figure 4.5
Primary task
fields.

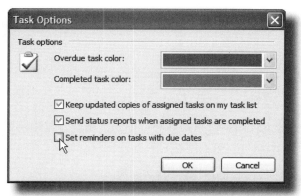

I recommend you do the same. In case this is new to you, reminders are small Outlook dialog boxes that pop to the front of your screen, often with a beep. These are very useful when assigned to calendar appointments for reminding you when that appointment is about to start. However the opposite is true for tasks, given the way we are using our daily tasks list; reminders for tasks are only a nuisance. They are distracting and serve no purpose if they pop up in the middle of other activities. Rather, using this system, as you find available time to work on tasks, you will develop a habit of reviewing your daily tasks list several times per day; this eliminates the need for a task reminder.

Categories Button

At the bottom of the Task dialog box, you'll see a Categories button. Clicking that button brings up a dialog box in which you can assign a category to the task. Why might you want to do this? Outlook allows you to filter on category types when you view tasks in any of the task views. However, I do not use Outlook Categories with *tasks*. In the pages ahead, you will see that there are many better ways to accomplish what categories achieve for tasks. I *do* use Outlook Categories extensively with e-mail and this is discussed quite thoroughly in chapter 7.

Details Tab

The second tab in the task input window is the Details tab. (See figure 4.6.) I completely ignore the fields in the Details tab when working with tasks. This is another case where fields are useful only when integrating Outlook with other Microsoft applications such as Microsoft Project, or perhaps when tracking billable time against a task.

Figure 4.6
Details tab of the Task dialog box, ignored in this task system.

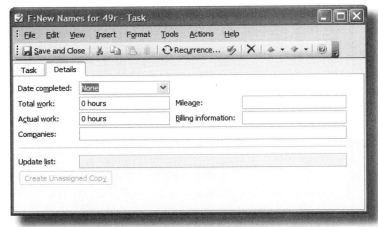

3. Using a Simple Prioritization System That Emphasizes Must-Do-Today Tasks

We All Prioritize

Whether intentionally or unconsciously, we all prioritize. We all create opinions about the relative importance of things on our plate. The trick is to use those intentions effectively, in a way that assists us in completing the right things at the right time.

I described the prioritization system in chapter 2 (pages 29-32). I mentioned that Outlook's Priority column is limited to three values (High, Normal, Low). I also mentioned that the High priority Outlook task category should be reserved only for daily tasks that are due today. Let's talk more about how to implement priorities in Outlook.

How to Set Priorities in Outlook

In case this is new to you, the way to assign the value of the Priority box for a task in Outlook is quite simple. From the TaskPad or from one of the Tasks folder views, you merely click on the task's Priority box (the one with the ! label above it) and the three Outlook priority choices will pop up; choose one of them and your task Priority box is set. (See figure 4.7.) Alternately, from within the Task dialog box, you simply use the Priority box on the task tab. (See figure 4.8.)

Figure 4.7
Setting the
Priority box in
the TaskPad.

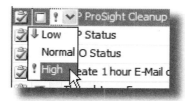

Figure 4.8
Setting the Pri-
ority box in the
Task dialog box.

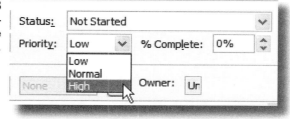

If you are accustomed to using FranklinCovey you may recall that system uses an A, B, C nomenclature to identify those three categories. Within that classification, FranklinCovey then adds a numerical ordering to each of these letter categories; numbers are appended, for example A1, A2, B1. The numbers indicate the order in which those tasks within the letter category should be completed.

However, Outlook's design pretty much precludes the use of the Franklin-Covey A1, A2, A3 prioritization approach, unless you add some special FranklinCovey software. Reason: Outlook does not enable the appending of numbers to those priorities. But that's perfectly fine because in the system I'm teaching you, three levels is plenty. In fact, two levels would probably be sufficient.

Other Ways to Represent Priority

This is because we are also assigning various levels of priorities implicitly by the other ways we process our tasks. If you think about it, you have at least two dimensions of priority: how important in absolute terms is the task to you, and how important from a time perspective is it. The way we have configured Outlook in this book allows you to consider both these dimensions easily and intuitively, in a number of different ways.

For instance, in your daily list, when you set the due date to a future date, you are in essence assigning that task a lower priority with regard to time.

And when you assign a task as a master task you are assigning it a low level of absolute priority. Furthermore, within the master tasks you have the same three Outlook priority values available. In chapter 5, I will show you additional ways to indicate task priority.

Sorting on Priority

You can sort any of the Outlook Tasks folder views on priority by clicking on the Priority column heading. In fact, you can sort those views on any column merely by clicking on the title of any of the columns (and note that clicking more than once on the same column title will alternately sort the list ascending and descending). This sorting technique applies to virtually any table style view within Outlook. You will see in the chapters ahead why it is useful to sort on various columns in these views.

The TaskPad view is, due to our settings, sorted by default on the Priority column, with most important tasks at top; and then on Due Date. We defined it that way when we created the custom view definition for the TaskPad in chapter 3 (pages 67-72). Unlike with Tasks folders, there is usually no reason to sort on any of the other columns when using the TaskPad.

You may occasionally accidentally sort your TaskPad on one of the other columns by inadvertently clicking on the column heads. Therefore, you will need to occasionally return the TaskPad sort order to our preferred *priority descending, due date descending* sorting. It is important to do so because you always want to focus first your must-do-today items. To return to our configured sorting do this: click on the column title of the Priority box as described above. Then shift-click on the title of the Due Date field, to put a secondary sort on it.

Side Note: *See page 221 of chapter 9 for further discussion of making this reconfiguration. See also the section titled Prioritizing within the Medium Priority, immediately ahead, for a discussion of why we are using this type of sort.*

Must-Do-Today Tasks

The Priority box in Outlook is most useful when assigning a daily task to be a must-do-today task; you do this by assigning a high priority in the Outlook Priority box. This puts a red ! within the Priority column for that task and sorts the task to the top of the daily list.

More than anything else that I do, I keep my eye on those must-do-today tasks throughout the day and constantly look for opportunities to complete them early in the day. Using Outlook priorities to ensure I complete my urgent tasks is perhaps the strongest value that my task management system provides me. It allows me to leave work at a reasonable hour knowing that my most important commitments for the day have been completed.

Cautions When Using Must-do-Today

You need to use this must-do-today designation with caution, however. It is tempting to, out of enthusiasm, assign a high priority to a task that is really not due today. If you start doing this, you will dilute the impact of seeing a red ! on a task, and you may start to ignore it. So commit to holding firm to the true meaning of this assignment. One good test before you assign a high priority to an item is to mentally ask yourself, "What is the impact if this task does not complete today?" If the answer is "not much," don't make the assignment. Rather, use other ways to mark the importance of that task. For example, use the GOAL: designation described on page 92 (see inset: Artificial Hard Due Dates). Or try the prioritization techniques described immediately ahead.

Most Tasks Are Medium Priority

Something you will notice after a few days or weeks of using this system is that most of the tasks on your daily list have a medium priority assignment. This makes sense because most low priority tasks have probably been moved to your master tasks list. It also makes sense because on most days you will not be able to complete all of your medium level tasks. As a result, the medium priority tasks will auto forward to the next day, and they will tend to increase in number over time. These older medium priority tasks will merge in with new medium priority tasks appearing for the first time on their assigned start days. As a result, you can quickly build up quite a few medium priority tasks on your TaskPad. We will cover in the daily planning section of chapter 5 (pages 108-117) strategies designed to handle this.

Prioritizing within the Medium Priority

Note that there is an implicit prioritization within the medium priority group on your TaskPad. This is because we have configured our TaskPad in chapter 3 to sort first on Outlook priority (high at the top) *and second on due date* (newer dates at the top). So within your potentially long list of medium tasks the ones with the freshest due date will be sorted to the top of that subgroup. We have configured the TaskPad this way so that you are encouraged to notice deferred tasks when they first arrive on your next action list. Furthermore, the fact that a task can go many days without completion often indicates that its true importance is lower than first thought; this sorting acknowledges that trend by placing tasks lower in the list as they age.

This sorting on date within the medium priority group gives you another level of prioritization within the TaskPad. Items sorted higher are noticed first. You can manipulate this sorting to your advantage: if in your long list of medium items you see some you want to emphasize, just reset the due date to today, and they will move to the top of the medium list.

Also note that, per our configurations, when a task due date is equal to today's date it will appear underlined on your TaskPad, giving it a bit more urgency. See the section called Prioritizing within Your Medium (Normal) Level Tasks, in chapter 5, page 115, for more discussion.

Using Low Priority in Daily List

I use the low priority in the daily list for items that are timely, but not important if they do not get done. They are not appropriate for the master list because in a week or two they will expire. Example: read the weekly communication from your HR department this week. Try to get tickets for the new movie this week.

Priorities in the Master List

Priorities are treated somewhat differently in the master list compared to the daily list. A high priority in the master list obviously no longer means must do today; rather you need to think of these priorities in a different way. Here's how to use priorities in the master list.

Use the low priority as a wish list category. These are projects or tasks that you would like to do someday but don't expect to get to right away. I call this my Ideas list—this is a great place to store ideas you do not want to lose but you doubt you will get to soon. Seeing those ideas during the weekly review allows you the opportunity to incorporate them when business conditions become right.

Medium priority I reserve for most master tasks and for miniprojects (described below).

And high priority I reserve for very high priority master tasks (tasks I expect to promote quickly to the daily tasks list) and for separately managed projects. Miniprojects and separately managed projects are described in the next best practice.

4. Writing Only Next Actions on Your Daily List

This best practice can be summarized simply as follows: place only the very next physical action for a task on your daily list.

Starting on page 32 in chapter 2, I describe in some detail the concept of *next action*, which was adapted from David Allen's excellent work. If you are not clear about this, I suggest you review those pages quickly before proceeding. Here is a summary of that section:

Recap of the Next Action Concept

- Many seemingly single-step tasks really require many steps to complete.

- You need to identify the very next action for a multistep task, and put only that on your daily list.

▪ The very next action should be the next physical thing you need to do to advance the multistep task. Examples:

"Garden Landscaping" is wrong; "Call Ted's Landscaping for Quote" is better.
"Jones report" is wrong; "E-mail Michael for copy of old Jones report" is better.

▪ If a task requires more than one sitting to do, it should not be placed on your daily list; instead convert it to a miniproject in your master tasks list and place only the very next action on your daily list.

The next action concept is an extremely powerful one—deceptively powerful. It leads to tasks written in a format that you can act on quickly, in the heat of a busy day. Otherwise, if you need to stop and think about a task, you will probably skip over it.

And using this will advance many of your tasks that seem to get "stuck." If a task hangs out for days or weeks on your TaskPad without action, examine it and see if it can be written in a clear next-action language, or see if a more specific next action can be extracted. Doing so will most likely allow the task to get unstuck.

Implementing in Outlook

Okay, enough review. How do you implement this in Outlook? There really is no magic to translate this to an Outlook methodology because this is more of a process point. It's a thought process you should go through as you write tasks on your TaskPad.

Visualizing Your Actions

But here is some additional help for writing next actions. One way to approach identifying next actions is to think in terms of visualizing an action to accomplish the task. Before you write the task, try to picture yourself accomplishing the task, and picture the very first steps needed to do that. When you are confident you have the very first step in mind, then picture yourself doing that step. Then write down words that best summarize that mental image. This may sound complicated but it really only takes a nanosecond. And the outcome of this simple process is remarkable: during the day when you see the task on your task list you are able to immediately act on it. There is no question about what you need to do; you just do it because you can see in your mind's eye the action steps you need to take.

The reason this is so important is that in the heat of the busy workday, you need to stack the deck in your favor when it comes to tasks, and this visualization technique accomplishes that. As a result, you'll find yourself knocking off tasks much more quickly than you have with any other type of to-do list in the past.

Here are some additional points to remember about next actions:

- Do this with daily tasks only, which is where next actions should be applied. In contrast, the purpose of the master tasks list is to list summary level or long-range items (though next actions on the daily list that lose importance may be moved to the master tasks list for later consideration).

- That said, if you have a project in the master list, in the text box of that project it makes sense to think about and list next actions. This is for later movement out to your daily tasks list (see next section).

- Think in terms of next actions, both as you first enter tasks on your daily list and as you review your tasks, throughout the day and during formal planning periods. When scanning your daily tasks list you may realize that a task is not written as the very next action; at that moment rewrite the task.

- Since next actions can usually be accomplished in one sitting, when you create the next action task, set the due date to be the day you want to do the task, or the first day you want to *consider* doing the task. In other words, set the due date to be the first day you want to see the task appear in your daily list. Ignore the start date, or set it to be the same as the due date. Remember that the task will automatically forward from day to day in Outlook's TaskPad until you complete the task.

Easy Habit to Make

After using next actions for a while, you will find them remarkably easy to keep up with. It will become a habit to use them. What happens is you become accustomed to writing tasks in action language. Tasks you do not write that way stand out to you as not making sense.

Identify Miniprojects and Place Them on Your Master List

I introduced miniprojects on page 35 in chapter 2. If you are uncertain about the concept, I suggest you review that section quickly before proceeding.

As you create next actions, you will invariably find that many tasks really require multiple steps to accomplish. So an important part of the next action best practice is to identify that set of multiple steps as a miniproject and place only the very next step on your daily list. And since we do not want to lose track of that miniproject, an entry representing the miniproject should be placed on your master tasks list, marked there as a project. This is particularly important if the multiple steps are likely to occur on different days and so may lose momentum in process. Storing a reference to your miniproject on the master list ensures that you will revisit this miniproject during your weekly planning.

Again, there is no special methodology for applying this within Outlook because this is more of a process point. It's a thought process you should go through as you add tasks to your list. There *are* some specific considerations in Outlook, however.

Labeling Miniprojects

It is useful during your weekly planning to be able to see all of your miniprojects grouped together in the master list. That way you can see an overview of your multiple projects and quickly take a higher-level perspective of what is on your plate. I enable this by how I label the miniprojects in the master list. I place a "P-" in front of the name, for example: "P-Risk Management Document." See figure 4.9 for more examples. Using this labeling, sorting the master list alphabetically groups labeled miniprojects together.

An alternate way to do this is to use the categories capability of Outlook, creating a Projects category and assigning that category appropriately. Both are

Figure 4.9
Example of miniprojects in Master tasks list.

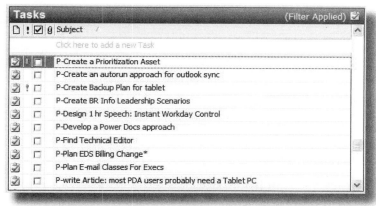

effective, although I prefer using the "P-" label on the subject line. This is so that when I am viewing my master list in a view that does not display categories, I can quickly see projects and consider them accordingly. There are also some related techniques described in chapter 9, Advanced Topics, that you will find easier using this labeling method.

Using the Text Box to Brainstorm Next Actions and Final Outcomes

When you create a miniproject, you often do so while brainstorming the multiple steps needed to accomplish it; after all, this is usually how you create a miniproject. For an instant you will have a mental image of most or all the major tasks necessary to accomplish it. Do not lose that image! Rather, record those brainstormed steps at the *moment* you have them. Doing this is simple. If you double-click the new task and open it, there is a large text box in the bottom portion of the resulting Task dialog box. Simply type your visualized steps there, quickly. Do a brain dump of the steps you just visualized, without analysis. The idea is not to try to be accurate or precise, rather just get some ideas written down loosely and casually. You'll be amazed how valuable this information becomes later when, during your weekly planning, you start thinking through the next steps on this miniproject.

Perhaps even more important is to clearly write down what the expected outcome of this project is. Why are you doing it? What will be produced when it is done? Use this text box to make a clear outcome statement for the overall activity.

I sometimes forget which tasks I've made entries in the text box for. To remind me, I put an asterisk at the end of the subject line. See figure 4.9 above, third item from the bottom, for an example.

Generating Additional Next Actions

One of the primary values of recording your miniprojects is using your miniproject list to periodically think through additional next actions to put on your daily list. I will cover this in detail in the next chapter, but briefly, the idea is this: many of your miniprojects are start and stop projects. As you complete tasks for them, subsequent tasks may not be needed immediately, and the miniproject holds for a while. By having a list of miniprojects that you review during your weekly review, you can periodically brainstorm ideas for how to progress each of your projects further. Sometimes the best natural cycle for start and stop projects like these is to make some progress, let the miniproject incubate, brainstorm and identify additional tasks later, then move those out to your daily list. Having a miniproject list, reviewed periodically, enables this.

Managing Larger Projects

A miniproject is usually created when looking at a task on your to-do list and realizing that it really takes more than one step to accomplish. So they tend to be very small projects; after all you originally thought this was one simple task. This is bottoms-up project identification.

But this concept of recording projects on your master list is also extremely useful for other, larger projects. At the other extreme from miniprojects are large, formal, separately managed projects with dedicated teams. These projects usually have a project manager assigned to them, possibly full time. They probably have full-time staff assigned to work the many tasks of the project. If they are managed well, they have one or more project team meetings per week dedicated to project management. Projects like these almost certainly use dedicated project management software like Microsoft Project to track. Does this mean they are not applicable to placement on the master list?

As a Project Manager

Actually no, just the opposite. But how you do this really depends on your role. If you are the full-time project manager, you should be spending considerable time each week thinking through the project and identifying next actions. So a useful thing to do is to make a separate entry in your master tasks list for each of the major subcomponents of the project, and use them as planning points during weekly planning. While your actual project plan will be the source of most major tasks on the project, you will need to track myriads of side activities that do not manage well on a Microsoft Project—like tool.

For example, project *issues,* which are formal identifications of situations where project plans have run into problems, need to be tracked outside of the project plan itself. Consider placing complex project issues assigned to you on your master list and continue to work them from that perspective; you can then identify and place next actions on your daily list to help progress solutions to the issues.

As a Manager of Multiple Project Managers

If you are a senior manager, program manager, or departmental lead over multiple project managers, the master list is an excellent place to track those multiple projects from the perch of your senior perspective. For instance, throughout the week as I have periodic encounters with the various project managers I am responsible for, I collect thoughts and recommended actions on each of those projects. Sometimes I record them directly on my next action list (the daily list). But sometimes the actions are not for me; they are thoughts that I want to pass on during the next project meeting that I attend. So having an entry in my master list for these separately managed projects is very useful. It gives me a place to enter thoughts I want to bring up at the next meeting (I use the text box of the project entry in the master task). Use this in addition to the delegation techniques covered in chapter 8.

If you are a departmental lead or manager of multiple projects, you may not have specific project-level tasks assigned to you for those projects. You do have, however, a team role to play. Probably your most important role is to help clear management, bureaucratic, and funding roadblocks so the project can progress. And to keep the project aligned with business goals. So with that role in mind, placing that project on the master list serves as a reminder to review the project periodically (during the weekly planning described in the next section). During that review, you may think of immediate clearing tasks you need to act on to assist the progress of that project. You should treat these like any other next actions and move them out to the daily list.

By the way, I use the Priority box for projects in the master list in the following way: active miniprojects I give a medium priority to; larger separately management projects I give a high priority to; and projects that I want to do someday but are not yet ready to activate I give a low priority to. This way when I sort my master list by priority, my large projects with extensive resources dedicated to them are the ones I look at first during my weekly review. This, after all, is really where my attention should go first.

Background Projects

Falling in between my large separately managed projects and my very small miniprojects that started out as tasks, are what I call background projects (see also page 35 of chapter 2 for a discussion of background projects). These are small- to medium-size one-person "projects" that have been formally assigned to me but that are too small to warrant formal project planning. These are the slow burn initiatives that you do in your spare time, for which you may need to periodically report progress upward to management, but that tend to start and stop as you wait for replies from people, completion of related tasks, and so on. Treat these background projects the same as miniprojects. Make entries for each one on the master list, brainstorm activities within the text box of that task entry, and periodically move next actions out to the daily list. As when managing multiple project managers, these projects are aided by the delegation techniques covered in chapter 8.

Review Your Projects and Miniprojects Regularly

Finally, there is no sense in recording projects and miniprojects if you don't periodically review them and decide on next steps. Plan to review your project list at least once a week during your weekly planning sessions, described in the next chapter.

In Reality, My Miniproject List Is Small

Over the years, I have found my tendency to create miniprojects from tasks comes and goes. What happens is this: when I work the next action in my daily list that week, I then automatically identify the subsequent step and record that in my daily list. I then never need to refer to the item in the master list because it is progressing and on track. I have sometimes gotten in the habit then of knowing that I do not need to write certain kinds of tasks as a miniproject because I know I will cycle through all the subsequent tasks naturally, once I start the first next action. The power of the next-action language is what makes this possible; it gets me started solidly and kicks in at each stage when identifying next steps. In the end, I find that I breeze through completion of all components.

So should you write down miniprojects? While you are getting started with this new system, my recommendation is this: write down all multistep tasks as miniprojects and try the system for a while. You will soon adapt your own most efficient techniques as time goes on.

Summary

This chapter introduced the first four best practices:

1 Tracking all tasks in Outlook Tasks System

2 Using a master tasks list kept separate from your daily tasks list

3 Using a simple prioritization system that emphasizes must-do-today tasks

4 Writing only next actions on your daily list

Review of Key Learnings

In these first four best practices, a few points are worth repeating.

- Focus on the task Due Date field in Outlook; the due date is your "do" date, your action date, the day you plan to work the task or first want to first see the task on your daily list. Since next actions can be done in one sitting, the due date is also the start date.

- In this system we do not populate the task Start Date field.

- For tasks with a hard due date, place the word "Due:" followed by the date, at the end of the task Subject line. Use this rarely — only when consequences to missing the date are significant.

- Clicking on a future date within the calendar will not change the tasks displayed in the TaskPad; they always display relative to today. To view tasks scheduled to appear on future days navigate to the All Daily Tasks view within the Tasks folder.

- You can convert a daily task to a master task merely by removing the date entries. And you can convert a master task to a daily task by adding a due date entry.

- If a task requires more than one sitting to do it should not be placed on your daily list. Instead convert it to a miniproject in your master tasks list and place only the very next action on your daily list.

Next Steps

You now know how to enter daily and master tasks. You know how to use date fields and the Priority box to indicate importance and timing. You know the difference between miniprojects and next actions. You know what belongs on you daily list and what on your master list. So presumably you are now busy collecting and recording your tasks.

But what do you do when your daily list reaches twenty or more tasks long? Try to work them all? When do you actually do something about all those master tasks you have collected? There are the topics of daily and weekly planning. These are the next best practices to discuss. The domain is a big one and so the entire next chapter, chapter 5, is devoted to it.

Chapter Five

Planning and Working Your Tasks in Outlook

In this chapter we cover Best Practice 5: Daily and Weekly Planning.

Working Your Tasks

Up to this point I have explained how to identify tasks, how to classify them in a way that's most useful for accomplishing them, and how to enter them effectively into Outlook's task management system.

The Value of the System

But what good is listing tasks if you don't actually work them? Assuming you have time, and have applied the principles of this system, working them should be straightforward. This is especially true of your daily list because, if entered using this system, your daily list is mostly a set of actions that individually should be readily doable. The system is designed to encourage that. If tasks are written correctly as a *next action*, then when you're ready to work those tasks, the title of the task itself describes the action you need to take, and you just do it. And because we have put so much initial effort into configuring Outlook and applying best practices toward classifying tasks, this means that when you finally do glance at your daily list, the most important and useful tasks are the ones that you see and do first.

Note, however, that throughout the week and even throughout the day, due to changing situations, the right tasks to work on, and the amount of time available for them, can easily change. So your job is also to periodically assess and ensure that the tasks at or near the top of your daily list are the ones with the highest yield and the most benefit for a given day, and that they are the ones appropriate for the time allowed. And you may need to decide to make additional time available to work them. This sort of decision making you do moment to moment, intuitively, as you examine your appointments, and tasks, and decide which to do next. It is also decision making you should do during dedicated planning time when truing up your task lists.

Planning Your Tasks So You Can Work Them Well

Time is a precious commodity in a busy office. Finding the time to work your tasks is not easy. Ensuring that you have an adequate balance between tasks on your list and task time available can require some planning. The idea is to get your tasks done during the day so you can leave work on time and get your life more into balance. To make this possible you need to periodically spend time cleaning up your task list and identifying time in your day when you will work the tasks.

It is important, for those moments when you can escape from meetings and appointments and get to your tasks, that only high value and clearly stated tasks be presented to you. You need to periodically true up and calibrate the list so that only the most appropriate tasks are listed and worked. You should display on your daily list only tasks that you can run with throughout the busy workday. And if your day does not "add up" in terms of tasks needed versus time available, you need to fix that.

To accomplish this you should set aside some quality and quiet planning time to adjust your list; trying to use small gaps the middle of the business day is not the best way to do that. That's what daily planning time is for.

Daily Planning

Daily planning is the act of going through your daily list (the TaskPad) and truing it up. It is when you make judgments about what needs to be on the list for consideration during the day and week, and what you need to remove from consideration. It's the time you evaluate how much of your task list you think you can accomplish that day or week and, if needed, it is when to allocate more time in your schedule to work the tasks.

When should you do daily planning? First thing in the morning is best. The way I do it is this: I schedule no meetings before 9:00 A.M. and try to get into the office enough ahead of 9:00 to get settled, accomplish some quality daily planning, read some e-mails, and knock off a few tasks. If that doesn't work for you, you should actually block out half an hour first thing in the morning to do this daily planning.

Take this time seriously. If you are having difficulty fitting this in, read the section Don't Skip or Postpone This Daily Planning on page 114.

Rule Number 1: Keep Your Daily List Short

Understand this: you cannot possibly do every task you think of, or every task that someone hands to you. This is also true even of those items that you choose to place in your TaskPad (your daily list). You will quickly get to the point where more items are on your daily list than you can possibly do in a day, and more than you want to even *consider* for the day.

If your list is too long (figure 5.1) it is unusable; a long list is difficult to scan for a high-level view. It is difficult to grab appropriate tasks quickly. A very long list is demoralizing; you'll find that you psychologically give up if there's too much in front of you.

I try to keep my TaskPad list short enough so that I can see the entire list without scrolling, and preferably much shorter. I want to be able, within a normal and natural attention span, to digest the contents of the list and make decisions about what to do next (figure 5.2).

Figure 5.1
Daily tasks list that is too long.

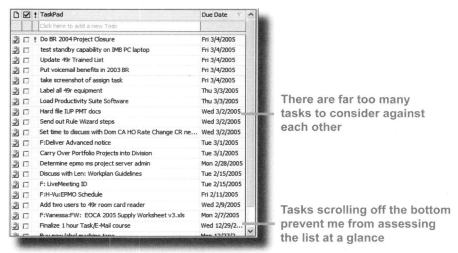

There are far too many tasks to consider against each other

Tasks scrolling off the bottom prevent me from assessing the list at a glance

Figure 5.2
Daily tasks list that is of reasonable length.

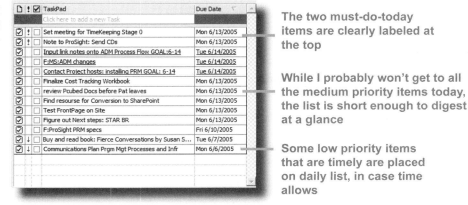

The two must-do-today items are clearly labeled at the top

While I probably won't get to all the medium priority items today, the list is short enough to digest at a glance

Some low priority items that are timely are placed on daily list, in case time allows

Even if you know you will not get to the entire list that day, you need to be able to *consider* the list at a glance. You also need to feel that it is of reasonable size so you feel good about your day, so you feel that you have not set impossible goals for yourself. Otherwise the list will appear impossible, and will be discouraging to work with.

Neither of these can happen if your list is too long. So during daily planning I recommend that you quickly assess which tasks to consider for today, and for the days ahead, and move the rest off the list (I will show you how in a moment).

Next, I recommend you decide whether you will add more dedicated task time to your day, either by canceling appointments or extending the day. Do this based on the importance and urgency of the remaining tasks.

Get these decisions done in the morning, when your mind is clear and you have time to contact people who may be affected by necessary changes in plans. Create a plan for the day that you can accomplish; create a plan that allows you to leave work at a reasonable hour with a feeling of success. And by a *plan* I do not mean a time-consuming step-by-step schedule of what you're going to do for the day. Rather your plan consists of nothing more than your trued-up daily tasks list and a validated appointment schedule that may show a block of time scheduled for task work. The steps below show you how to do this. While these steps may seem time consuming at first read, you will quickly, through practice, be able to accomplish all the steps in minutes, nearly automatically.

Confirm Your Must-Do-Today Tasks

▪ Focus first on your must-do-today tasks (marked with an Outlook high priority) and confirm that they are really needed today; if not, immediately lower the priority. Remember, do not succumb to the temptation to mark something as must do today just because you are enthusiastic or hopeful about it. These should be the tasks that could keep you from going home that evening if not completed, so guard this category carefully or it will lose its effectiveness (see figure 5.3).

Figure 5.3
Must-do-today
tasks.

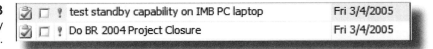

▪ Then scan through the rest of your medium priority items and decide if any of them must also be done today. Look first for any that have a due date in the subject line and check to see if that date is today's; remember if it is, it means you need to convert that task to a must-do-today task.

▓   Next, look for any item that is underlined and consider its importance; recall that these represent deferred tasks that are appearing on your list for the first time today and so they may represent timely tasks for the day.

▓   Once you have rationalized your must-do-today list, look at your sched-ule—at your appointment calendar for the day. If it is a typical day with a mixture of meetings and time available to accomplish tasks, confirm that you really can accomplish your must-do-today tasks in the time you have available.

You may be stretching your capacity if you have more than three to five must-do-today tasks on your list. If so, take time to consider their actual durations and the amount of task time available on your schedule. Not enough time? Then decide which ones you will postpone and make the necessary arrange-ments (contact the stakeholders and renegotiate the deadline). If the tasks cannot be postponed, figure out how to make more task time available on your schedule. You may need to cancel a meeting or an appointment. You may need to get some additional people to help you. Or as a last resort you may need to schedule evening work. Let's aim for you having time for both all your must-do tasks and many of your medium priority ones as well.

Then Look at Your Medium Priority Tasks

Next, consider the remainder of your medium priority list. Think about what this medium list represents—your top priorities for the next few days or even the full week. It represents tasks that you may or may not get to today but that you wish to get to if you can. It may also represent items that are not quite must-do today but that may be close to that level of urgency, and so you intend to try your best to fit them in today (you'll see how to mark those in a moment).

These also represent lower urgency items that you may want to scan several times a day to see if synergetic situations present themselves, situations that make the task easy and natural to do. Maybe that's because you are going to be in a meeting with the right person, or because the right information has arrived to move the task forward, or even because the right energy or inspira-tion has finally arrived to tackle the task in the moment. And if none of those situations present themselves, you still know that simply working from the top of the list down gets you closer to your goals.

Rationalize and Shorten Your Daily List

If this medium list gets too long it will be difficult to work with. While we have agreed that it is okay to let medium priority tasks forward from day to day, you do not want a *long* list of tasks staring at you throughout the day. It makes it difficult to scan the list and it is demoralizing to see so many items that you cannot possibly do.

Certainly it is good to have a few more items on your list than you think you can do in the day. This will keep you challenged and allow you to maintain momentum. And it makes sense to include items that you are waiting for the right moment in the week to attack; you can allow them to forward along visibly day to day until the right timing presents itself.

However, you do not want to have *so* many items that the list becomes unusable. Therefore, you need to ask yourself some questions. Are items on there that really are not important? If so move them to the master list. Are important items on there that have lingered for days? If so, decide which of these tasks you think you should try to take a stab at today, and raise their priority within the medium portion of the list (see Prioritizing within Your Medium (Normal) Level Tasks, page 115). At the same time, consider whether you need to block additional amounts of time on your appointment calendar to ensure that you can accomplish these.

All this assessment, with practice, can be done in a few minutes.

Scheduling More Time

It is easy to get in the habit of doing only must-do-today tasks and letting your important but not urgent tasks build up without completion within your medium category. To prevent that, schedule some additional time on your calendar now to knock a few of those off (see Time Management: Finding Time to Work on Tasks, below). If no time is available today, schedule blocks of time for later in the week to complete these tasks, before the rest of your week fills up with appointments, and move these tasks to the daily list for those days. You need to get ahead of your important medium priority tasks, so start thinking now how are you going to do that.

Additional Efforts

One hopes the above analysis and moving of tasks will leave you with a match between your daily tasks list and your available time, allowing you to start the day with a list of reasonable length. If the remaining items still make your list longer than you can see, do not try to start your day with your list in that condition. You need to make additional efforts.

Scan your list and consider applying the following strategies to selected tasks to shorten your list. In all cases, use your knowledge of changing business conditions, and your intuition, to make quick but thoughtful decisions. You can make each of these decisions in a few seconds:

1   If an individual task has been on your list for a while, ask yourself if the written task truly represents the very next action for the task. If not, rewrite it. Many tasks are not completed for that reason alone. Once rewritten, you may be able to complete it easily today.

2 Delegate it (and be sure to follow the delegation process described in chapter 8). Delegation is perhaps the best way to multiply your time. If you have staff, make use of them.

3 If the task is important and a relatively big one, find time on your calendar today or later in the week and actually schedule it in on your calendar. Blocking out time to work tasks is sometimes the only way to get the big ones done. And scheduling time on your calendar for tasks well ahead of time keeps colleagues from dropping meetings into those empty slots. But once you have scheduled the task time do this also: keep the task on your daily tasks list with a due date assigned to the same day as the day you're going to work on the task. That way if your scheduled time gets blown away, you don't lose track of the task; it remains on your list and forwards on to subsequent days until complete.

4 Move it to your master task by setting the Due Date to None. This represents a decision that you will rethink this task at your next weekly review. Moving a task here implicitly means it can be put off a few weeks. If you have many medium priority tasks this may be your best option.

5 If you cannot afford to put a task off a few weeks then, instead of moving it to the master tasks list, adjust the due date ahead a few days. Some quick mental calculations will be needed on each task to decide if that is acceptable and where to put it. That way you can reconsider this item in your morning's prioritization when it reappears; the timing might be better. Occasionally the need to complete it fades over time. However, if you find yourself consistently using this choice, consider that this will catch up to you within a few days or weeks as tasks build up. As they do, it will be necessary to schedule more task periods into your normal work hours in the days ahead—or consider the sixth item just below.

6 Finally, consider if you can renegotiate and delete the task. Maybe you really can't get to it in the required time or really just don't want to do it. Renegotiate the task with the stakeholders (that may just be you) and take it off your list.

Again, this may seem like many steps, but this activity quickly becomes second nature. I can usually scan through and shorten a task list within five or ten minutes, while making good decisions. This small effort will pay back with a much more relaxed mind and hours of effectively focused time.

What This Does for You: Perfect Prioritization and Planning

The above activities are incredibly valuable. Think of what you accomplish when you do this: you have thought through your priorities for the day and indicated which must get done today and which additional ones you're going to try to do today. You have blocked time for the most important ones. You have taken some tasks off your list because you realize they really are not that important, or you may have sent notes to stakeholders telling them you need to delay agreed-to tasks you know you just can't get to. And you have done all of this before starting your work for the day. This is prioritization activity at its finest. You can start the day with the knowledge that only the most important tasks are on the plate for you to work on. You can work through your day with confidence you are focusing on the right things. And if at the end of the business day the must-do-today portion of your rationalized task list is all completed, you can leave work guilt-free, knowing that all your major commitments have been met. What better way to approach your business day and to improve your work-life balance?

Don't Skip or Postpone This Daily Planning

This is what your morning session allows you: nearly perfect prioritization and planning. However, make sure you really do this first thing in the morning. If you find yourself not getting through all the planning steps, figure out why. Are you jumping into tasks as you see them? Are you getting sidetracked? Prevent getting sidetracked by reading e-mail only after planning is done. Let your phone roll over to voice mail. If colleagues interrupt you, ask them politely to stop back in 30 minutes.

Don't decide "I'll do this planning later today." If you wait until the end of the day, when tasks are late and stakeholders are angry, you will make poor decisions and become fatalistic in your attitude to tasks and work. "I am expected to do way too much, this is ridiculous." Or: "It looks like I should be working all night every night to get this stuff done, and this is unfair." Rather, if you do the math in the morning and see the day just does not add up, you have time to start making realistic decisions about what your priorities for the day should be. Identify and plan to do the most important tasks first, and then share the math with the stakeholders who will not get what they need. You will be amazed at how reasonable stakeholders can be if you give them a heads up well in advance and allow them time to plan alternative solutions.

Ammunition Against Fire Drills

If your boss or colleague drops an urgent task on you in the middle of the day, having planned your day ahead of time allows you to show the plan and do the math with that person at that moment. Let your boss decide which stakeholders will not get their deliverables and even ask your boss to deliver the bad news. With such facts at hand, your boss may realize that your existing priorities outweigh the new request. Having your day thought through ahead of time provides valuable ammunition in these situations.

If You Must Skip

Clearly, there will be days you must skip planning. Perhaps you are traveling, or booked 7 to 7 with meetings. Or perhaps you have had a few slow days, and yesterday's planning still holds. The beauty of this system is that if you have been accurate in your must-do-today assignments, all you really *must* do is make sure your high priority tasks are attended to. Doing that should hold you a few days.

Balancing Importance

When cleaning your list in the morning to shorten it, you will find that deciding which tasks to move off your list and where to put them is a judgment call. Theoretically, any of the medium or low priority tasks are candidates for postponing. Your goal should be to assess the changing business situation around you and respond accordingly. You need to use your best intuitive and professional judgment to decide the right application of timeliness and importance as you look at each task. For instance, if a big project is due tomorrow and you know you need to work on it today to make a reasonable contribution toward tomorrow's deadline, even though it's not marked as a must-do-today task, that timeliness factor rules.

Also consider the importance factor. I strongly feel that you should work as many tasks as possible during the week that will help achieve your own important goals. You can get so good at the mechanics of scheduling and working tasks as they come to you that you forget to point your attention toward those tasks that are really important to you. So as you are examining your daily list and identifying tasks to postpone, make sure at least a few of your goal-oriented tasks remain near the top of your list. We will talk more about goals and how to work them into your task list in chapter 9.

Work Your Must-Do-Today Tasks

Once your list is of a reasonable size and you start your workday, now concentrate on your high priority, must-do-today tasks. These you should constantly look for opportunities to complete early, because these keep you from going home at night. Try to keep this list in front of you all the time so that you do not stray into time-wasting activities as holes in your schedule appear. Try to get them done early so that the pressure releases in the second half of the day. That way you have time to start working your medium tasks and getting ahead of your list, which creates a very satisfying sense of accomplishment. When the natural time arrives to go home, you can do so with a sense of satisfaction and with complete freedom from the nagging feeling that you have left important things behind.

Prioritizing within Your Medium (Normal) Level Tasks

As you begin to work your medium priority tasks (called Normal in Outlook), note this. Even after you have shortened your list, the majority of your tasks will still be medium priority, and you will probably not get to all of them today. In scanning these tasks in your TaskPad you will find some that are more important than others to get to first and so you may want to prioritize within that section of the TaskPad.

At first, it may seem like you have few mechanical options for marking the priority of items within a given Outlook priority classification. If you are accustomed to FranklinCovey, for example, you may be disappointed to find that Outlook offers no way to add a 1, 2, 3 after priorities, to rank within the three Outlook priority categories.

Actually you do have options for ranking your medium level tasks. One thing you can do is lower the priority of the *other* items by setting their Outlook priority to Low; this will cause them to sort to the bottom of the TaskPad.

Using the Due Date to Set Priorities

Another thing you can do to raise the positional importance of a medium priority task is to reset the Due Date field to today. Remember, because of our configurations done in chapter 3, this underlines the item and moves it up in the sorting of the list, just below the must-do-today (High) tasks. See figures 5.4 and 5.5 below.

Figure 5.4
A task before resetting the Due Date to today.

Figure 5.5
After setting the Due Date to today (2/19).

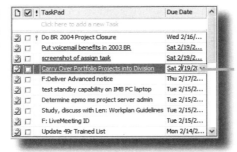

The task is underlined and sorts to the upper portion of the medium priority tasks

This works because our configurations were designed to sort medium tasks with the freshest due dates to the top of the medium category. And tasks with a Due Date of today are underlined. We originally configured the TaskPad this way so that you were encouraged to notice deferred tasks when they first appeared on your next action list. Nevertheless, you can also use it as a prioritization mechanism.

To reorder the list further, change the Due Date field of an item that just appeared today, but that is not very important, to an earlier date. This causes it to sort lower in the list.

There is nothing wrong with resetting the Due Date field of a daily task to today, or setting the due dates of others to be earlier than today, to reorder the visible list. Recall that in this system, the Due Date field is merely an indication of when you want to *first* see the item and consider doing it. It is not the true due date. It is the first "do" date (review the section titled Use of Date Fields, on page 89 of chapter 4, if this concept is confusing to you). So once the date in the item's Due Date field has arrived and the item is visible, the temporal nature of its displayed Due Date field becomes insignificant and you should feel free to change it. Prioritizing the order of your list is one reason to do so. Note of course that setting the Due Date to a date in the *future* does have significance: the task will be removed from the TaskPad until that date arrives.

Another way to emphasize certain tasks is to place the word GOAL: followed by the date you want an item done right in the subject line. Use this for soft due dates that will not keep you from going home, but that still have date significance. Review the discussion on page 92 of chapter 4 (see inset: Artificial Hard Due Dates).

Remember, though, prioritizing within the medium category is optional. If you keep your TaskPad list short enough, you should be able to read the whole list at a glance and let your intuition guide you on next priorities. I go weeks without ever prioritizing within my displayed medium category list. The daily planning activity of moving items to the master list (or into the future), and keeping today's list very short, is all the prioritizing I usually need.

Side Note: *If your underlined tasks do not automatically sort to the top of your medium task list in the TaskPad, then you have lost the sort order you configured on your TaskPad in chapter 3. This is easy to accidentally do; if you accidentally click the column head of one of the columns in the TaskPad, then the view will re-sort on that column, and the preconfigured sorting will be lost. See chapter 9, page 221, for a discussion and quick solution. Also see page 222 for a discussion of other ways to set the order of tasks in the TaskPad.*

Complete Your Planning before Working Your Tasks

Again, do this daily TaskPad processing first thing in the morning. It may seem like a lot of steps but it quickly becomes intuitive and automatic. It's also a great way to take a high level view of all the things on your plate. Such planning time is well spent; take advantage of it.

Also be sure that you complete your planning before you actually jump into your tasks. In planning and reviewing your TaskPad first thing in the morning, it will be tempting to jump into the tasks as you see them, before you completely reprioritize them. Do not let this happen. If you do, you will quickly lose your planning time before full prioritization is complete and end up with a nonprioritized list to work from the rest of the day. If you work low priority tasks at the expense of more important ones then you truly have wasted your day. Clearly separate planning time from doing, and guard your planning time well.

If during planning you see something that seems urgent and you are tempted to jump right on it, instead use and trust your system. Immediately mark the item as must do today or raise its medium priority (see above), and know that it will be one of the first things you work on once you start your tasks.

Weekly Planning

Once you start using a master tasks list, weekly planning becomes important. This is when you review your lower priority tasks and your projects and miniprojects list and discover additional next actions for your daily list. It is also a time to review your goals and to make sure that activities toward those goals make it onto your daily schedule. It is important that you schedule an hour or so a week for weekly planning and use that time effectively.

How to Do Weekly Planning

In Outlook, weekly planning is really just a matter of examining your master list (and All Daily Tasks list) and making intelligent decisions based on what has occurred in the past week. In your weekly planning session, you will:

- Step through the projects—the projects and miniprojects part—on the master tasks list and ask yourself for each: "What is the next action needed to move this forward?" As you find next actions create them in your daily list.

- If you have separately managed projects (remember, we marked these as a high priority in your master tasks list), review them.

- Review individual medium priority items that you may have moved to the master tasks list when your week was too busy; perhaps next week has more time to work them, or their urgency has become higher.

- Review items in the master task view marked with the Outlook low priority symbol (I call this my ideas list) to determine if the need for any of those ideas has matured enough to warrant moving them to the daily list or to the project level of the master list.

- Review your goals, and look for opportunities to place activities against those goals into your schedule or daily list for the following week (see chapter 9, page 209).

- Review your daily list (the TaskPad) and true it up if necessary.

■ Review the All Daily Tasks view for future daily tasks you have scheduled and see if their urgency may now be higher; you may need to pull the date in.

Let's take a more detailed look at each of these activities.

Review of Projects and Miniprojects during Weekly Planning

I like to take a top-down approach when reviewing my master list, so I always start with my projects and then my miniprojects. This is where the master tasks list offers considerable value. To do this, first open the Tasks folder in Outlook and navigate to the Master Tasks view. Then simply sort by subject (click on the word Subject in the header portion of the master list) and then scroll down to where the "P-" items start.

Side Note: *If you have lots of "P-" items, shift-click the Priority column to enable a sub-sort on Priority. That sorts your large, separately managed projects to the top of the group.*

Spend a moment or two on each project and miniproject. If you have been putting thoughts inside the text portion of the project tasks throughout the week, open each project and examine that text. It amazes me how many good ideas that I collect during the week in that space (and completely forget about) end up helping me greatly in progressing the project.

For lightly managed miniprojects review the goal of the project. What is the outcome going to look like when you successfully complete this project? Write that down or change what you had previously written if needed. If you have multiple outcomes write each of them down. Now brainstorm tasks necessary to reach those outcomes. Focus on those that you need to do next, your next action tasks. You may have a very next action for each outcome. Once you feel that you have done all you can in the few moments of thought, move the very next action items out to your daily list and put appropriate dates on them.

Side Note: *Unless there is any reason not to, I always set the due date for such next actions to the next business day. One reason not to do that may be that you already know that day will be a hectic day with no time to do tasks. So if your identified actions can wait (they are not must-do-today tasks for the next business day) feel free to distribute the due days into subsequent days in the week; that way on the morning of your next business day you're not overwhelmed with a huge daily tasks list.*

Also, brainstorm ways to delegate the tasks you have created. You will quickly generate many more tasks than you alone can accomplish so start thinking of whom you will assign these tasks to. I go over delegation techniques and notations in Outlook in some detail in chapter 8.

Review of Separately Managed Projects

For your larger, separately managed projects (first described on page 102 of chapter 4) you should also pull your physical project folders and update the formal project plan based on the Notes fields of these items in your projects list, if anything was recorded there during the week. Alternatively, use this time to plan agenda items for the next formal meeting on that project. Create any daily tasks you may see you need.

Individual Tasks Floating in the Master List

Throughout the week, you may have moved daily tasks out to your master tasks list as you realized they were not yet important. Some may have been sitting there for a while. These individual tasks may be important in the future, so take them seriously; this may be the week to move them to your daily list.

Review Your Ideas List

You also may have been dropping *ideas* into your master tasks list throughout the weeks. Remember that you assigned a low priority to ideas that you hoped to get to eventually, so you can look at all of these at once by sorting on the Priority column and scrolling to the bottom of your master list. Some of these ideas may be ripe for action.

Keep in mind, though, that many of the ideas you dropped on your master tasks list will probably be found to be miniprojects if you analyze them. That is, they probably each would require many steps to complete. So if you decide a particular idea has matured, don't just instantly drop it on your daily tasks list. Rather take a moment and think the implementation through and parse out the next action first. Remember, the text box of an Outlook task is an excellent place to record any brainstormed intermediate steps you may identify.

If I am short on time, I do not review this ideas list every week. Reviewing it monthly is a fair goal.

Review Your Goals

We will talk more about goals in chapter 9, but for now let's say this: one hopes some of your miniprojects represent important goals you have. During weekly planning, make sure you give those goal-based projects as much if not more importance than projects that may have been assigned to you by others. You want to make sure that tasks from those goals become assigned to your workdays throughout the week ahead. Either schedule appointment time for them, or place them on your daily tasks list.

Review Daily List

Review the daily list and revise the dates on anything that has not been completed in the week just finished. This is the time to take sober stock of what you did and did not accomplish in the week. In the heat of the week's activities, things may have been moving too fast to understand fully the best steps for each task. So now take the time and do that. You can learn a lot from this review.

If you continually find that many important tasks are not completed, it may be the time to do some simple capacity planning. I will cover this in detail in chapter 9, Advanced Topics, but essentially this is estimating the time to complete each task, totaling the time available in the week, and adding additional task work time or renegotiating commitments as needed. See page 199 for a full discussion.

You should also reprioritize. Within the existing daily list you may need to convert some medium items to high if they have been postponed so long as to become urgent. Or you may move some medium priority items back to the master list, recognizing that their importance has waned over time.

Look Ahead on Your All Daily Tasks List

Open the All Daily Tasks view and look in particular at any tasks that are going to start in the week ahead. Remember, these are tasks whose due date you set into the future. You did that either because they truly were associated with that date (like a weekly status report) or because they were lower priority tasks you moved out to clear up a busy day earlier in the week. You may as well verify that these forward-dated tasks still make sense since they will soon be popping up in the middle of your week ahead. In the heat of the battle during the coming week, you may not have time to think about their importance. So it is good to remove unnecessary distractions now if possible. Use the time you have now to weigh your priorities and decide if the tasks are needed this week. Or you may decide that some tasks scheduled for later in the week need to have their due dates pulled in a bit, because their urgency has increased since you last looked at them.

Time Management: Finding Time to Work on Tasks

Just as important as deciding *what* to do is deciding *when* to do it, and making sure time is available. Everyone's work patterns are different. Some of you have endless meetings all day long. Others of you may sit at your desk working assignments most of the day. Or you may have operational responsibilities scheduled throughout the day. Some of you may travel extensively. And I'm sure there is everything in between. So you will need to appropriately design your approach to making time for working tasks.

If you are at your desk all day and are not devoted exclusively to operational activities, you may not need to set aside dedicated task working time; your workday is your task day. If you are in meetings most of the day the opposite is true; you are going to need to identify periods of time in the day when you will accomplish your task list, and schedule those periods on your calendar.

Setting General "Tasks" Appointments

My typical day falls somewhere in between the above scenarios. I am often 50 to 60 percent booked with meetings, so I usually have time in between those meetings for working tasks.

During busy weeks when meetings are more prevalent, I need to schedule specific time for working tasks, and I have no problem doing so if I do it ahead of time. When needed, I place one- to two-hour appointments on my calendar labeled simply "Tasks." During those appointments, I work down my daily tasks list trying to complete as many tasks on my list as possible.

There are other weeks when my meeting schedule is so intense that I find it takes some effort to schedule task time.

And at the far end of the scale, it is not unusual to meet executives whose every workday every week consists of endless meetings. After teaching them these task techniques, they concluded that they needed to specifically schedule task time every day of the week, well ahead of time, to prevent the open slots from being claimed by appointment seekers. You may find this works for you too. It is something you should strongly consider because it prevents your only available task time from being after-hours time. Many of the meetings that subsequently cannot be scheduled probably were not critical anyway.

Using Task Time Effectively

If your task time is limited, you may need to protect it to prevent the time from being consumed by interruptions. Task time is usually worked at your desk and so is prone to drop-by visits. You may need to establish some understanding with your team on when your uninterrupted work hours are, and that you wish to be undisturbed during those times.

Note that it is also very easy for you to create your own distractions and use such time for unimportant activities. Many of us (myself included) tend to take appointments scheduled with others more seriously than appointments scheduled with ourselves, which is what this time really is. We may tend to "relax into" the general task time and lose productivity. This is particularly likely if you have intense meetings all day long and find these task periods at your desk to be your only time to slow down and unwind. The section titled Cleaning Up Your Task Time in chapter 9, Advanced Topics, explores some specific ideas to optimize your scheduled task time.

Another remedy is to schedule these task times for periods when you are fresh and not in need of unwinding, as discussed next.

Time Mapping

One technique highlighted by Julie Morgenstern in her book on time management, *Time Management from the Inside Out*, is something called time mapping. This expands upon a best practice recommended by nearly all the time and

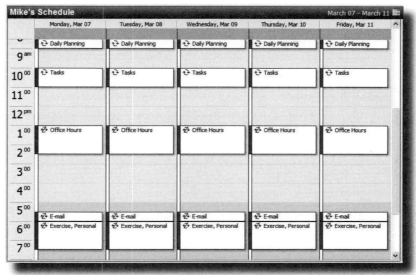

task management experts: identify the times of day that you are best at doing certain activities, and schedule those times throughout the week for their optimum usage (see figure 5.6).

So for example if you like to do tasks in the morning when your mind is clear, make sure that you have a standing meeting with yourself on your calendar for task processing every day at that same time. If you like to keep open office hours after lunch when you enjoy conversations with colleagues and subordinates, schedule a block of open time in your calendar every day at that time. In other words, map each day the same throughout the week. This is often difficult to pull off completely due to previously set standing meetings (figure 5.6 is an idealized example), but to whatever degree you can, you will optimize your natural cycle.

Giving Yourself Priority

Scheduling the Time

And while setting aside time for tasks why not also set aside time for yourself? Have you been promising yourself to make visiting the gym a regular occurrence? Use this time-mapping approach to block out your exercise time regularly on your schedule when that works best. How about making time for your important personal roles and responsibilities, like family and friends? This is the way to do it; start blocking your time now and living by your priorities.

Your first complaint about this idea, of course, is that it removes time from your schedule for work and so how are you now going to get your work done? The answer is that you are never going to have enough time to do all the work that you and others send your way. So you need to set your highest work and personal priorities first and then allow the lower priority ones that don't fit to fall off the bottom of your list (renegotiating with stakeholders as needed). If this idea is troubling or unclear, reread the section called The Working Late Syndrome on page 30 of chapter 2.

Using the Time

You also need to give yourself permission to use that personal time when you see it on your calendar. In the split second of deciding whether to leave for the gym or continue working, it is sometimes easy to keep working; you know that is what is expected of you, and you want to get all your "stuff" done. Especially if you work in an office where everyone works late, the peer pressure can be enormous.

This is more of a psychological question than an operational or technique question. Entire books have been written about solving dilemmas like this. Again, I refer you to Stephen Covey's *First Things First*, in particular chapter 9, Integrity in the Moment of Choice. The gist of the solution is this: you need to decide what is "right" in life and then believe in your decision. You need to convince yourself that you and others will accept and actually respect this integrity-based approach to life, and then you need to start living that belief.

If you can force yourself to make those tough decisions several days in a row, the right actions become habit and yes, you will soon start leaving for the gym every day at the same time. This is why time mapping works if you really can make the appointment every day; it relies on making the decision a habit.

Specific Task Appointments

For Large or Tough Tasks

Occasionally you will come across a task that is accurately recorded in your daily list as a next action and yet it is clear that it will take several hours or more to accomplish. Or perhaps you have a task that has a hard due date that you need to ensure gets done. In cases such as these, rather than scheduling general "task time" on your schedule, it is better to schedule the specific task by name on your calendar. In general, if you have trouble getting tasks done working off only your task list, this is one possible solution. Do this scheduling during your daily or weekly planning.

This technique has advantages and disadvantages. Among the advantages are that it is a great way to make sure specific tasks have task time set aside for them. It also highlights the importance of a task.

A Word of Caution

However, it can be an inefficient use of time as well, and so you should be careful with it. Why? Because you will tend to fill the time allotted even if the full time is not needed. You may tend to overestimate the time slot needed and then "relax" into the time when it arrives. The advantage of a daily tasks list is that you always have a next task down the list that you can jump to when you finish the first one, and so you work through them more quickly. My recommendation is to use the one task per appointment approach only when needed for stuck or urgent tasks, and normally to work off your next action daily list.

Converting Tasks to Appointments in Outlook

To speed the operation of converting a task to an appointment, note that you can do this by simply dragging the task from the TaskPad to the appointment calendar. The new appointment window pops up ready for editing. You will need to enter the start and stop times by hand; Outlook does not set the times by where you "drop" the task.

Also note that if you right-click before you drag you can choose to move the task rather than copy it. However I do not recommend doing that. Moving a task deletes the task from the task list and you don't want to do that; otherwise, if the scheduled work time gets away from you due to distractions, the task is no longer on your task list day after day reminding you to try again later.

Here's a hint: when writing the name of the task appointment, record the name of the deliverable that must be complete at the end of that appointment time. So instead of "Review Jim's performance," write: "Complete Jim's performance review document." While the difference seems subtle, using a deliverable name in the action statement ensures the time is more focused.

Summary

You will find over time that if you have set up and written your daily tasks as next actions, then working tasks is nearly automatic. You will find that you no longer need to struggle to get individual tasks done during the day because the actions pop right out at you. That is the beauty of the next action approach to tasks; the title of the task itself tells you what to do next.

So your primary job becomes controlling what tasks appear on your daily list. You need to make sure high value tasks are there, and that the size of the list is not overwhelming. And you need to ensure that you have allowed enough time on your schedule for tasks that are important to your job and to you. Making those decisions and right sizing your daily list result from daily and weekly planning.

I recommend that at first you make daily planning a formal step at the start of each morning. After a while, you will find that you will fit it into your day unconsciously; it will be the logical thing to do when you first glance at your task list for the morning.

Keep weekly planning as a formal appointment on your schedule; it is very easy to postpone this activity, so take a little effort to make sure you get it done. The rewards of weekly planning are enormous; try it and you'll see what I mean.

Review of Key Learnings

This chapter covered best practice number 5, planning. A few key points in this chapter are worth repeating.

- Do your daily planning first thing in the morning, to start your day right.

- Try to keep the TaskPad list short enough so that you can see the entire list without scrolling, and preferably much shorter.

- Once you have scheduled a task as an appointment on your calendar, also keep the task on your daily tasks list; this is so you do not lose the task if your appointment is canceled.

- Use the Due Date field to prioritize within your medium level tasks. Set it earlier than today to move tasks lower in the list; set it later than today to remove tasks from the visible daily list until that day arrives.

Next Steps

This completes the suite of task-management-only best practices. Next you will learn how to merge e-mail into your Total Workday Control system.

Chapter Six

Converting E-Mail to Tasks and Using Workflows

Getting Your Inbox Under Control

Your Outlook Inbox is probably out of control. This is true for most e-mail users; it's usually only the degree of disarray that varies. Outlook has powerful built-in but rarely used features you can learn that help solve this problem. These solutions, when combined with task management principles, complete the suite of Outlook activities you need to learn to get your workday under control.

This chapter provides an overview of Outlook e-mail management, specifically looking at best practice number 6: converting e-mails to tasks. The chapter then focuses on using best practice workflows as part of your Outlook e-mail management. Chapter 7 will cover best practices for *filing* e-mails.

The Problems with an Out-of-Control E-Mail System

Letting lots of mail sit in your Inbox leaves you with that nagging feeling of unprocessed to-do items. It will probably lead to dropped tasks and replies. And it will complicate your search for important saved e-mails.

Not acting promptly on e-mails frustrates the goals of team collaboration. It lowers the impact of your interactions with outside business associates. And if sloppy e-mail handling becomes common behavior in an organization, it hinders the effectiveness of the organization.

And while better e-mail processing is not a task management topic per se, it will greatly impact your ability to get tasks done. Setting up an effective e-mail processing workflow is an essential step toward increasing your effectiveness with your tasks. Making a near-empty Inbox one goal of this processing goes a long way toward helping you know that you can finally focus on important but not urgent activities (like strategic thinking, or going home on time to see your family).

Most People Know Their E-Mail Is Out of Control

Nearly everyone agrees there is a problem with their e-mail. These are some common complaints:

- I get just too many e-mails each day to possibly be able to process them all adequately.

- It takes too long to read and process e-mails.

- My colleagues do not respond to the e-mails that I send them.

- Too many of the e-mails I get are of low value and are a waste of time for me.

- My Inbox is out of control... I promise to clean it out soon... I sense important things are in there that I am not attending to.

- I feel overwhelmed and behind on all these e-mails.

- I have a filing system for e-mails, but I can never find stuff after I file it... and I am behind on filing, so I am not sure if stuff is in my Inbox or in one of my folders.

- (And extending into related problems) I have too many meetings and too much work to do so there is no time to read all my e-mails.

The reality is that the problems listed above are not the cause of out-of-control e-mail; rather, they are the symptoms. There is nothing inherently wrong with e-mail, nor with large volumes of business-related e-mail. In fact, just the contrary: using e-mail correctly is a phenomenal way of increasing your accomplishments at work, of getting your tasks done more quickly, and of avoiding working late hours trying to get everything done.

E-Mail Advantages

Here are the advantages of e-mail:

- Using it batches up communication processing, which allows you to focus for longer periods of uninterrupted time on dedicated work.

- Sending e-mail prevents you from needing to interrupt or distract yourself and your coworkers every time you need to pass on information or seek it out.

- It speeds communications because you can send a message without starting a live discussion, which usually takes longer.

■ It speeds communications because you do not need to wait for appropriate times to deliver a communication.

■ E-mail tracks communications because a record is left of every sent and received e-mail.

■ It clarifies communications because the well-written word often leaves little room for misunderstanding; the reader can reread a message as often as is needed to fully understand the communication.

All of these advantages, when fully realized, will contribute to getting your tasks done more quickly and accomplishing more.

E-mail is becoming increasingly critical in the business world. It is now the substitute for most formal memos. It is the format for most written business communications. I suspect that you now get far more e-mail than you do paper mail in your business. To not have a well-oiled process for dealing with your e-mail is to not have a smoothly flowing business routine.

When Your Inbox Is Out of Control

When e-mail gets out of control and becomes ineffective all the advantages listed above largely disappear. If you and your coworkers do not use e-mail effectively, then:

■ It leads to more meetings or phone calls, since live communications are the only option when people do not respond to e-mails.

■ It leads to a need to interrupt people at their desk, again since e-mail is being ignored.

■ It leads to poor individual task processing since tasks are often lost in the e-mail.

■ It leads to dropped workflow next steps, and stalled initiatives, since the flow of collaborative work through e-mail gets interrupted.

■ It leads to dropped business communications and opportunities with external business associates.

The message is clear: when e-mail usage is ineffective, team effectiveness drops and team collaboration becomes sluggish. Your business will suffer.

Best Practices and Workflows

Each of the above e-mail weaknesses can be eliminated by implementing e-mail best practices and workflows. While you may not be able to convert your entire team to good e-mail habits, you certainly can set an example by adopting good habits yourself. And most of the advantages of good e-mail usage flow one way; you will benefit greatly even if others do not.

What follows is a discussion on how to implement best e-mail practices within Outlook so that you can use e-mail to its fullest advantage. You will learn a workflow that eliminates tasks from being lost in your e-mail. You will learn a workflow that greatly improves your ability to file away read e-mails so that you can find them later and they do not clutter your Inbox. These best practices and workflows accomplish three main goals:

- Processing your e-mail quickly and providing prompt responses,

- Clearly identifying tasks in your e-mail and getting them into your task list, and

- Having a clear, uncluttered Inbox and being able to find filed e-mails promptly.

Processing Quickly and Responding Promptly to E-Mail

Processing quickly and responding promptly to e-mails you receive is essential to encouraging fluid collaboration within your team and organization and with your outside business associates. Getting through your e-mails quickly frees you for other important business activities.

Prompt replies eliminate many of the negative outcomes listed above of poor e-mail processing. It is the grease that lubricates a well-oiled team machine. It makes a huge difference in the productivity of your organization. Getting quick answers speeds the job you're focused on. And when you can rely on quick e-mail answers to your daily collaboration activities, then you do not need to rely on slower in-person meetings and phone calls to get your tasks done. Your team should establish a reasonable standard for e-mail reply time and stick to it. The workflows described below enable rapid e-mail replies.

Converting E-Mails to Tasks

A huge number of tasks these days arrive via e-mail, either as explicit tasks from your boss or colleagues, or as implicit tasks represented by required follow-ups the e-mails generate. Tasks embedded in e-mails are one reason many people do not clean their Inbox; they know that important e-mails are in there with activities they need to act on or information they need to remember. So to be safe nothing is tossed or filed. But then those embedded tasks get lost in the huge collection of old e-mails; not only do they not get done, but the e-mail Inbox becomes an unusable mess.

Converting e-mails to tasks is the solution. It is so important that most of this chapter, starting with the section below, has been devoted to it.

Clearing Your Inbox by Filing

Clearing your Inbox has huge benefit in multiple ways. First, it removes from your psyche that feeling of clutter and unattended responsibilities that haunts you whenever you glance at your overflowing Inbox.

Next, it saves you time because it allows you to clearly delineate between mail that needs further processing and mail that you no longer need to read; without clearing your Inbox you'll be constantly glancing through old mail in search of to-dos and unfiled information. In contrast, with the Inbox-clearing workflows taught in this chapter and the next, you need to reread your e-mail much less frequently.

And finally, using a good workflow for clearing your Inbox prevents you from allowing responsibilities buried in e-mail items to get away from you. Capturing and processing while clearing your Inbox acknowledges those responsibilities quickly and efficiently and allows you to respond in a timely manner.

Converting E-Mails to Outlook Tasks

The Most Important Best Practice

For the average knowledge worker, the most important of the eight best practices is number 6: convert e-mails that require later action to tasks. If it is so important, why didn't I make it number 1, you ask? This is because, to make use of this best practice, you need to have a strong task management system in place. You need to have learned and be using best practices 1 through 5 successfully so you know what to do with those tasks that you create from your e-mails. Assuming you have not skipped the first part of this book, you are now ready.

I cannot emphasize enough how critical the best practice of converting e-mails to tasks is. It makes a huge difference in your ability to use e-mail productively. It provides a major step in successful task management and in getting control of your busy workday. And it is a principal requirement to allow you to empty your Inbox quickly.

Why This Works So Well

Identifying tasks embedded in your e-mail and clearly converting them to distinct Outlook tasks is tremendously powerful. One reason is that it removes a nasty ambiguity that we are often faced with when trying to act on or clean our Inbox. How many times have you stared at an e-mail and sensed that it was important, but you had no clear quick next step for it? The ambiguity usually exists because, to do the mail item justice, it would take far more time or steps than you had in mind at the moment. In such cases we have a choice of plunging into the implied action, and in so doing, derailing our efforts to proceed quickly through our Inbox. Or we can leave the item in the Inbox and come back to it at some undetermined later time (which we suspect may be much later or never). Because neither choice seems appropriate, the mind becomes conflicted and usually freezes on such items. Often, after an uncomfortable pause, we just move on to the next item leaving this one sitting in the

Inbox, since we can't figure out what to do with it. Repeatedly misprocessing task-laden e-mails like this leads to a number of problems:

- An overflowing, out-of-control Inbox.

- Working low priority items first: working on activities as you see them in your e-mail often leads to working on low priority items first at the expense of high priority items.

- Slowness in processing e-mails.

- Multiple readings of e-mail.

- Trying to use the Inbox as your task list, and then losing or wrongly prioritizing the tasks.

- Stalling on an e-mail, or action paralysis: "What should I do with this?"

- Skipping over e-mails and promising to come back to them.

- And finally, a negative or fatalistic approach toward your Inbox: "I'm never going to get through all of these."

An Easy Solution

The solution to this problem is remarkably easy: simply convert task-laden e-mails into explicit tasks and move them into your task list. The task list is where these items belong because you can prioritize and work these tasks when you are focused on doing tasks rather than when you have decided you should be reading mail. It is important to separate these two styles of activities.

And if you think to yourself, "I will still have to work on these later, I have not gained anything," you are wrong. This remarkably easy solution is also remarkably powerful. By putting these items in your task list you have placed them where they can and will be worked in the proper time, priority, and mind frame. This clear allocation of intention results in far superior outcomes.

And more importantly you have removed the ambiguity — you can now quickly move on to the next e-mail, without being dragged down by the uncertainties of identifying how and when to do the task-heavy mail item. This allows you much greater speed in clearing your Inbox with the confidence that these important tasks will not be lost.

Use Built-In Tools

When you find an action item in your e-mail you could create a new task by hand. Sometimes all the instructions or background information that you need to complete the task are in the e-mail you received, so you could copy and paste the text of the e-mail into that new hand-created task.

Outlook 2002 and 2003 offer easier methods to convert e-mail messages directly into tasks, however, with all enclosed e-mail information intact. If you are planning to make this a regular habit then you should take advantage of these methods. Since they are so simple, they will encourage you to actually create tasks when needed. Those methods are covered below and are simple to learn.

This simplicity of converting e-mails to tasks is one of the most powerful features of Outlook. From the perspective of task management, it's a fantastic way to make sure tasks get entered into your task system. From the perspective of e-mail management, it's a fantastic way to get e-mails out of your Inbox. By converting e-mails containing implicit or explicit tasks to actual tasks, you enable the removal of that e-mail from your Inbox; it has now been "handled" and the original message can now be filed away.

Methods of Converting E-Mails to Tasks

When you convert an e-mail to a task, the entire text of the mail is stored in the text portion of the new task, and the subject line of the task takes on the subject line of the e-mail (which you can then easily edit). There are two different ways to convert an e-mail into a task: one is best for e-mails without attached files, the other best for e-mails with attached files.

Creating Tasks from E-Mails Without Attachments

After deciding that an e-mail *without an attached file* contains a task that is important to you, close the e-mail and do these steps:

1 From within your regular e-mail view click the e-mail item in your e-mail list view and drag it over to the Tasks folder icon in the navigation area of Outlook. Depending on which version of Outlook you have and how you have configured it, that Tasks folder icon might be located in the Outlook Bar, as in Outlook 2002; it might be in a Folder List pane; or it might be at the bottom of the Navigation Pane as in Outlook 2003. See chapter 3, pages 48 to 50, for a complete discussion of where to find the Tasks folder icon.

2 Once you drag it there, release the mouse and a new Task dialog box will open. The beauty of this approach is that the new Task dialog box will contain the entire e-mail text, and the task name will equal the name of the e-mail. That means you have very little typing to do to complete the conversion. But you should at a minimum do the following steps immediately:

3 Change the title of the task to a title that is in next action format. This is an essential step; you must extract from the e-mail the core next action it implies and write that into the subject line, overwriting the old e-mail title.

4   Set a due date for this task. Set it to today if you want to see it in the Task-Pad now, or defer it to a later date. Or leave it without a date if you want to make the e-mail into a master task.

5   Then click Save and Close in the upper left corner of the new Task dialog box.

That's it! Your task has been saved in the task database inside Outlook. If the Due Date field was set to today, then you can see the new task appear right now in your TaskPad.

This simple built-in feature of Outlook, being able to quickly convert e-mails into tasks, is one of the single most important task management capabilities that Outlook provides. It greatly improves your ability to identify and process important tasks, and it allows you to clean your Inbox in ways you have never been able to do before.

Note that converting an e-mail to a task by this left-click and drag method will not save any e-mail attachments into the new task. Nor will it allow you to easily convert the task back into an e-mail. If you want to do either of these follow the steps below.

Creating Tasks from E-Mails with Attachments

If your e-mails to be converted to tasks have attachments that you wish to save within the final task item, or if you may want to convert the task back to an e-mail someday, then do this: when you start to drag the mail item to the task folder simply right-click the item first instead of a left-clicking it. This causes, on release of the mouse button over the Tasks folder icon, a shortcut menu to open. From this menu you should choose: Copy Here as Task with Attachment. In Outlook 2003 this is the second item in the menu; in Outlook 2002 this is the third item in the menu (see figures 6.1 and 6.2).

This operation saves the complete e-mail as an attachment inside the task, appearing as a simple icon in the task body (see figure 6.3). Any attachments to the original e-mail are left intact nested inside this attachment. Immediately retitle the task to indicate the core next action.

To open the original e-mail simply double-click the e-mail icon inside the task item; the e-mail that opens is a fully operational e-mail with all its original attachments. Note that you are able to reply to this e-mail if you wish. That makes this right-click technique useful even for e-mails without attachments, if acting on that task might require resending the original e-mail.

This technique is a great way to create follow-up tasks for important e-mail responses you are waiting for, discussed next.

Side Note: *Some people don't like having to double-click an icon when they open their Task dialog box in order to see the task text and attachment. So if you really want to see the text of the e-mail and see the attachment, do this: create the task using the text-only method described first; then open the original e-mail and drag the e-mail attachment from the e-mail to the newly created Task dialog box. This way you get both the e-mail text and the attachment visible when you open your new task.*

Figure 6.1
Outlook 2003 conversion of e-mail to task with attachment menu choice.

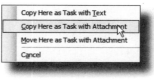

Figure 6.2
Outlook 2002 conversion of e-mail to task with attachment menu choice.

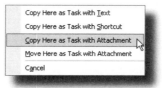

Figure 6.3
Result of creating a task with the original e-mail saved as an attachment.

Attached original e-mail

Also note that when you right-click before you drag you can choose to *move* the e-mail into a task rather than *copy* it. However I do not recommend doing that. Moving an e-mail deletes the e-mail from the e-mail list which is undesirable because you may need to refer to it again later after it is filed.

Create Tasks When You Are Waiting for Important E-Mail Responses

When I send an important "request" e-mail I often set for myself a corresponding follow-up task to look for a reply. Reason: I am sometimes frustrated by colleagues and staff who fail to respond to simple requests I send them; I suspect you are too. Often their one-minute effort to respond will advance my miniproject immeasurably.

Saving All Sent Mail

You should confirm that your copy of Outlook is configured to automatically create an entry in the Sent Items folder for all mail you send. This will become important when creating tasks from sent mail. There are two places to do this. The first is under E-mail Options as shown in figure 6.4; the setting shown is the default setting, and correct, so just be sure you did not turn this off. To confirm this configuration, open the Tools menu, choose Options, click the Preferences tab, click the E-mail Options button, and ensure the Save Copies of Messages in the Sent Items Folder option is selected (figure 6.4).

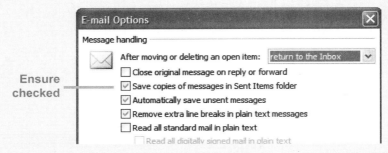

Figure 6.4   Ensure the Save Copies of Messages in Sent Items Folder is checked.

If you are using Outlook 2002, you should also adjust your system is set to save *all* sent mail to this folder, even mail sent as replies to locally saved mail. Unfortunately, a default setting in Outlook 2002 is to save reply mail sent from a personal folder (like your Processed Mail folder) into the same local folder, not into the Sent Items folder. To remove this unfortunate setting, do this: open the Tools menu, choose Options, click the Preferences tab, click the E-mail Options button, click the Advanced E-mail Options button, and in the dialog box that opens, clear the check box titled: In Folders Other than the Inbox, Save Replies with Original Message, as in figure 6.5 below.

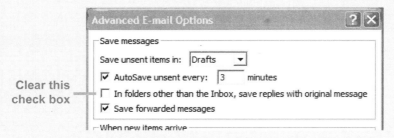

Figure 6.5   To ensure that all sent mail is saved in the Sent Items folder, clear this setting in the Advanced E-mail Options dialog box.

The trouble is that to be polite I usually give them a few days to respond, and by then I have forgotten that I am waiting. I often only realize I've received no response on the day my miniproject is due. It's too late by that time, and then with many in this situation the blame game starts ("Bill never got back to me; I would have completed this if he hadn't dropped the ball").

While this problem is fairly common, it is especially common with "background projects" first discussed on page 35 of chapter 2. In those cases the staff usually don't work for you and so deprioritize your requests. And if you are juggling five or ten background projects, like many managers are, it is impossible to keep all the loose end requests that are hanging out there in your head.

So if you are on the hook for completing a multistep task, and if a key step of that activity requires you to receive an e-mail response from someone, do the following. At the moment you send the e-mail request, set a follow-up task for yourself to remind that person later, in case they don't reply. Set your task to appear on your daily list at some reasonable number of days into the future but well before the due date of your multistep task. That way if they drop the ball on getting back to you, you are reminded to escalate this while you still have time to get your task done.

To do this easily in Outlook, immediately after you send the e-mail, open the Sent Items folder and find the item (it will be at the top of the date-sorted list); then right-click and drag the item to the Tasks folder icon. When you drop the item there a popup menu appears from which you should choose: Copy Here as Task with Attachment, as described in the section above.

Side Note: *To make all this possible, be sure you have made the settings described in the inset on the facing page: Saving All Sent Mail. Otherwise, you may have no sent mail records to work with.*

Then set the due date to a reasonable day to send them a reminder. And set the subject text to start with an "F:" to signify this is a follow-up task. A complete subject line annotation system is described in chapter 8, Delegation.

Side Note: *If the e-mail and follow-up task is the result of acting on another task that now must wait for the reply, you may want to forward date that original task to after the reminder date, so you don't keep seeing and considering it.*

When the due date arrives and the follow-up task appears in your task list, if your request is unfulfilled, you can open the message from within the task and resend it as part of your escalation with the recipient. Even better: when you open the message from inside the task, *reply* to your own message (adjusting the To: field back to the recipient) and write a sentence such as "Wondering if you received my e-mail below and had any thoughts." The reply action inserts a header above the old mail that clearly shows the recipient that the message was originally sent addressed to them, and the date it was sent (presumably some time ago). This is usually pretty effective at jogging some action.

For those who may have used a "waiting for " list in the past to track items like this, I find the above approach much better because the follow-up item actually contains all the information needed to remind the tardy staff. And more importantly the item does not appear until it has aged an appropriate amount. There is nothing worse than bugging someone about a request without letting them have time to work on it. It also avoids you having to do a mental calculation every time you look at a waiting-for list to decide whether action is needed on the items in the list. And finally, it avoids you having more than one daily list to track. Rather, the follow-up task appears on your single daily tasks list (the TaskPad) and at just the right time.

Use of Follow-Up Flag Tool

I have one exception to the rule of not leaving anything in the Inbox as you clean it, and that's this: if the action needed for an e-mail is simply to reply to it, and yet you know you don't have time to do it quickly in the moment (say because it will take more than a minute or two to compose your reply), it is silly to convert it to a task. Rather, I recommend that you flag this message with an Outlook follow-up flag. This is a small (usually red) flag that sits in the margin of the e-mail message list. Then, when you collect and move your e-mails into the processed e-mail folder, just avoid the flagged items; leave them in the Inbox. The advantage of leaving such pending reply mail in the Inbox is that it ensures you will see it often. This keeps the reply task a high priority. It's either that or convert it to a high priority task, which takes a few more steps. You should however make a commitment to yourself to return and reply to those messages before the end of the day.

The way you add a follow-up flag to a message is to select the message in the mail list, right-click, and choose Follow Up from the shortcut menu. In Outlook 2003 that menu opens submenus in which you can choose the color of the flag; I normally choose red (see figure 6.6).

I find I very rarely use the follow-up flag: replies are usually delayed due to need for some action, and so conversion to a task is usually much more appropriate.

Ways Not to Use the Follow-Up Flag

There are a lot more things you can do with the follow-up flag, including setting alarms to remind you of follow-ups. Some people use follow-up flags as a form of task list within their e-mail. I strongly recommend *against* using these capabilities because they get you in the habit of leaving tasks in your e-mail Inbox, and the Inbox is not a good location for tasks. Reason: once you collect more than five or six flagged e-mails they are difficult to keep track of. While you might be able to change the title of an e-mail to a next action phrase, this could make your e-mail history confusing, so it is best not to. Without doing

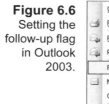

Figure 6.6
Setting the
follow-up flag
in Outlook
2003.

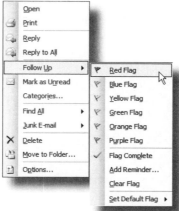

so though, if you leave tasks in your Inbox without action titles, you will be constantly guessing what the flagged e-mails are really for; you will need to open each e-mail and reread it to figure out what the task actually is. And there is no provision for master tasks in this scenario.

So even though the follow-up flag may seem versatile, using it to mark tasks in the Inbox is really only a stopgap for those using less effective Outlook approaches, where e-mail is left for weeks or months in the Inbox. Rather the much better practice is to convert all action e-mails to tasks and use the follow-up flag only for the limited purposes described above—to mark delayed replies.

Recommended E-Mail Processing Workflow

All of the recommendations above should come together when you sit to read and process your Outlook e-mail Inbox. There are many different ways to combine these tools and you will develop a preferred method over time. Until you do, let me suggest an idealized workflow that incorporates all the elements of e-mail processing best practices.

The details of all the steps in this workflow have been covered in this chapter, except for step 6 (filing), which will be covered in the next chapter.

The structure of the steps should help your thinking as you start to put all the elements of this system together. But if not, if the multiple steps here just complicate things for you, the most important element of all can be summarized in one simple statement:

If an e-mail indicates that an action is required and you can't do it now, immediately convert the e-mail to a task.

If you remember and act on this alone, you will be miles ahead of your e-mail issues.

And now, study the detailed e-mail workflow on the facing page (this workflow is copied in the back of Appendix C, so you can clip it out and place it next to your computer).

Try to Empty Your Inbox

When completed with this workflow, the only read-mail left in the Inbox should be mail that is flagged for a later reply. And commit yourself to processing those flagged replies within a day. If your immediate reply to an e-mail is "I will get back to you in a week" then also create a task from it now to do so and process the mail out of the Inbox. Any mail that requires a later action other than a simple reply that day should be converted to a task.

There is a tremendously satisfying feeling once you have completely cleaned your Inbox, so I urge you to work toward that goal. It clearly signals that you are completely done with that batch of e-mail. It frees your mind to move on to the next activities at hand. And it ensures that you do not drop or misplace any activities. So if after processing your Inbox completely you see any messages in there (without follow-up flags), you are not finished; keep working until the Inbox is empty.

Thoughts about the Workflow

Isn't This Complicated?

This may seem like a lot of steps, but after a little practice you will speed through these steps almost instantly, and you will only spend a few seconds per e-mail on processing actions. In fact, once you get the hang of it, your e-mail processing will go dramatically faster than your previous methods. This is because you now have a very crisp decision-making process with which to treat your e-mail. You have removed ambiguity from your e-mail processing. Using this workflow there are rarely any questions about what to do with a given e-mail; it is indecision that slows e-mail processing, and this process removes indecision. You will find you rarely need to reread e-mails. The net result is much faster e-mail processing, and an Inbox that gets fully emptied. And batching your categorization (discussed in the next chapter) speeds this even more.

Refrain from Working Your Tasks until After the Inbox Is Processed

As stated in the task chapters of this book, you need to get out of the habit of working a task the moment you see it delivered to you. Otherwise you'll never get to your high priority tasks. This principle works with e-mail too. When processing your Inbox you are going to see a lot of things that seem to need immediate attention. Make a pact with yourself that unless that action can be accomplished in a minute, you will convert the action to a task in your TaskPad (or perhaps to an e-mail flagged for follow-up reply later in the day). Stick with this pact, or you will never get through your Inbox. Only when you

The Total Workday Control E-Mail Workflow

Read Each E-Mail, and...

1 Delete: Decide if the mail has no action and no later value and should be deleted (junk mail, useless banter, and so forth). If so delete it immediately. Don't spend much time on this. If you are uncertain, plan on keeping it and move on to the next step.

For All E-Mail You Decide Not to Delete...

2 Act on it now: Decide if the e-mail generates the need for an immediate action and if that action can be done quickly (completed in one minute); if so just do it now. That action might be to reply to the e-mail, forward it, make a quick call, send a new e-mail to someone else, and so on. Choose this option cautiously though, because that one minute can easily expand to five or ten.

3 Mark for reply: If the only action needed is to reply to the e-mail but it will take more than one minute to do so, flag it with an Outlook follow-up flag (right-click on the message and choose Follow Up), and leave it in your Inbox until you can reply. These should be the only items left in your Inbox. If, however, the reason you cannot reply immediately is because some other action has to happen first, follow the next step instead.

4 Most important—Convert it to a task: If an action other than a simple reply is needed but cannot be done now, create an Outlook task and copy/convert the mail to a task using the steps described in the sections above.

5 Set follow-up task: If your action is to make a quick reply or send a new message, after you do so, consider whether you need to set a follow-up task for that message, following the instructions in the section above titled Create Tasks When You Are Waiting for Important E-mail Responses.

6 File it: Assign Outlook Categories as appropriate or as desired, using the techniques in the next chapter. Do not spend too much time on this; if no appropriate category jumps out at you leave the e-mail uncategorized (occasionally the right step here is to create a new category). And if more than one category seems appropriate choose each of them. In actual practice you'll probably delay step 6 and do your filing in batches as described in chapter 7. Or you may decide to skip categorization in your workflow altogether.

In all cases except mail flagged for pending replies, the next step is to move the processed mail item out of the Inbox and into the Processed Mail folder.

are done processing your Inbox and you have seen and prioritized the entire task list—only then start working the tasks from your TaskPad.

Deleting and Archiving E-Mails

You would think that given the goal of reaching a near empty Inbox, one of the best things you can do to an e-mail is delete it. That's true; if an e-mail is obviously junk then throw it out immediately. But use some caution here: if it takes you more than a second or two to determine that an e-mail should be deleted, then don't bother. I have seen people torture themselves for minutes over whether to delete an e-mail or not, and this defeats the process.

Rather, to keep your e-mail processing going quickly, I recommend you keep all e-mail that you have any doubts about. Disk storage is cheap these days, certainly cheaper than your time. And Outlook has excellent AutoArchive features built in. Appendix B includes strategies for archiving and deleting aged mail and instructions for using the AutoArchive features.

Sent Items Folder

One other point. Your Sent Items folder, as it fills, may drive your Exchange mailbox over its size limit. Remember, if your organization has imposed a limit on your Exchange mailbox size, you will get these messages. What I do when I see the size limit warning message is this: I open the Sent Items folder, sort descending by date, select the bottom half of the messages, and drag them into the Saved Sent mail folder (you will create this folder in chapter 7). Others choose to delete their older sent mail; do whichever fits your work style.

Whether you work with an Exchange Server or not, if you do save all your sent mail, again, take a look at Appendix B for strategies on archiving and deleting aged mail and instructions for using Outlook's AutoArchive features.

How Often to Use This Workflow?

Use steps 1 through 5 whenever you read an e-mail, even if you have only a moment at your computer. They only take a second.

Try to do step 6 (filing) at least once a day; if you are very busy this step can be put off for a few days without too much impact. The problem with putting step 6 off too long is that when you come back to categorize the e-mail you will have forgotten the contents of many of your e-mails, and you may need to reread each to classify them. So it is better to include a filing session whenever you engage in an extended session of e-mail reading. Once you get ahead of your Inbox, looping back at the end of each e-mail reading session to categorize and completely empty your Inbox becomes easy. And the smaller the amount of mail you need to process at once the easier this becomes.

Granted, in-between meetings, when you glance quickly at your Inbox for important messages, you will not have time to do a full processing. But commit to yourself that you will at least engage steps 1 through 5 *every time you read mail*; those steps are quick, and using them will have a remarkable impact on improving your e-mail efficiency. Absolutely commit to doing step 4.

If you are out of the office and miss a few days without processing, do not despair. I agree that returning from a day or two of travel and facing multiple screens worth of e-mail can be demoralizing. However I am continually amazed at how quickly several screens full of e-mail can be processed using the workflow. Even today, I find myself surprised how quickly I can empty a seemingly overloaded Inbox after many days of neglect. Because this workflow provides such a rapid decision-making framework, you will find that your mail processing goes much more quickly than in the past.

Getting Started with the Workflow

When you first start this system, if you are like I once was, you probably have a huge Inbox containing months of historical mail. If so, you have two choices.

You may want to take a Saturday and process and empty your entire Inbox. Doing so will give you lots of practice on the workflow. It will also give you time to think about, set up, and experiment with using the e-mail categories method of filing described in the next chapter. That way when you return to your normal busy workday you will be proficient with processing your mail and can fit the system in without issue. Note the section in chapter 9, Advanced Topics, on automating assignment of categories; this method works equally well on e-mail already in your Inbox and so will speed your bulk processing job.

If you do not have a large block of time available for dedicated catch-up e-mail work, or just don't feel like doing it, your other choice is this: create a second personal folder called Mail Older Than [date], and drag all read e-mail older than that named date, a date that is say five days ago, out of your Inbox and into that folder. Then start your processing on the mail that is left in your Inbox and be sure to empty and keep up with your Inbox from that point forward (don't add any more mail to the Mail Older Than folder). You can always look through your Mail Older Than folder if you think important mail is there. As time passes and the mail in there ages, it becomes less impactful; eventually you will stop referring to that folder. That said, in the weeks of work ahead you might even see if you can periodically dip into the top of the Mail Older Than folder and process a little of your old mail at a time. This is your decision. What's more important though is that you start afresh and stay ahead of your new mail; moving your collection of historical e-mail into the Mail Older Than folder allows this fresh start.

Tape a Copy of This Workflow Next to Your Computer Screen

To get started with this new workflow I recommend you tape a copy next to your computer screen. You can either copy page 141, or go to the extra page in the back of this book that duplicates this workflow and clip it out. After a while the workflow will become second nature and you will not need the list any more. But for now consider yourself in training, and refer to it often.

Remote E-Mail Access: Impact on Workflow

If you also read your mail while away from a full copy of Outlook the above workflow requires a little modification. For example, if you use Outlook Web Access (OWA) or a handheld device like a Blackberry, you cannot use many of the Outlook features needed for this workflow. Reason: many of the special views are not available. You cannot easily categorize and file. And most importantly, you cannot automatically convert e-mails to tasks.

Side Note: *You can drag e-mail to create tasks using OWA but the functionality is different from the full Outlook client and unsuitable for our system.*

Not being able to convert e-mail to tasks is by far the most critical problem of these non-Outlook tools because you do not want to allow tasks that arrive in your e-mail to remain scattered among your read mail. This leads to dropped tasks and the need to reread all your e-mail before you file it, frustrating the intentions of the new workflow. So my recommendation is this: when using remote e-mail readers, find some way to create a task by more manual means. Using Outlook Web Access you can at least copy the text of the e-mail into a manually created task. And if you use a handheld you can create the task by hand in the handheld and sync it later.

If all else fails, find a way to mark a task-laden e-mail when you are finished reading it so that when you return to your main copy of Outlook you know to reread it and convert it to a task then. Mark it either with a distinct follow-up flag, or if that is not possible, as unread. That way you will read it again when you return to your desk later, and convert it to a task then.

Most other aspects of the workflow are not significantly affected by remote access. You can reply, take action, and delete. And you can always do your categorizing and filing when you return to your desk.

Summary

Immediately converting e-mails to tasks as soon as you see an action in them removes the primary source of an out-of-control Inbox. If you do that consistently, and you have established a good task management system per the earlier chapters in this book, the majority of your Inbox woes will evaporate.

Establishing a repeatable e-mail processing habit is essential for creating a successful task management system and essential for keeping your Inbox under control. It will prevent you from losing track of tasks that arrive by e-mail. It will increase the collaborative flow of productive work within your team.

You will be amazed at the sense of relief and control that you get once you have a sustainable e-mail workflow in place that allows you to stay ahead of your Inbox. Your attitude about e-mail will change dramatically. You will begin to appreciate fully the value e-mail brings to you as a work tool, and you will no longer experience that nagging feeling of unattended responsibilities every time you look at your Inbox. And once mastered it may even allow you to leave work at a reasonable hour without feeling that you have left a stack of unfinished work to do.

Review of Key Learnings

- For every e-mail you read, ask yourself what is the action needed for this; if more than a simple reply is called for, convert the e-mail to a task immediately, with the next action in the name of the task.

- Learn to use all the convert-to-task tools built into Outlook.

- Create follow-up tasks for e-mails you send that require action by the recipient.

Next Steps

Now that you have learned how to convert e-mails into tasks and you understand the e-mail workflow, next you need to learn how to clean your Inbox by filing e-mails that you have read and are done with. This is the topic of chapter 7.

Chapter Seven

Filing Your E-Mail Using Outlook Categories

Filing Your E-Mail

I consistently refer to many of my old e-mails as I work through my day, so I appreciate having a good topic-based filing system in place to facilitate finding stored e-mail.

However, topic-based filing is not for everyone. It takes time. Many people rarely look at their old e-mail. And by no means is it a requirement for regaining workday control. Why? Because once you have extracted explicit or implicit tasks from incoming e-mail using the techniques in chapter 6, what you do with it after that is, by comparison, low priority. Compared to taking action on e-mails or converting them to Outlook tasks, filing e-mails by topic is way down the scale. And if you are happy using the powerful Outlook e-mail search tools available, topic-based filing is almost unnecessary.

But even if you do not file e-mails by topic, you will probably want to retain read e-mails in bulk for at least a little while, to enable the occasional revisit of history. You never know when the text of an old message will bail you out of a mess or provide critical reference information to advance a project. So most people do store at least some old mail.

If you keep your old e-mails, you should not store them in your Inbox. Old e-mail stored there will clutter your Inbox and clutter your workday. Some filing system, even very simple, is needed to get old mail out of sight.

Clearing Your Inbox

There is a reason why the place that Outlook stores your incoming mail is called the "Inbox." You may recall the old two- or three-level tray system of processing paper that many office workers once had on their desks. While these systems varied, the top box was always called the "Inbox." And the meaning of this box was simple: it is where new, unprocessed mail and memos were placed. And the rules of most of the systems were this: as soon as you read an item in the Inbox it never went back into the Inbox. Rather it was filed, or disposed of, or placed in one of the lower boxes indicating that the item was "in process." There was great value to these systems and they generally worked well if you knew how to use them.

This idea of using the Inbox only for new unread items has unfortunately been lost by most e-mail users. The Inbox now not only has that receiving function but has also become the place to store read, "in-process" mail that you have additional actions in mind for, as well as being a bulk filing location for old mail. No wonder the Inbox has become so useless to so many people. You just cannot mix all these functions together and hope to make sense of your e-mail.

The simple filing methods that follow mend this problem. Central to these methods is this: the Inbox should only be used for new unread mail. *Once the mail has been read and action taken, or deferred action items converted to Outlook tasks, all mail should be processed out of the Inbox, either by deleting it or by filing it in a searchable way.* This commitment, combined with a commitment to read new e-mail promptly, will generally lead you to a consistently near-empty Inbox.

Filing by Topic Is Optional

The most important lesson here is get read mail out of your Inbox, by either deleting it or filing it out of sight. A less important lesson is how to file mail by topic. In fact, filing by topic is purely optional. Many of my students choose not to categorize e-mail as they file it, but instead file it in bulk. They either rarely search their old mail or use Outlook search tools to find the mail by keyword.

If this description fits you, then at least study the sections ahead that tell you how to get old mail out of your Inbox and into a single saved location. If at a minimum you convert e-mail to tasks and file in bulk, you will be well ahead of any e-mail problems.

However, many if not most of you will probably also want to file your e-mail by topic, which is the subject of most of this chapter.

Filing in Multiple Folders: Not My Preferred Solution

I once held mixed opinions about the importance of filing e-mail by topic as a way of keeping the e-mail Inbox near empty. While the results were usually worthwhile, it often seemed like it required too great an effort. However, in recent years I have become a complete convert.

The reason for my earlier mixed opinion was the lack of a good workflow and my mixed success with filing e-mails in Outlook folders. This latter point—

storing old e-mail within multiple Outlook folders—has been recommended by Outlook experts for years; it is generally the preferred method for storing old mail.

This is one place I break from generally accepted practices because I found they just don't work very well for me. Over the years I discovered and have implemented much better techniques, techniques that I have found are much more successful than filing in folders. I now have no problems keeping my e-mail Inbox empty while still being able to retrieve old mail. And I have taught this technique to scores of other users who find it easy to implement and absolutely worthwhile.

Problems with Filing in Multiple Outlook Folders

The commonly recommended approach to processing and emptying your Inbox is to create a series of custom Outlook folders and to file your e-mails in those named folders as you process the Inbox. I suspect you may have tried this as well. However, using that approach I was never able to achieve this goal of consistently keeping my Inbox even close to clear.

Side Note: *Many Outlook users who successfully use multiple folders still swear by it and find they prefer it to the category method taught here. Your experience and preference should be the final guide.*

The reasons I'd never succeeded is that every time I attempted to clean up the Inbox by filing into multiple custom Outlook folders, I experienced several negative outcomes:

- Before having a good task system, I would often use my Inbox as one of my task lists and so would leave mail there as reminders and not file them.

- Even after establishing a useful task system, I was never really sure when I was "done" enough with an e-mail to file it away. Often I had a vague sense of uncompleted tasks associated with an e-mail that made me want to let it sit in my Inbox until I was sure it was ready to be out of my line of sight.

- Sometimes it seemed like the item belonged in several different folders. Using folders required me to decide on one and only one folder to file it in. In my indecision, I'd leave the item unfiled or waste time and get frustrated with the process.

- Once filed, I would often forget which folder I stored items in and would get frustrated with having to hunt through multiple folders to find them.

- Because of my frustration with folders, I would often not completely file for days or weeks at a time. Then when I needed to look for mail, I would not know whether to look in the folders or in my Inbox and so would waste time searching both.

■ Finally, whenever I instituted the filing system, I regretted no longer having one view of all my collected e-mail. I often locate an e-mail by approximately how far in the past it arrived and by proximity with other events. Or I like to view all e-mails from one individual. I missed the ability to scan through my entire Inbox, sorted either by date or by sender. Having my saved mail split among multiple folders precluded that.

Side Note: *Filing in multiple folders also complicates the use of the Outlook AutoArchive feature, which is covered in Appendix B.*

For these reasons, I have always given up on filing e-mail into a collection of various category-driven Outlook folders. Yet there remained many times that I wished I did have a good filing system for my Inbox.

Better Outlook Filing Solution: Using Outlook Categories

Outlook has another approach that accomplishes a folder-like role but overcomes these shortcomings to filing in folders. This solution uses Outlook Categories combined with either of two Outlook features: Show in Groups or Search Folders. The solution is a godsend for keeping your Inbox clear and enabling you to find important e-mails. It allows you to store your e-mail in a single chronological folder yet view all mail in a folder-like structure. With this approach, all the shortcomings described above are eliminated and a fluid system of filing and finding e-mails is possible.

Outlook Categories

Outlook Categories are simple filing criteria that you can quickly and easily assign to any of the multiple item types used in Outlook. For your e-mail filings solution you will be assigning Outlook Categories to e-mail in your Inbox, and then dragging the mail out of your Inbox into a single Outlook folder. When you want to view your collection of e-mail during searches for mail, you will then open that folder and use Show in Groups or Search Folders to display a folder-like collection of mail grouped by your categories. Following are more details about this solution.

Side Note: *If you are currently using a multiple folder filing system or no system at all, and you wish tips on how to transition to this new category-based system, see the section at the end of this chapter (page 184) called Transitioning.*

Show in Groups and Search Folders

These two features, Show in Groups and Search Folders, while very different, accomplish roughly the same results for our category filing purposes, and so you can use them interchangeably (though I have my preference). Both features are present in Outlook 2003; Outlook 2002 users can use only the Show in Groups feature, as Microsoft first introduced Search Folders in Outlook 2003.

Both Show in Groups and Search Folders allow you to store and view virtual collections of e-mails — collections that you create based on classification criteria. This allows you to view virtual collections that meet criteria like "Web Project" or "Personal," which you assign through Outlook Categories. And since these are virtual collections, you can associate individual mail messages with multiple categories and view them in multiple collections. This critically important capability frees you from the angst of choosing one and only one category assignment at processing time, and so it greatly speeds your ability to file the e-mail. You get the best of both worlds: a clean Inbox and a flexible filing system.

Since this is a virtual collection, all e-mails can remain actually stored in only one folder enabling you to search one folder by date or by sender if you wish. We don't want that one folder to be the Inbox, however, since the function of the Inbox should remain in keeping with its name: a place to store only new mail as it arrives. So rather we are going to create a new folder called "Processed Mail." Once a category is assigned to mail in your Inbox (and other workflow operations described in chapter 6 are engaged), you simply drag the e-mail out of your Inbox into that folder. If you ever want to see one chronological- or sender-sorted view of all your old mail you simply open that Processed Mail folder; it will all be there. If you want to view your folder-like collections of categorized mail you simply open the category view or search folder for that category. This system achieves all of our filing and search goals and it provides a way to clear out the Inbox rapidly.

Side Note: *A side benefit of using Outlook Categories for filing mail is that assigned categories stay with the message during round-trips through an Exchange Server, so e-mail is essentially self-filing the next time you get a reply to a reply.*

Figures 7.1 and 7.2 display how your categorized e-mail will look once opened in Show in Groups and Search Folders respectively.

Five Steps to Implementing an E-Mail Filing System

There are five steps to implementing our e-mail filing system in Outlook.

1 Learn to use Outlook folders.

2 Create a new personal folder called Processed Mail.

Those filing in bulk will stop at end of step 2. Those filing by topic continue:

3 Understand and use Outlook Categories.

4 View your filed mail using Show in Groups.

5 Alternatively, view your filed mail using Search Folders.

In the pages ahead, we will take a look at each step, one at a time.

Figure 7.1
Outlook 2002
with Show in
Groups in use
to display filed
e-mail category
groups (all
categories col-
lapsed).

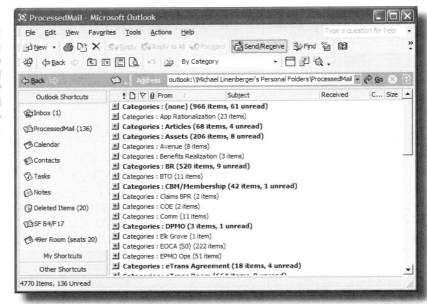

Figure 7.2
Outlook 2003
with Search
Folders in use
to display filed
e-mail.

Side Note: *In figure 7.2 above, the Search Folder called Book Mail is selected on the left and its contents displayed on the right.*

E-Mail Filing Step One: Using Outlook Folders

Showing Outlook Folders

Before you can use Search Folders and Show in Groups correctly you need to learn how to show and use folders in Outlook and specifically how to set up a personal folder for your saved e-mail. You may already be quite experienced at this and already have a personal folder set up for saved e-mail. Even so, stay with this discussion because you are going to need to create a new personal folder in a specific place and way.

I introduced folders in chapter 3 pages 43-55, but only briefly; there is much more to learn. If you are uncomfortable using folders in Outlook, or have never fully understood how they work, I recommend this: place-mark this page and jump ahead and read Appendix A: Understanding Outlook Folders. I think you'll find this to be an excellent explanation of what for many is a mystery. Reading the appendix however is purely optional, and so feel free to plunge ahead now with the steps below.

Folders in Outlook are hierarchical storage areas very much like the folders you see on your hard drive. They differ in that they are visible only within the Outlook system and meaningful only to Outlook (they do not represent actual folders on your hard drive or network, but rather represent separate storage areas within the Outlook data file system itself).

Side Note: *Depending on whether you're working in a Microsoft Exchange Server environment typical for large organizations or in an Internet mail environment (common for home or small office deployments), and depending on whether you've added additional personal folders to Outlook, your folders may look a little different from what you see in the figures ahead. Appendix A explains many of these differences.*

Showing Folders in Outlook 2002

Out of the box, Outlook 2002 hides the folders pane, relying on the Outlook Bar instead for navigation between the folders. Whether you display folders or not, you are using them whenever you switch between the major views in Outlook; all of your tasks are stored in your Tasks folder, all of your contacts are stored in your Contacts folder, and so on. So in Outlook 2002 every time you click on a shortcut on the Outlook Bar to switch major views you're actually switching the folder you're looking at.

However, you can choose to explicitly show the entire list of folders very easily; simply go to the View menu and select Folder List. After you do this, your window will look like figure 7.3. Note that the folders list shows a lot more folders than what is displayed in the Outlook Bar, and this is the main reason I suggest you display it—so you can see the personal folders you will create, and so you can understand how they fit in with your other folders.

Side Note: *In fact, many Outlook 2002 users choose to view only the Folder List and hide the Outlook Bar; this frees a little space on the screen. It also makes navigation slightly*

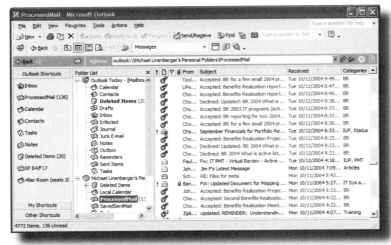

Figure 7.3
Outlook 2002
with Folder
List pane and
Outlook Bar in
place.

more complex because the Folder List pane is a bit more difficult to read. If you want to do this, simply go to the View menu and uncheck the Outlook Bar selection.

Showing Folders in Outlook 2003

Outlook 2003 by default shows the e-mail folders only in its Navigation Pane, as in figure 7.4 (you may need to click first on the Mail banner button as shown at the bottom of figure 7.4 to see this).

If for some reason the complete left panel view is missing from your Outlook window, simply go to the View menu and choose Navigation Pane (this will open the left side navigation area) and then click the Mail banner button; this will display the e-mail folders.

Multiple Folder Lists in Outlook 2003

With Outlook 2003 there are actually four folder lists. The first folder list is dedicated to mail (as described above, called All Mail Folders). The second is a slightly expanded folder view called Folder List (figure 7.6) which is similar to the folder list in Outlook 2002. You reach this expanded view by clicking the Folder List button in the lower right portion of the Navigation Pane (figure 7.5).

Note that the title just above the top of the folders changes to All Folders when you do this. The difference in content of this folder view is subtle (it includes nonmail folders) and not too important for our purposes; you can feel free to use either view. One advantage of using the All Mail Folders view is that it opens a third folder view—a shortcut folder list at the top (called Favorite Folders, see top of figure 7.4). You can drag into this copies of your favorite mail folders for quick navigation, including any personal folders you create (this shortcut list is the third folder list). This is useful and a good

Figure 7.4
Outlook 2003
All Mail Folders
view.

Click here to view the
e-mail folders

Figure 7.5
Opening
Outlook 2003
Folder List.

Click here to open the Folder List

reason to favor this All Mail Folders view; again, you activate this view by clicking on the Mail banner button near the bottom of the Navigation Pane.

Shortcuts in Outlook 2003

The fourth of the four folder lists is the Shortcuts list. This is similar to the Favorite Folders list described above, but that list only shows *mail* favorites. If you wish to have a *multifunction* shortcut capability where you can list mail, task, contacts, and other items (like the Outlook 2002 Outlook Bar), you can also reveal the equivalent in Outlook 2003, called Shortcuts.

Do this by clicking the small shortcut icon at the lower right of the Navigation Pane (figure 7.7). On first use this only opens an empty shortcuts collection.

You then need to add shortcuts by clicking the Add New Shortcut statement shown in the middle of figure 7.8. That figure shows the result of adding seven shortcuts in the top of the list. This shortcuts capability in Outlook 2003, rather than collecting a list of icons like in Outlook 2002, lets you, in effect, build a custom hierarchical folder list; it can be quite useful.

E-Mail Filing Step Two: Creating a New Personal Folder

Before using Search Folders or Show in Groups, you need to create one destination for all processed e-mails. This will be a single Outlook folder that all your e-mail, once processed, is moved to. This allows you to keep a single chronological list view of all e-mail but still process and clear your Inbox. It is within this folder that you will create your folder-like views.

Before creating a new personal folder, however, I highly recommend you read Appendix A: Understanding Outlook Folders. Doing so will ensure that you set up personal folders in a way that is most optimized for your environment. If time is short, feel free to proceed with the steps below; at some point in the future when you do read Appendix A you can change your configurations to better suit the environment your Outlook system exists in.

How to Create a New Personal Folder

These instructions work for both Outlook 2002 and Outlook 2003.

1 Examine your folders using the techniques in the previous section and identify whether you have a personal folders group or not. If you do, skip to step 2. If you do not, please follow the steps on page 243 of Appendix A titled Creating the Personal Folders File: The New Personal Folders Group. Then return to step 2 below.

Side Note: Do not forget to make this personal folders file part of any backup system you may have. Also, study www.workdaycontrol.com for other filing options.

2 Open the File menu of Outlook; choose Folder, and then New Folder from the submenu. The dialog box in figure 7.9 will appear. Note that depending on your setup, the folders in the bottom portion of this dialog box may look different.

3 Type the name of the new folder in the top field; name this folder "Processed Mail."

4 Then in the Folder Contains box, leave the current choice: Mail and Post Items.

5 Within the scrolling folders list at the bottom of this dialog box click once on the words "Personal Folder" so that it is selected. This tells Outlook this new folder will be created within the personal folders file. If you have

Figure 7.6
Outlook 2003's
Folder List is
similar to that of
Outlook 2002.

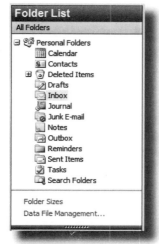

Figure 7.7
Opening
Shortcuts in
Outlook 2003.

Click here to open Shortcuts

Figure 7.8
Outlook 2003
Shortcuts, once
opened.

Figure 7.9
Create New
Folder dialog
box.

more than one personal folder file choose the one you use the most, or the top one.

6 Then click OK. You should see the new Processed Mail folder appear within the folder list in Outlook.

Side Note: *For those of you in a Microsoft Exchange (or IMAP) environment, you have a choice as to where you create this new folder – either in the Mailbox (Exchange) section of your folder list or in the personal folders file section. I recommend this folder be created in the personal folders section as described above. See Appendix A for more details. The exception to this is for those who use Outlook Web Access (the web-based version of Outlook). If you do, study the folder setup options described at the book website: www.workdaycontrol.com.*

Create a Saved Sent Mail Folder

If you work in an Exchange environment and if you have not already created a folder in your personal folders file section to save your old *sent* mail, then do so now. While this is not an integral part of my task and e-mail management system, it's something you should do so that you can periodically clean out your Sent Mail folder on the Exchange Servers but still save the sent mail. This is to prevent messages from your IT department periodically warning you about an oversized mailbox. To create this folder, just repeat the instructions above for the Processed Mail folder and substitute the name "Saved Sent Mail" every place you see the name "Processed Mail." Once created, periodically drag older messages out of your Sent Mail folder into this folder; your IT department will appreciate you for doing this.

If Filing in Bulk, Stop Here

If you have decided not to file by topic, stop here. You can use your new Processed Mail folder, with the workflows presented in chapter 6, to start processing your Inbox. Skip ahead now to chapter 8.

E-Mail Filing Step Three: Assigning Categories to E-Mail

If you want to be able to file and search for e-mail by topic, you now need to learn how to use Outlook Categories. You will be assigning categories to mail just before you drag them into the Processed Mail folder.

Adding the Categories Column

So that you can see your category assignments, you need to add a categories column to your Messages view in your Inbox. To do this, open your Inbox, right-click any of your column headings, and choose from the bottom of the shortcut menu the menu choice: Customize Current View... (Custom... in Outlook 2003). In the dialog box that opens, click Fields... and in the next dialog box (called Show Fields, figure 7.10) click on the word Categories in the list on the left to select it. Then click Add (in the middle of the dialog box) to add that field to the bottom of the list on the right side as shown in figure 7.10. Click OK and then OK again.

If you have any trouble finding the Categories field in the list on the left, try selecting All Mail Fields in the selection box titled Select Available Fields From:, and then look again at the scrolling field list. That should display it.

Once back at your Messages view, you may need to resize the width of the new Categories column to make it more readable. Do this by dragging the margin of the column heading.

Figure 7.10
Show Fields dialog box, after adding the Categories field.

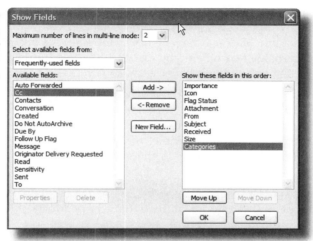

Deciding on the Categories List

What categories should you use for your filing? You will almost certainly not use the default list that comes with Outlook so start thinking about your filing system. You can create categories ahead of time or as you go. Unless you are for some reason synchronizing e-mail with a Palm there is nothing wrong with creating many categories (at the time of this writing, the Palm operating system limited the number of categories it could import to about 15). However if you create way too many, scrolling through the list in Outlook while assigning categories will be slow, so use some sanity. I'll show how to create them below.

I recommend you let your list grow organically. Discover which categories are most useful. Create whatever categories best help you search and find your e-mail.

You can always assign multiple categories to an individual e-mail, the more the better. Such messages will show up in multiple Search Folders or Show in Groups displays. This is a very useful behavior because it eliminates difficult decisions on where to file mail and increases your chance of finding mail later. If two categories apply, just assign it to both.

Creating and Assigning Categories in the E-Mail Inbox List View

Here's the easiest way to create and assign categories. Right-click any e-mail item in your e-mail Inbox list. From the shortcut menu choose Categories (see figure 7.11).

A Categories dialog box opens, displaying whatever category list is currently populated in your system (see figure 7.12).

Click one or more categories you wish to assign, and then OK. If none of the categories in your category list fits your needs and you want to add another category, click the Master Category List... button at the bottom of the window. This opens a dialog box where you can add additional categories or delete existing ones in the category list (see figure 7.13).

You add a category by typing the new name in the top field and clicking Add; then click OK. This returns you to the previous dialog box. Stay there for a moment because after you create a new category you still need to assign it to the e-mail. In the list, find your new category, and select the check box next to it. Repeat for any other category that applies to the message and then click OK.

While you have the Master Category List dialog box open, I recommend you remove the default categories in there that shipped with Outlook. Most are not useful for the business world.

Side Note: *One other constraint with using categories is that there is no quick way to rename a category once it is assigned to mail, at least not in one step. See chapter 9, page 219, for instructions on how to do this.*

Assigning the Same Category to Multiple Messages at Once

Prior to right-clicking an item in the e-mail list to assign a category, note that you can shift or control-select multiple e-mails at once in an e-mail list. Whatever assignments you make in the Category dialog box are then assigned to all the selected e-mail items. This is useful to speed category assignment to batches of e-mail, something I describe below.

Assigning Categories by Dragging and Dropping

If you have used custom folders in the past to store e-mail, then you know the easiest way to store the e-mails in those folders is to drag and drop each e-mail onto the folder you want to store it in. A similar operation is possible for category assignment using Show in Groups; this is covered on page 187.

Automatic Assigning of Categories

One more point about assigning categories: you can easily create an Outlook rule that will automatically assign a category to all incoming mail from a

Figure 7.11
Assign categories from the e-mail list view by right-clicking the item, and choosing Categories... from the shortcut menu.

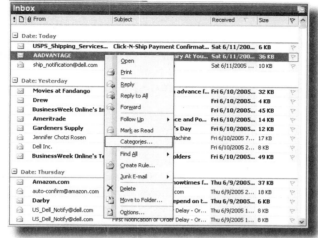

Figure 7.12
The Categories dialog box is where you can assign one or more categories to an e-mail.

Figure 7.13
The Master Category List dialog box is where you can edit the categories you are able to assign.

particular sender, or to mail with particular keywords in the subject line or body of the message. For example, I have created a rule to assign the Personal category to mail from family members. Categorizing in this way saves quite a few steps later. Instructions for doing this can be found in chapter 9.

E-Mail Filing Step Four: Finding Your Mail Once Filed, Using Show in Groups

Here is the reason for assigning all these categories: finding your mail. This is your filing system, your folder replacement system. This solution allows you to keep all processed mail together in one list but still view your mail as if filed in multiple folders. Sure, you could use the Outlook search feature to find your mail by keyword instead. But there is something so much more user friendly, more accessible, with glancing down a chronological list of items in a folder of like-subject mail. And keyword searches never seem to work the way I expect in Outlook. So I still like my folder-like collections.

Some Points about Using Outlook Categories

Setting Category Standards. If multiple individuals in your organization intend to adopt this e-mail processing system then I recommend you agree together on common category names for similar subjects. Reason: e-mail arriving from colleagues using this system may occasionally display your colleagues' categories; you may need to change the category to match one of yours. You all will save time if you agree to use the same category names. See chapter 9, page 220, for more discussion.

Miscellaneous Category. You may be tempted to create a category called Other or Miscellaneous to file e-mail that doesn't fit other categories. However, if you are going to be using Show in Groups as I recommend, then don't create one of these catchall categories. The reason: Show in Groups automatically creates, assigns, and displays such a category (called None) for all uncategorized e-mail. There is more discussion of this below.

Category Hierarchy. There is no provision using Outlook Categories to create a category hierarchy. So if you are accustomed to using a nested folder filing system, sorry, you can't do the equivalent with categories. The ability to assign multiple categories somewhat makes up for this. Frankly though, I think hierarchical e-mail filing systems are too slow to use and too hard to maintain. I encourage you to try the single-level-category system for a while and see what you think.

Turning Off AutoPreview

Outlook contains an optional configuration called AutoPreview that displays the first three lines of every e-mail right in the e-mail list view. I recommend you not use that feature because it makes assigning categories to multiple e-mails more difficult. You can turn this off by opening the View menu and deselecting AutoPreview. I also avoid in Outlook 2003 using the Reading Pane in its right-pane configuration, as this often causes e-mails in the list view to occupy more than one line (primarily because the width of the mail list pane becomes constrained), which slows down the assignment of categories to multiple e-mails. Again, use the View menu to make these changes.

Assigning Categories to an Open E-Mail

If you are reading an e-mail and ready to make the assignment (or if you have just written a new e-mail and want to categorize it), you can categorize it directly from the e-mail editing window. These steps are a bit cumbersome, though, so I rarely assign categories from an open e-mail. In case you are interested, here's how:

With the e-mail open, choose Options from the View menu. In the middle of the mail options dialog box you will see a Categories button. Click that and the same Categories dialog box as in Figure 7.11 opens, ready for category assignment.

Assigning categories to outgoing mail is purely optional and something I rarely do, but it has two benefits. The category stays with the mail in the Sent Items folder, making finding mail there easier. And if the mail is sent to an Exchange user, any replies to that mail you receive back retain the original category; no need to assign the category later when processing that reply.

In Outlook 2003 You Have a Choice

Since Outlook 2003 has both Show in Groups and Search Folders (described below), you have a choice of which to use. Show in Groups by Category produces similar results to using Search Folders but does not require the multistep setup that Search Folders does. Once set up, Show in Groups can be a little slower to use than Search Folders because if any of the categories are expanded you will need to scroll down the category/mail list to find the category group of interest to you. However, if you have many categories, Show in Groups requires less setup time than Search Folders. After years of using both, I have come to prefer Show in Groups. In Outlook 2002 it is your only choice. Let's start with Show in Groups.

Show in Groups

Why Show in Groups Is Useful

The Show in Groups feature is a way to view collapsible collections of mail assigned to a specific category. It is available in both Outlook 2003 and Outlook 2002. It is the only way in Outlook 2002 to view collections of e-mail grouped by various criteria. In Outlook 2003 Microsoft combined Show in Groups with a new feature called Arrangements, which allows Show in Groups to group more intelligently. When you first opened Outlook 2003, Show in Groups/Arrangements was probably already activated in your Inbox, sorted on the Received column. If you are seeing your mail grouped in groups like Today, Yesterday, Last Week, then this is it (see figure 7.14). (Outlook 2002 lacks the Arrangements feature and so cannot group like this on the Received column.)

Grouping by Category

What Show in Groups also enables (among other things) is using your Processed Mail folder as a view grouped on Outlook Category. If you do this (I'll show you how in a moment), your Processed Mail list is now grouped by e-mail category and each category group is clearly labeled. The list-view contents of each category can be collapsed or expanded like an outline view. Figure 7.15 is such a view with all category headings collapsed for Outlook 2003, and figure 7.17 is similar for Outlook 2002.

Figure 7.14
Typical use of the Show in Groups Arrangements feature in Outlook 2003 is to group your mail intelligently by day.

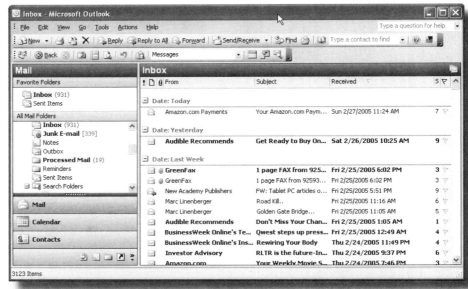

Clicking on the plus sign next to any category expands that category list underneath the heading, showing the mail that matches the category. For example, if I click on the plus sign next to the Personal category, the mail within expands below that category label (see figures 7.16 and 7.17).

If a message has more than one category assigned to it, the message will show up multiple times in this list, once under each category group.

Figure 7.15
The Show in Groups feature can be used to group your mail in category groups, which can be expanded and collapsed like an outline view.

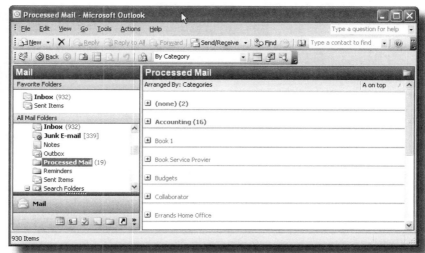

About Views

To set up Show in Groups, first you need to understand the concept of default and custom Outlook views. I first introduced views in chapter 3. They are saved, configured displays of data in a folder, with varying parameters such as sort order, displayed fields, grouping, and even filtering (to remove display of messages that fail to meet certain criteria).

All Outlook folders have a set of default saved views that are delivered out of the box with Outlook. The most important default *mail* view is the Messages view, which is the simple chronological list of messages you are accustomed to seeing.

Views and Show in Groups

Views are the key to using Show in Groups. There are two ways to set up Show in Groups views in Outlook. You can manually reconfigure an existing default view, or you can define a new saved custom view. I recommend the latter because you usually want to leave the existing default views unmodified for later use.

Figure 7.16
Show in Groups feature in Outlook 2003 with the Personal group expanded to see the items inside.

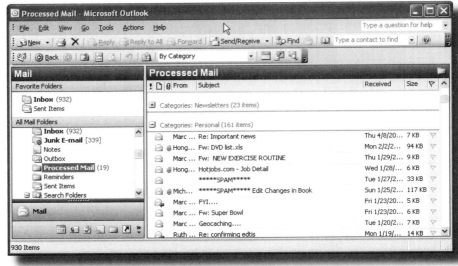

Figure 7.17
Show in Groups feature in Outlook 2002 with a group expanded to see the items inside.

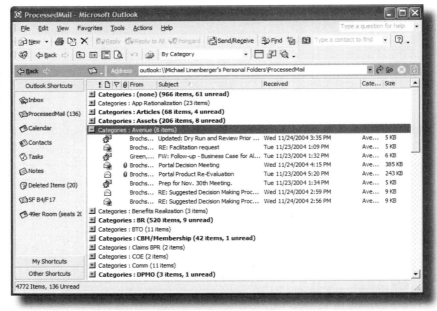

That said, let's review the manual approach first so you can see how it is done. You will probably need to use this manual approach occasionally for special needs, such as to fix your defined views when they are accidentally modified.

Manually Configuring Show in Groups in Outlook 2003

We will be doing this within whatever view your Processed Mail folder is currently set to. It is probably the Messages view, which is the standard e-mail default view. Note this: making manual changes to an existing view permanently changes that view. So after trying this, be sure to undo these steps, as described next, to return this view to its original configuration.

To configure Show in Groups manually, grouping by categories, do this:

1 Open the Processed Mail e-mail folder. The default view called Messages will probably open (as labeled in the Advanced toolbar, which we added in chapter 3); if not use whatever view is current.

2 From the View menu, choose Arrange By, and select Show in Groups, near the bottom of the choice list, so that it is checked (see figure 7.18). If the Show in Groups option is grayed out or already checked, your view is already in a Show in Groups configuration, so skip to the next step.

3 Immediately go back to the View menu, choose Arrange By again, and now select Categories so that it is checked.

You have now configured Show in Groups, grouping by categories. Assuming you have already assigned categories to some e-mail (if not, assign some categories now) you will see a collection of category headings.

The new view may open fully collapsed or with some categories expanded. To see the view with all categories collapsed (so you can find a specific category quickly) do this: from the View menu, choose Expand/Collapse Groups and then choose Collapse All Groups. The view hierarchy will fully collapse, as in the earlier figure 7.15. You can then scroll through the group list and expand the group of interest by clicking on the plus sign next to it.

These steps constitute just one of many ways to manually configure and use Show in Groups within an existing mail view in Outlook 2003. You can also group on a field by right-clicking the column heading above the field column you want to group on, and then choose Group By This Field. There are other ways to do this as well (for example, using the Group By Box). I leave experimenting with this to you.

Manually Removing Show in Groups in Outlook 2003

Configuring Show in Groups manually within an existing view like Messages permanently destroys the purely chronological list Messages was designed

Figure 7.18
Configure Show
in Groups from
the View menu
by clicking on
the Arrange By
command.

for, so be sure to undo the above steps. In order to undo those steps, you need to reverse the steps almost exactly. Here's how:

1   Open the View menu and choose Arrange By.

2   From the Arrange By submenu select Date (at the very top of the list),

3   Then go back into the Arrange By submenu and clear the check mark next to Show in Groups.

That should remove Show in Groups from the current display.

Manually Resetting a Default View in Outlook 2003

You can also remove manually added changes to any default Outlook view (like Messages) by following the steps below. This is useful if you lose track of changes you make and want to start fresh.

1   Open the View menu and choose Arrange By.

2   From the Arrange By submenu select Current View, then Customize Current View...

3   Then in the lower left corner of the Customize Current View dialog box click Reset Current View (click OK when asked if you are sure).

Creating a Saved Show in Groups View in Outlook 2003

The steps described above for configuring Show in Groups is the manual way to create this view; it was done by modifying an existing view. I showed those steps because you may need to use similar manual steps some day to repair a misconfigured view. That is not my recommended method for customizing views. Better is to create a saved view that you can navigate to and from by name, instantly, using the Current View selector. Once created, using a saved view is quicker. And creating the view this way leaves the default views undisturbed.

You will need to create the following saved view (named By Category) to use this system. To create the saved By Category view in Outlook 2003 do this:

1 Open the folder you want to view. This will probably be your Processed Mail folder.

2 Open the View menu; choose Arrange By, and from the Arrange By sub-menu choose Current View.

3 From the Current View submenu, choose Define Views… the following dialog box opens:

4   Click New… and within the resulting dialog box, in the field called Name of New View, overtype the words "New View" with "by Category."

5   Leave the other settings as they are and click OK; the following dialog box opens:

6   Click Group By… and the following dialog box opens:

7   Clear the Automatically Group According to Arrangement check box; then from the Group Items By list, choose Categories.

8   From the Then By list, choose Received.

9   Select again the check box titled Automatically Group According to Arrangement. This will dim your previous choices, which is okay.

10   Click OK to close that dialog box.

11   Back in the Customize View dialog box click Fields... and in the dialog box that opens (called Show Fields, see next page) click on the word Categories in the list on the left to select it. Then click Add (in the middle of the dialog box) to add that field to the bottom of the list on the right. Click OK.

   If you have any trouble finding the Categories field in the list on the left, try selecting All Mail Fields in the selection box titled Select Available Fields From:, and then look again at the scrolling field list. That should display it.

Side Note: *In the Show Fields dialog box shown in the figure at the top of the next page, the Categories field is already added to the list on the right. Note that a field name will not be found anywhere in the list on the left if that field has already been added to the list on the right. The list on the left only shows unused fields.*

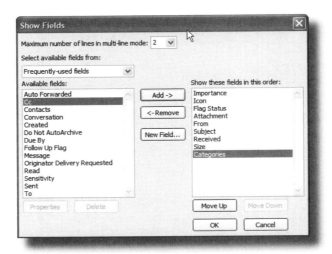

12   Then click OK again to finish definition of the new view. Then click Apply View to see the new view.

Using the New View

You now have created and saved the view you need to examine your saved mail by categories. You will come to this By Category view whenever you want to look up older mail in a category setting. From now on, you can select the By Category view whenever you need to; just use the Current View selector tool on the Advanced tool bar (discussed in chapter 3 and below in Showing Custom (and Default) E-Mail Views).

Note that when using the view, if you click on any of the column headings, the view will regroup around whatever field heading you click on. If you do this (either accidentally or by choice) simply click again on the Categories heading to get the correctly sorted view back.

Creating a Saved Show in Groups in Outlook 2002

I am going to skip the manual way to configure this view in 2002 and jump right into creating the saved view. Show in Groups in Outlook 2002 behaves and configures nearly identically to Show in Groups in Outlook 2003.

To create a Show in Groups, By Category saved view in Outlook 2002, take the following steps.

1   Open the folder you want to view. This will probably be your Processed Mail folder.

2   From the View menu, choose Current View.

3   Then choose Define Views… the following dialog box opens:

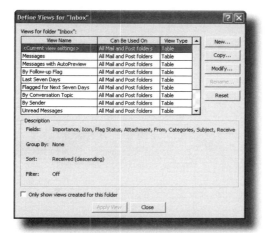

4   Click the New... button and within the resulting dialog box type the name By Category in the box called Name of New View.

5   Click OK; you should then see the View Summary dialog box.

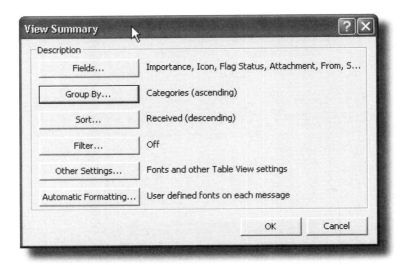

6 Click Fields... and in the Fields dialog box that opens, add the Category field to the bottom of the field list on the right side. (See step 11 on page 171 for some additional tips on how to do this). Click OK.

7 Back at the View Summary dialog box, Click Group By... and in the Group By dialog box that opens, group by Categories.

8 Do not modify any other settings.

9 Click OK on this dialog box. Confirm the current Sort is shown set to Received on the next dialog box, if so click OK (if not, set it that way by clicking the Sort... button). On the final dialog box click Apply View.

You now have created and saved the view you need to examine your saved mail by categories. You will come to this By Category view whenever you want to look up older mail in a category setting. Follow the instructions below to switch between this view and others.

Showing Custom (and Default) E-Mail Views

Selecting Between E-Mail Views in Outlook 2002 and 2003

To select custom e-mail views first decide with which folder the view is associated. In this book all our custom mail views are associated with the Processed Mail folder, so choose that folder from the Folder list (or All Mail Folders list), first.

Side Note: *Throughout any given workday, you will be routinely alternating between your Inbox folder for viewing new mail and this Processed Mail folder for viewing saved mail.*

Then you should choose the view you wish to use within that folder. To do this, simply choose the view name from the Current View selector on the Advanced toolbar (see figure 7.19; if the Advanced toolbar is not present, choose the View menu, select Toolbars, and check the entry next to the Advanced toolbar).

Figure 7.19
The Current View selector on the Advanced toolbar.

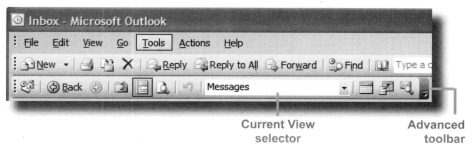

Current View selector   Advanced toolbar

To start the By Category view with all categories collapsed (so you can find a specific category quickly), do this: from the View menu, choose Expand/Collapse Groups and then choose Collapse All Groups. The view will open fully collapsed. You can then scroll through the group list and expand the group of interest by clicking on the plus sign next to it.

When viewing saved mail in the Processed Mail folder, you will be routinely using two views: this new custom By Category view, to view mail grouped by category, and the Messages view. Recall the Messages view is the raw, simple mail view; it is a default view that Outlook created automatically when you created the Processed Mail folder. This is the view you will use to see one chronological list of all your saved mail.

Show in Groups in Outlook 2002 versus Outlook 2003

I prefer Outlook 2002 over Outlook 2003 for the way it treats Show in Groups. Here's why:

■ In the fully collapsed view, the heading height of each category in 2002 is much smaller than in 2003; as a result, in 2002 you can see more categories listed, which is more convenient when you are quickly scanning for a given category to expand.

■ In Outlook 2002 when viewing an expanded category while in Show in Groups, if you click on one of the column headings, the mail will sort on that heading within the expanded category. This is nice behavior because users often want to sort on the From field within a given category and that is what this allows. In contrast, in Outlook 2003 if you click on a column heading, the entire Show in Groups view will re-sort or regroup by the column you clicked on. While this can be useful, it eliminates what was a more intuitive way to sort inside a group easily, compared to 2002. You can still do this in Outlook 2003, however, with a trick described in the next inset.

Sorting within a Group in Outlook 2003

In the inset above, I mention that Outlook 2002 has an easier way of sorting within category groups. So in 2003 how do you do this? While not as simple as 2002, it is still pretty simple. You need to use a trick. When you are ready to sort inside the group, hold down the Shift key before you click on the column title. That's it. Some points to remember when doing this:

■ Do not forget that each click inverts the sort direction (ascending versus descending). A little triangle forms in the column heading that indicates the direction of the sort.

■ Also note that if you click on another column while still holding down the Shift key (say because you clicked the wrong column first), you will get a second level sort added to the first; this double sort within the group is probably not what you intended. So if you change your mind on which column you want to sort on, click a column head once *without* the Shift key held down, to clear the sort, and then try again.

■ Since a little triangle forms in the column heading when a list is sorted on that column, it tells you which column(s) is currently being sorted. When you inadvertently create a double sort, as described above, you will see a triangle in *two* columns; this is a clue to what's going on.

Side Note: *You will probably also sort this Messages view on other columns like the From column (just click on the column heading above the From field). If you do that a lot you may want to create another view like it called By Sender which opens sorted on the From field. I leave that configuration to you.*

Side Note: *A Messages view also exists within your Inbox. It is the default view there as well, and you normally use it when viewing Inbox mail. So do not get confused when you see the name "Messages" at the top of the screen while in the Inbox; this is the same view but within a different mail folder, so different messages are displayed.*

Another Way to Choose Views in Outlook 2003

Outlook 2003 has an additional way to select views right on the Navigation Pane. To activate it: from the View menu choose Arrange By, and from the Arrange By submenu check Show Views in Navigation Pane. From now on, if you scroll down within the All Mail folders section of the Navigation Pane, near the bottom you will see a subsection called Current View, and within that a list of all your custom and standard views for mail. Choosing from this list is identical to choosing from the Advanced toolbar. (See figure 7.20).

Figure 7.20
A Current View
selector can
be added to
the Navigation
Pane (Outlook
2003 only).

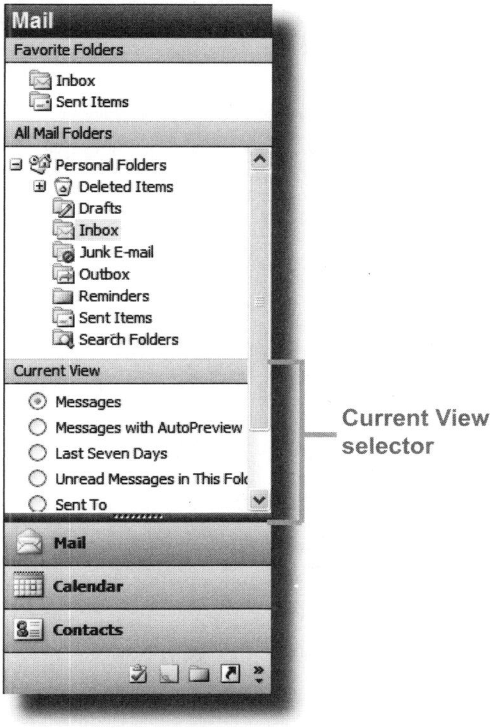

Current View
selector

E-Mail Filing Step Five: Finding Your Filed Mail Using Search Folders (Outlook 2003 Only)

Search Folders are an Outlook 2003 feature that allows creation of virtual folders in your folder list. They can be used instead of Show in Groups (though I prefer to use Show in Groups). They appear within and under the Search Folder master folder, right in the All Mail Folders pane or the Folder List pane of Outlook (see figure 7.21). In this sample, eight Search Folders are shown.

Search Folders are virtual folders that populate with an entry for every mail item that matches certain search criteria, criteria defined at the time the particular search folder is created. You create one folder for each set of search criteria. The best criterion to use for our purposes is collecting mail that has a given Outlook Category assigned; many other search approaches are also possible. Once created, clicking on the folder opens a view of all matching mail in a folder view, as if it were a real Outlook folder.

The advantage to using Search Folders over Show in Groups is this: they look and act nearly identical to regular Outlook folders. If you are accustomed to using the folder view for manipulating saved mail, Search Folders create a very similar view for your collection of category-assigned mail. When you

Figure 7.21
Search Folders are virtual Outlook 2003 folders that appear and act like "normal" Outlook folders.

double-click a search folder, it opens just like any other folder, displaying the mail contained within. So there is a familiarity factor at work here which many find comforting.

There are two disadvantages. One is that unlike real folders, you cannot drag mail items into the search folder to place them there. Rather, using our system, you need to assign categories the same way described above: right-click on the mail item and choose the Categories menu, and then pick the categories from the scrolling list. Then drag the item into your Processed Mail folder. Only then will the item appear in your search folder.

The other disadvantage of Search Folders is that unlike Show in Groups, you must explicitly create a search folder for each category you are using. With Show in Groups, as soon as you create a new category in your master categories list and start using it, the new category and associated mail will appear in your categories view. Not so with Search Folders; you need to go through a somewhat cumbersome set of steps every time you create a search folder.

Side Note: *You cannot create nested Search Folders (no subfolders).*

Even with those disadvantages, there is a certain elegance to using Search Folders; the folder-like appearance right in the Outlook folder list is quite satisfying. If you have a relatively small and stable set of categories, you may prefer the elegance of this approach.

Creating Search Folders

Creating Search Folders around categories is a moderately complex process, with four levels of nested dialog boxes to open and set criteria in. This is not difficult, though, and the full steps are shown below. Once created, they are very easy to use.

1 From the File menu in Outlook 2003, choose New, and then Search Folder. The dialog box on the left of figure 7.22 appears.

Figure 7.22
Configuring Search Folders.

2   Scroll to the bottom of the scrolling list and click once on the very last choice, called Create a Custom Search Folder, to highlight it as shown on the right side of figure 7.22.

3   Then click the Choose... button that appears in the lower right corner (see right side of figure 7.22; note that double-clicking the Create a Custom Search Folder item has the same effect as clicking the Choose... button).

4   A small Custom Search Folder dialog box appears.

Enter the name of your Search Folder within the Name field at the top of that dialog box. This name will display on the folder, so choose a name that reflects the category you will be accumulating (for this example I labeled the folder "My Projects Mail").

5   Next, set the source folders the Search Folder draws from. In the lower portion of this window, you will see a field named Mail from These Folders Will Be Included in This Search Folder. Next to that is a Browse... button. You use this field and button to indicate the actual folders from which you want this virtual search folder to collect. Do you want to include mail from all folders? Or include only mail from inside your Processed Mail folder? To set choices like this, click Browse...

6a If you are in an Internet e-mail environment (if in Exchange environment, skip to step 7) you will see a mail folder selection window with the Personal Folders folder at the top of your folder hierarchy, selected by default (see next figure).

Think about this carefully. If you leave this default set as it is, your search folder will collect items from all your Outlook folders, including Sent Items, Deleted Items, and even nonmail folders. This is not a good choice for our intentions. I recommend instead checking just Inbox and Processed Mail (see below).

Side Note: *The check box at the bottom of this dialog box, Search Subfolders, can be ignored in this case (set either way) since the Processed Mail folder and Inbox have no subfolders.*

6b Be sure to uncheck the Personal Folders check box at the top of the list. Then click OK. Skip ahead to step 8.

7   If you are in an Exchange environment, this list will look different. You may see both the Exchange Server folders and your Personal Folders. However Search Folders are limited in an Exchange environment: you will only be able to choose from one mail store, either the Exchange Server or your Personal Folders. I recommend choosing from the Personal

Folders mail store. Choose the equivalent of your Processed Mail folder; uncheck everything else and click OK.

8   After you click OK (at end of steps 6b or 7) you will return to the Custom Search Folder dialog box. Now you need to define which category to look for. This is what really defines this particular Search Folder. Click Criteria... and you'll see the Search Folder Criteria dialog box open.

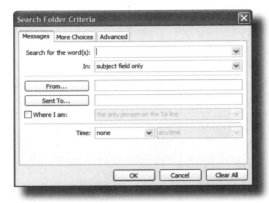

9   Select the second tab called More Choices.

10   Click Categories..., and you will see the by-now familiar Categories selection dialog box. Choose the category of interest (Projects for this example), and click OK. Then click OK in the Search Folder Criteria dialog box, click OK in the Custom Search Folder dialog box, and finally click OK in the New Search Folder dialog box.

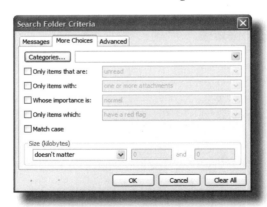

Now Examine Your Folder List

You should now see the new search folder added to the Search Folder hierarchy within your Outlook Folders List view. For this example, the My Projects Mail folder is now visible, as in figure 7.21. If you open that search folder, you will see all mail that you have assigned to the Projects category.

These folders self-update, so if you assign the Projects category to more mail later, that new mail will also appear in the previously created Search Folder. Once you create a Search Folder, there is nothing you need do to maintain it.

Deleting Search Folders and Mail inside Search Folders

Search Folders are a virtual view of your mail. The actual mail sits in real Outlook folder(s) such as the ones you defined above as the source of your search (Processed Mail, most likely). So if you are done using a Search Folder, you can delete the folder and the mail itself is not deleted but is retained in the Processed Mail folder.

However, while viewing individual mail inside a Search Folder *the opposite is true*. If you delete an individual e-mail item from within the Search Folder, the actual mail item is *deleted* from its source folder (in this case, the Processed Mail folder). Any operations that you perform on individual e-mail items (delete, change category, or edit item, for example) within a Search Folder are made on the actual item wherever it is located.

Thoughts on Using Show in Groups and Search Folders

If you are like me, you will probably actually search for maybe 5 percent of the mail that you file. Does that make this filing process a waste of time? Absolutely not. The act of filing a piece of mail forces you to think about the usefulness of the mail, which is a good exercise. In so doing you may realize that there is actually a task associated with the mail.

And you get a certain peace of mind when you can logically file a piece of mail and get it out of your Inbox. Even though you may not search for a specific piece of mail, being able to glance visually through all the mail associated with a particular topic often helps reconstruct the history and resolve an uncertain information search. How many times have you suspected that a certain piece of information exists somewhere in your e-mail around a given topic, but you could not recall enough to use a keyword search effectively? Often all you know is roughly how long ago you got the information and the major topic area, or the topic and who the message was from. Being able to search through virtual folders of related e-mail, chronologically, or sorted by sender, will usually save the day.

Show in Groups versus Search Folders

If you are using Outlook 2003 then you have the choice of either Show in Groups or Search Folders. So which should you use? The advantage to Search

Folders is that they act like the folders you may already be using to store mail. They appear right in your Outlook folders list with other folders. So there is a certain elegance and sense of familiarity that they afford.

I have come to favor using Show in Groups. This is because I often create a new category every month or so (and more often at the beginning of using the system); with Search Folders quite a few steps are needed to create each new categorized folder. Show in Groups in contrast requires no steps to create a display area for your new category; Outlook adds the new category automatically. Furthermore, if you have many categories, your Search Folders folder tree can get quite large. Show in Groups behaves better with a long list of categories. And Show in Groups allows a drag and drop category assignment (discussed next) that Search Folders does not allow.

Tips on Using Categories

Transitioning

From a Multiple Folder–Based Filing System

If you are already using a multiple folder–based filing system for e-mail you may wonder what the recommendations are for transitioning to a category-based system. My primary recommendation is this: start fresh. There is no reason you cannot add a Processed Mail folder to your existing multiple folder system and start using the category system with mail that is currently in your Inbox. Then retain your current system for the old mail you have already filed.

The useful life of most old mail passes fast; in no time the only mail that you'll be looking at will be the mail filed by category, and your old folder-based filing will be a rarely touched a system. At some point you will feel confident to archive that system and refer only to your category-based Processed Mail folder. And this is a good way to try out the Category filing approach. If you do not like it you can always drag the mail back to your old folders.

Side Note: *If you do combine with an old folder system, you may want to name your Processed Mail folder something like: _Processed Mail, so that it sorts to the top of your folders.*

From No Filing System

Whether you are currently using a multiple folder filing system or not, chances are good that your Inbox is quite overcrowded with perhaps months of old mail. How do you get started? Do you need to commit yourself to classifying all of your months of old mail? My answer is no.

Again, what I recommend is to take a fresh start. In this case, as I described in chapter 6, I recommend creating an additional personal folder called Mail Older Than [date]. Decide on a reasonable date in the past, say one week ago, and then copy all mail older than that into that folder. Mail newer than that you commit to processing into your Processed Mail folder immediately. Then, as time allows, dip into the Old Mail folder to classify and file the mail there if you wish. But digging into the Mail Older Than folder is purely optional; what is important is that you empty your Inbox quickly, so you can experience the benefits of doing so. And then keep maintaining it.

Should You Categorize Everything?

Is it necessary to categorize every piece of mail in your Inbox? Absolutely not. If you stare at a piece of mail for more than a second or two and no category jumps out at you, then waste no more time on it. You need to balance the advantages of the system against the imposition of the system on your time. One of the goals of this system is to get you out earlier at the end of each workday; you won't do that if you spend too much time using the system. I find I can assign categories to two full screens of mail in about five minutes or less. Once you get good at this, if it takes you longer than that, you are spending too much time choosing your categories. It is probably better to leave more mail uncategorized (and/or reduce your number of categories).

Integrating Categorization into Workflow: Batch Processing

The workflow presented in the previous chapter in which each e-mail is read individually, then categorized, and then filed was, for simplification, an idealized one. In reality, I usually batch process my e-mail by grouping the steps

What Happens to Uncategorized Mail?

Whether you assigned a category to mail or not, you should drag all your mail out of your Inbox into your Processed Mail folder. So what happens to the mail that you do not categorize? Of course, it goes into your Processed Mail folder with everything else, and you can see it by using the Messages view. How is this e-mail treated in Search Folders and Show in Groups? This is another place where Show in Groups has an advantage: Show in Groups automatically creates a category called None and all of your unfiled mail can be found in that group. This is the equivalent of creating an Other category and actively filing mail there, but it is better because the filing is done automatically. The None category is listed at the top of the Show in Groups By Category view that we created earlier. I end up categorizing only about 75 percent of the mail that I save so the other quarter ends up in this None category automatically. Search Folders has no such default collection.

of that workflow. I will read and take action steps for e-mail whenever I work my e-mail (steps 1–5 on page 141), no matter how short the period is. I place a particular emphasis on making quick replies and converting embedded tasks immediately into Outlook tasks. I'll then come back to that read e-mail and do step 6 (set categories and drag to Processed Mail folder) on blocks of e-mail together. Step 6 I may do hours or even days later depending upon how busy I am.

In reality, this matches how most of us process e-mails in normal life. When we have a few minutes here and there we read some e-mails, acting on those we can at the moment and deferring action on others. And every so often we try to go back and clean up the Inbox.

The difference with this improved workflow is this key one: as soon as you read an e-mail, before you close it, you should *immediately* make a decision—is this a task, a quick-reply-now, or a reply-later e-mail? And once you decide, make sure you act accordingly before you move on to the next e-mail: convert it to task, reply immediately, or flag it for later reply. In other words, if an e-mail requires action, act or plan the actions immediately when you first read it. That way, when you return to your e-mail Inbox later to clean it up, your only needed action will be to optionally categorize the mail, and then drag all mail to the processed mail folder. This removes nearly all tension you may feel about old mail sitting in your Inbox because all actions have been taken.

How Often to Categorize?

You can if needed delay the categorization step because you have taken all the really needed actions, as described above. Try to categorize at least once a day. If you are very busy, this step can be put off for a few days without too much impact.

However, the problem with putting categorizing off is that when you come back to categorize the e-mail later, you will have forgotten the contents of some of your mail and you may need to reread them to classify them. So it is better to include the categorization step whenever you engage in an extended session of e-mail reading. Once you get ahead of your Inbox, looping back at the end of each e-mail reading session to categorize and completely empty your Inbox becomes easy. And the smaller the amount of mail you need to process at once the easier this becomes. When you do categorization just after reading and acting on a block of mail, there will be no need to reread any e-mails. Just quickly go through your Inbox and categorize in blocks, based on titles (see below). The crisp decision-making process and read-once policy are what makes this Inbox workflow so speedy.

Speeding up Category Assignments

One of the most common early complaints I hear from first-time users of this system is "Assigning categories is harder than dragging to folders, it takes several steps to right-click the mail and pick a category from a dialog box, this seems slow." If you do not use any of the tips below, this is true. But the tips below, if used selectively, usually clear up any objections.

Categorizing in Blocks

Categorizing e-mails in blocks is a way to make assigning categories go more quickly. For example, if I see a number of messages scattered about the Inbox that fit the Personal category, I will control-select the group (hold down the

Control key and click discontinuous items with my mouse), then I will right-click *one* of the items in the selected group, and set the Personal category classification. This operation sets the category for *all* the selected mail. Then, while the group is still selected, I drag the group into the Processed Mail folder. I'll then repeat this operation for other groups of categories I might see. After the obvious like groups are gone, I then pick off and categorize the single items that are left in the list. This works for me; you will find your own preferred way of batch processing your mail.

What may make this even quicker for you is this: try sorting on the From column before you apply your categories in batches. Often e-mails from the same person all categorize the same, and so you can select adjacent items together (using the Shift key) before setting the category.

Assigning Categories by Dragging and Dropping

If you have used custom folders in the past to store e-mail, then you know the easiest way to store the e-mails into those folders is to drag and drop each e-mail onto the folder you want to store it in. With the category filing system recommended in this book, you may miss this capability. You might think that Search Folders would enable this capability since they act like folders; unfortunately that is not true—you cannot drag e-mails into Search Folders.

Interestingly though, you *can* drag e-mails to create category assignments using Show in Groups. To do this you need to open and arrange two mail windows; since this is a little inconvenient, I would only do this if I were filing a large amount of mail at once. And a large monitor is definitely a help.

Here are the steps to set this up:

1 With your Inbox open, right-click your Processed Mail folder in your Folder List pane, and choose Open in New Window from the shortcut menu.

2 Once open, select your By Category view for this window, and collapse all headings.

3 Now resize and position your two Outlook windows so you can see them side by side (or top and bottom, whatever your preference).

You can now drag e-mail out of your Inbox over to your Processed Mail window and drop the e-mails onto the category heading of your choice. This operation will both assign the category and file the mail in the Processed Mail folder in one step—a nice feature. The only disadvantage to this method is that you cannot assign multiple categories. You can however drag and categorize multiple e-mails into the same folder at once. And if you quit Outlook using Exit from the File menu, rather than by closing windows, the two windows will reopen the next time you start Outlook.

Consider Creating Category Assignment Rules

In chapter 9, Advanced Topics, I describe how to set rules in Outlook so that mail arrives in your Inbox precategorized. Once you have used the e-mail workflow and have been assigning categories to your mail for some time, I recommend you take a look at that section and give it a try. It takes a little work to set it up, but it will speed your Inbox processing tremendously. Nearly 70 percent of my filed mail is automatically categorized because of my frequent use of this feature.

Summary

Filing e-mail by topic is an optional activity you will probably want to do. Over the years, filing by using categories has proved to be an effective way to get e-mail out of the Inbox and into a place where you can find it easily later. Show in Groups and Search Folders are excellent ways to create folder-like structures from a collection of categorized e-mail. Once you configure Outlook appropriately and gain a little practice, using categories to file mail will become second nature.

Review of Key Learnings

- Once the mail has been read and action items completed or converted to tasks, all mail should be processed out of the Inbox, either by deleting it or by filing it in a way that you can find it later.

- Using Outlook Categories instead of multiple folders provides a much more usable way of filing e-mail.

- Show in Groups automatically creates a category called None that collects and displays all uncategorized e-mail.

- You need to balance the advantages of the system versus the imposition of the system on your time. If you stare at a piece of mail for more than a second or two and no category jumps out at you, then waste no more time on it. Leave it without a category assignment.

- In practice, it is easiest if you separate time spent on identification of action items from time spent on e-mail categorization. Identify action items first and convert to tasks, then come back to categorize and file your e-mail in batches.

Next Steps

Now that you have learned how to file mail, it is time to go back to the workflows at the end of chapter 6 and start putting it all together. This filing skill is the very last step of that workflow. Your suite of e-mail tools is now complete. Start using them.

Chapter Eight
Outlook-Based Delegation

The Eighth Best Practice

Delegating tasks effectively is an essential means for clearing tasks off your list, freeing time to focus on activities that are more important and more appropriate to your role. It is also good for the staff you delegate to because they learn as you assist them through increasing levels of skills; it can and should be a win-win arrangement. Many new and even experienced work managers have trouble delegating effectively. As a result, too many tasks that should be delegated end up remaining self-assigned.

Failures with delegation often stem from lack of good systems to assign, track, and follow up on delegated tasks. When a due date arrives and the delegated task has not been completed, too often managers blame the delegated staff: "That person can't seem to get things done for me; if I need something done I'd better do it myself," and tasks end up back on the manager's list. It's highly likely that the failure was due to the delegation methodology, not due to the staff the task was delegated to.

Delegation of tasks can represent handoffs to subordinates or "requests" to colleagues. Both can be managed the same way.

Successful Delegation

It's amazing how much respect and attention staff will give you and the tasks you assign if you provide three things:

- An honest and thoughtful discussion of the reasons the task is important and why this person may be the right one to work on it.

- Plenty of lead time on the due date of the task.

■ Consistent and reasonably spaced check-ins while waiting for the task to be completed.

It's when you fail to manage assigned tasks without providing these things that tempers get short and staff feel overburdened.

It's no wonder managers are so bad at using these. They have a large pile of their own tasks to manage, so how can they be expected to consistently assign and track the task list of others? In the earlier chapters of this book, you have learned best practices for getting your own tasks under control; in this chapter you will learn best practices for delegating tasks to others.

The Task Delegation Approach

My approach to task delegation is a three-step process:

1 **Identify**: At the moment the task and need to delegate arises, enter and annotate it in your task system as one to be delegated and indicate to whom to delegate it. Do not actually communicate the task until the next step.

2 **Get Buy-In**: Use a face-to-face or phone meeting to gain buy-in and acceptance from the staff or colleague and to set a due date for the task. Update the system to indicate acceptance (if achieved), and schedule your first check-in time frame.

3 **Follow Up**: At the scheduled check-in, follow up on the assigned task, provide help if needed, and set subsequent follow-up time frames. Escalate only after several follow-ups.

I like this approach because the staff manages their task their own way, and I use my task system to initiate regular personal follow-up activities. This avoids forcing my task management approach on other staff, yet it allows me a personal touch in my follow-up. I cover logistics for each of these steps next.

Identify and Annotate a Task for Delegation

In step 1, when I identify tasks that I intend to assign to others, I annotate the subject line of tasks in my task list. This helps me plan and initiate the assignment process. My assignment annotation system is simple: I place the initials of the staff that I intend to assign the task to in the very front of the subject line, followed by a colon, then followed by the subject itself. So a task I intend to assign to Joe Smith to provide network performance resolution would

appear with "JS:Resolve Network Performance" in the subject line. This is
for my use only; I do not give the task list to Joe. I may give Joe a head's up
e-mail that something new is coming to be discussed in the next meeting;
for big tasks the more warning the better. And I set the due date to the day I
intend to meet Joe to discuss the task assignment.

By using this annotation system, on the day I intend to meet with Joe I am
reminded to make this assignment. Or if I meet with Joe early, I can sort
alphabetically within the All Daily Tasks view of Outlook, scroll down to
Joe's initials, and collect the tasks that I propose to hand off in person.

Gaining Buy-In for the Task

A Valuable Step

Assigning a task to someone without prior discussion is largely discouraged
by management experts. An important element of delegation is achieving
buy-in from the staff that you plan to delegate to. During one-on-one meetings with my staff, I spend time discussing the value of the task. I try to share
the vision behind it. And if the task is an interesting one, I try to share my
excitement. If the task is urgent I make sure the staff shares my feeling of
urgency and the reasons behind it. I then make a point of asking the staff if he
or she is interested in the task and feels they can add it to their list. And very
importantly, can they complete it by the intended deadline. One hopes the
answer is yes to all of those questions. If working this task may cause other
delegated tasks to be late, now is the time to discuss that. You may have to
make some trade-offs in your list of delegated tasks for this individual.

Gaining such buy-in is incredibly important. It builds respect of staff for you
and your management techniques. It creates a sense of ownership between
the staff and the task. And it goes a long way toward ensuring the successful
completion of the delegated task.

Skipping this step leads to bad morale and incomplete assignments. There are
hundreds of ways to do this wrong. For example, dropping a task assignment
in someone's Inbox without prior discussion is one bad way.

Outlook's Assign Task Feature

It's for this reason that even though Outlook has an automatic way to delegate tasks, I recommend that you do not use that capability. Let me explain.

If your organization has a Microsoft Exchange implementation, then you can
use Outlook to assign electronically tasks to other staff. Automatic assignment
of tasks is activated by clicking the Assign Task button at the top of the task
input dialog (see figure 8.1). This feature is also available by right-clicking a
task in the task list view.

When you use the Assign Task feature, your copy of Outlook actually sends
a special e-mail with the task attached, asking the recipient to formally accept

Figure 8.1
Assign Task
buttons.

or reject the task assignment. If it is accepted, the task is added to the recipient's own Outlook task list, and you automatically get back a message saying the task was accepted. At that point your copy of the task is modified to show that a formal assignment has been made and to whom it was assigned. Subsequently you can request special Outlook-based status reports from those recipients (sent using the button just to the right of the Assign Task button shown above). And when you receive those status reports back, the status fields (Status and % Complete) will be updated in your own task list to reflect the progress of work that your staff has made on the task.

This is a great concept and a great implementation. However, every time I've tried to use it I've found that for various reasons, usually people-related, the team stops or never fully starts using this approach. There are two main problems:

■   If not used carefully, it encourages the classic "dump and run" approach to delegating tasks. Dropping a task assignment in someone's Inbox is not consistent with gaining staff buy-in.

■   Many staff prefer not to use Outlook's task system to manage their tasks.

That said, it is a well-implemented technology. One scenario where it could be used effectively is this: your entire staff is already using Microsoft Outlook to manage tasks, and you agree not to use the Assign Task button until *after* you've had your discussion with your staff about a task assignment. You may want to try that out. The following discussion assumes that you do *not* use Outlook's automated assign task functionality.

Methods of Follow-Up and Buy-In

Meeting with Your Staff to Review Assignments

I have one-on-one meetings weekly with all my key staff to discuss and assign tasks and to check the progress of previously assigned tasks. But if the next one-on-one is too far off and the task urgent, I set a separate short ad hoc meeting to have the discussion. Before that meeting, I use my All Daily Tasks view to pull up tasks quickly for that staff: I review all tasks that are outstanding and all tasks that I intend to assign. I sort alphabetically on the subject line so that all tasks that have that individual's initials on them sort together. I bring that list with me to the meeting for review.

The best way to do this is to use a Tablet PC or a laptop and bring it with you to the meeting. If you don't use a laptop or a Tablet PC you can instead print that list and bring the paper copy.

I discuss with the staff tasks that they have not yet agreed to and, if needed, reprioritize and redate the outstanding ones to reflect newer priorities and meeting outcomes; I input those changes immediately or when I return to my computer. Again, this is even easier if you bring the laptop or a Tablet PC with you to the meeting. Having a PC with you is an effective way to keep up with a rapidly changing landscape of assigned tasks—particularly if you have many staff. And assuming that during your discussion about the status of each task you may have changes to make to those tasks (for example, marking the subject for follow-up, extending the due date, or checking the task complete) you can edit the tasks right in this window, in the meeting. You can either do this in-line within the list view, or double-click the task and edit it within the Task dialog box. If you are using a PDA and synchronizing your tasks, this operation is also possible (but more difficult). If you are not using any mobile devices you can mark up your paper printout of tasks and make the changes when you return to your computer.

Following Up on Delegated Tasks

Once the task is accepted, it is essential to schedule and engage in regular follow-up activities. Consistent and reasonable follow-up is the key often-overlooked point. We are tempted to think that once a task is assigned, the recipient "should" do it. Even if we agree that check-ins are needed, it is easy to forget to do this well before the due date. New managers are often afraid to disturb their staff about assigned work.

This is an essential step of task delegation. It is good management practice to track delegated task assignment progress regularly, well before the task is due. It is bad management practice to wait until the task is due for the first check-in.

The solution is to adopt a system whereby the next "fair" date for the check-in is negotiated at the assignment and clearly scheduled in your task system as an activity for you to do. And then a very proactive follow-up is taken by you when that time arrives. Using Outlook tools, this is an easy operation; you simply create a dated follow-up task for each outstanding delegated item.

Creating the Follow-Up Task

Creating such follow-up tasks is made very easy if you do the following: convert your task entry for the intended assignment into a follow-up task at the time the task is accepted.

Here is how this works. Recall the task that I intended to assign to Joe Smith to resolve network performance issues. Remember that at the time I decided to assign it I marked it: "JS:Resolve Network Performance." This notation indicated I intended to assign this task to Joe but that Joe had not yet accepted it. Once I discuss this assignment with Joe and he accepts it, I then immediately modify the annotation of the same task as follows: "F:JS: Resolve Network Performance"; the added "F" stands for follow up. That way before or during my weekly one-on-one with Joe, I can sort separately on those tasks he's accepted already and on those that still need discussion to establish buy-in.

And at the same time I add the "F" for follow-up to my task I also change the Outlook Due Date field of the task to be the day I want to be reminded to check in with Joe. I set the priority to be either high (must do today) or at least a medium; this priority level ensures I take action on the day the task appears on my daily list. Again, I avoid the use of Outlook reminders or alarms for tasks (I only use them for appointments). Rather the appearance of a brief check-in task at the top of my daily list nearly always leads to my taking action on that check-in the same day it appears. In fact, check-in tasks are among the quickest tasks to accomplish, so engaging them is a great way to knock a number of your tasks off your list for that day, which always feels good.

For those who may have used a "waiting for" list in the past to track items like this, I find the above approach much better because the follow-up item does not appear to you until it has aged an appropriate amount. There is nothing worse than pursuing someone about a request that you just gave them without letting them have time to work on it; this avoids that. And it avoids you having to do a mental calculation every time you look at a waiting for list to decide whether action is needed on the items in the list. Rather, the follow-up task appears on your action list at just the right time. Also, a separate waiting for list is one more list you have to remember to check daily. It is so much easier if your follow-up tasks appear automatically in your daily tasks list, on the day that they are due.

Assign Partial Deliverables for Check-In Points

You may also wish to negotiate a specific partial deliverable on a follow-up date. If the final task includes creating something tangible then a rough draft or first pass at the final product is a good target deliverable for the check-in. This helps prevent the check-in date from merely being an agreed-to reminder date. And often a great deal of discovery can occur in creating a first draft. Requiring an early rough draft forces discovery to occur early enough to allow time to adjust plans. For this to be effective you need to convince your staff that you will be very lenient in judgment of that rough draft; otherwise, they will spend too much time polishing something that may be wrong.

I put the agreed-to final due date of the delegated task either in the body of the text of the task or in the subject line if delivery day is urgent (see page 91 of chapter 4 for a discussion of using the subject line for due dates). If that day is approaching and the task is still not done, on my morning review of open tasks I convert it to a high priority (must-do-today) task.

This follow-up task system really does work. I find it is amazingly effective at clearing my subconscious of loose-end concerns about assignments and for guiding me in appropriate follow-up activities. At any given time I can have twenty or more open assigned tasks that are neatly scheduled for follow-ups. They remain out of sight until exactly the right scheduled check-in point, freeing my psyche for more important activities. Without a system like this I might forget to check in, and then the task becomes an emergency. I might even check in too often which is unnecessary and irritating to staff. The system brings order and calm to an otherwise chaotic mess.

How to Follow Up on Delegated Tasks

When the due date of the follow-up tasks arrives (in reality, my informal reminder date) and the follow-up task appears at the top of my daily tasks list, I then have a choice in how I follow up.

I may schedule it to coincide with the next regular one-on-one meeting. For that meeting, using the All Daily Tasks view, I sort on the task name and scroll to the task list for the individual.

Avoid Following Up in a Group

You may be tempted to make follow-ups part of a regularly scheduled departmental or team meeting. This is probably the most commonly used technique in the business world today. I recommend you avoid this. Not everybody needs to hear everyone's tasks and where they are on them. Such sessions lack positive energy and often lead to useless posturing. They usually do not optimize the time spent. Use your one-on-ones instead.

Many tasks, however, move too fast to wait for scheduled one-on-one meetings. Or you may need to cancel a scheduled meeting. You may not have regular one-on-one meetings with your staff. And you may make many assignments to staff that aren't your subordinates; you may not meet regularly with these staff. This is the beauty of having the scheduled follow-ups as individual tasks on your task list. They trigger and appear at the top of your daily tasks list at just the right time, whether you look for them or not, and whether meetings are scheduled or not.

Following Up Outside of a Meeting

How to handle follow-ups outside of meetings can vary. If I'm really busy and the actual needed delivery date is not for a good number of days more, I may just shoot off an e-mail to Joe asking, "How are things going on the network performance issue? Let me know as soon as you can, the senior staff meeting is coming up in five days." If this is to a colleague I would be much more politic: "Hi Sally, just checking in to see if all is okay on getting the product overview presentation together by Friday. Let me know if I can get you any additional information or help in any other way. Really appreciate you working on this. That report is going to make the BigCo sale a success."

With my own staff though, better yet is to call or walk over to the staff's desk. The personal touch and one-task-at-a-time nature of this check-in is usually effective at getting the task moving. And you are raising the reminder while Joe is at his desk, at his tools, where he can actually act when he gets the reminder and thinks, "Oh man, I forgot about this, I better move on it."

Setting the Next Follow-Up

Whether you follow up in meetings or in between, there is one more critical step that you must do. In case you don't or can't get an immediate answer to your follow-up, or the answer indicates that the task is not yet complete, then decide and record immediately what day would be the appropriate next day to check in again. Immediately reset the due date on the follow-up task to that new date. This will cause the task to reappear on the task list on that day. If you send an e-mail or voice message as your follow-up action, then set the new date in the task at the moment you send the message (don't wait for a reply, otherwise you will forget). If your check in takes place in person, enter the new negotiated date into your system as soon as you finalize it at Joe's desk.

This is the key utility of using a system to boost your ability to get control of delegated tasks. Such tasks are too numerous and too fast moving to keep their status in your head. You need to keep the status of tasks up to date and in a system, and you need to make those updates immediately. Loose notes or memorized actions will not suffice; otherwise those tasks will fall through cracks. If you have a mobile device, you can do such a status reset right in your meeting with your staff. Whether that meeting is in the hall, in a conference room, or at your staff's desk, make sure you update the status immediately. Keeping tasks updated ensures a steady follow-up approach. It avoids forgotten agreements and sends a consistent management message to your staff. If staff learn from experience that you always follow up, they are less likely to relax on deadlines or take chances that you might not notice slipped deliverables.

Escalation

If the above reminder scenario repeats itself a number of times on the same task, however, you need to escalate management of this task beyond a simple reminder system. The weekly one-on-one meeting with your staff can be a good forum for this escalation because it allows time to brainstorm solutions to whatever is holding up completion of the task. Or if the deadline is too close, call an urgent ad hoc meeting to review impact of the problem and together plan out a course of action. The latter only happens after a few check-in points, so all involved will feel the escalation is fair. The beauty of this approach is that you can stay ahead of assigned tasks and manage them in a timely and fair fashion.

Summary

The positive effects of a good delegation system are remarkable. Staff that previously seemed forgetful or even irresponsible suddenly start responding positively to your assignments. People are human and can forget promises they make. This is particularly true if they do not have a good task management system in place themselves. As the sponsor of a delegated task it is up to you to usher the task ahead and ensure its completion. A good delegation system combined with your good task management system is a winning combination toward helping you succeed in delegating tasks.

Review of Key Learnings

- Effective delegation requires three important components: establishing buy-in, giving adequate lead time, and using effective follow-ups.

- You can implement an effective Outlook task nomenclature to accomplish successful delegation.

- Create follow-up tasks to ensure you check in with delegated staff on a regular basis.

Next Steps

Congratulations. At this point you are essentially done with your adventure. You have learned the basic task management system. You have learned how to convert e-mails to tasks. You have learned how to file e-mails once you are done with them, thus clearing your Inbox. And in this chapter you've learned how to use Outlook as the basis of an effective delegation system.

The next chapter explores a number of advanced topics. You may wish to work with the system for a few weeks before digging into that chapter. Or skim through it now and see if there are any pieces that you wish to start using immediately. You will find a wealth of time-saving ideas and insights there.

Chapter Nine
Advanced Topics

Doing the Math on Your Workweek

The Problem

If after following the approaches in chapters 4 through 8 you still find that you're not getting your tasks done, you may need to focus on time management. The top recommendations from the best books on time management are: avoid interruptions, manage the number of meetings you have, and schedule time to work on tasks. Generally, these are common-sense recommendations.

Note that at the basis of the third recommendation is an implicit assumption that we also do a fourth thing: figure out the amount of work time really needed to get all our tasks done. Most of us rarely do this, and from time to time we need to. If week after week you are consistently falling short on accomplishing your tasks, you probably need to do a simple five-minute exercise that I call "Doing the Math on Your Workweek."

Discovery

Here is how I came across this technique. After changing jobs and digging into a busy set of new activities, one month I found myself well behind on my important tasks. I was confused because I had all the tasks prioritized correctly, had deferred unimportant ones to the master tasks list, and scheduled ahead those that were important but not needed right now. And I had set aside and consistently used what seemed like a considerable amount of task time. Yet a number of my most important tasks were not getting done.

I finally decided to do something I generally didn't do, which is to apply some of my routine project management techniques to the collection of tasks that I had on hand. Project management techniques are usually not applicable to this system of ad hoc task management; in this case they were. Let me explain.

When managing projects one of the first things done after listing all the steps in a project is to estimate how long each of those steps take. The project manager uses that information to estimate the total duration and effort of the project, schedule the tasks, and assign people to the tasks. And while estimates are usually just that—estimates—even with some inaccuracies the result of doing the exercise will usually get the manager to a fairly accurate plan.

So I applied the same technique to my list of tasks. I simply stepped through all the tasks on my lists and estimated the duration of each, then summed them up. The results were surprising. Even though I had thought I had a good picture of the amount of work on my plate, I found myself amazed at how much the tasks I had signed up for actually added up to. My previous rough guess was under by a factor of three! Until I did the math, I had no idea how much work I had committed to.

Common Problem

As I work with more and more people on task management, I find that this is a common problem. People consistently underestimate the total amount of time it takes to accomplish the sum of the tasks they sign up for. Individually, the estimates for each of their tasks are usually not that bad; it is just that they never stop to do the math and add up how much *all* their tasks really require in a given week. There seems to be a psychological block we all have toward doing this math accurately. Maybe the human brain functions in a way that precludes us from doing this math intuitively. Or more likely, maybe this is just the result of our habit of optimism. Nonetheless, I see this again and again.

As discussed earlier, part of the problem is the "heat of the workday." As the research cited in chapter 1 points out, our brain functions differently when under stress or during intense activity. As work stress increases, we lose accurate perspective of the various dimensions of our work. Along with losing accurate measures of priority, one of the other perspectives we lose is an accurate measure of the time needed to accomplish work.

Easily Seen in Others

To see this more clearly, consider how you have often seen examples of this mistake occur with colleagues or your supervisor. For instance, how many times has this happened: your boss gets out of a stressful meeting with his or her boss, and in reaction to an urgent situation brought up in that meeting, assigns you a task to fix something. In your detached and calm perspective you estimate three days of work for this task. From your boss's emotional perspective he is amazed that it cannot be done in under a day. You both are experts in your field but you have amazingly different estimates on the effort required. The next thing your stressed boss usually does is accuse you of over-engineering the solution. In the end, the estimate done by calm analysis is the accurate one.

You often do the same thing to yourself. Imagine yourself in a stressful work-week where day after day you are collecting tasks on your next action list and not getting as much done as you had hoped. As the week progresses and you see the list of uncompleted tasks getting larger, what happens? You become more stressed and do an even poorer job of estimating the time that you need to get your work done. You are most likely consistently underestimating the time needed.

The way we usually make up for these errors is to work late into the evening. If done only occasionally in reaction to unusual peaks in activity, this works. But if your high workload is consistent and late nights are pulled night after night, the cumulative stress and fatigue only exacerbate the situation. You do not regain your clear perspective but rather, like Don Quixote, you keep chasing your impossible dream, in this case, of *doing it all*. You are getting more and more detached from reality in the process.

The Solution

The solution to this is remarkably simple. You just need to sober up for a moment, take five minutes, and do the math on your workweek. You need to figure out how many hours of tasks your have on your task list in the week ahead and how that compares to committed time. And if in this objective analysis you find yourself overbooked, then you need to take some measured and rational steps to account for that now, rather than hoping for a miracle to bail you out as the week progresses.

How far out should you do this math? For ad hoc tasks such as those studied in this book, a week's planning horizon is a good balance between near-term commitments and unknown future changes in priority and available time.

You can make this exercise as simple or as complex as you wish. I prefer to make it simple by doing the following.

Step by Step

1 First, create and use a new Tasks folder view that displays tasks due in the next week. I will show you how to create this view.

2 Next, reconcile the tasks in this list using the same steps you use to reconcile your daily tasks list (see pages 108-113 of chapter 5) but with one twist: don't leave anything on the week's task list that doesn't *really* need to get done in that period. Schedule everything else into a future week, or put it onto your master list. This removes lower priority tasks and leaves you with what *really* needs to get done; this is a reasonable activity if you are feeling behind on important tasks.

3   Then simply start at the top of your list and study each task for a moment, and do a rough estimate of the number of hours needed to complete that task. Don't worry about being terribly precise. I usually estimate in whole hours. Small tasks I usually list as 15 to 30 minutes each.

4   For each task, write the estimate for that task at the end of the subject line. For example: "Summarize staff meeting notes and distribute, 1 hr." Do this all the way to the bottom of your current daily list, as reconciled in step 2 above.

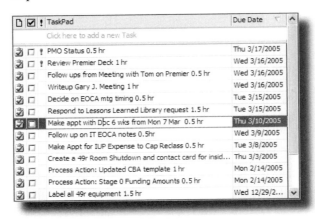

5   Then sum the total hours of tasks in that view (you can do that in your head) and write it down.

6   Compare that sum to the number of hours you have scheduled for task time in the week ahead. I suspect, if you are finding your week has slipped out of control, you will discover that the total hours needed for committed tasks is two to three times greater than the scheduled task time. If so, read on.

7   If not, if the two are roughly equal, you are probably in good shape. But if you find repeatedly that this is true and yet you are still not getting your tasks done, then see the section below called Cleaning Up Your Task Time.

You may at first balk at this exercise and think, "Estimating like this is very inaccurate; how can this really help?" My response: sure, individual task estimates may be off a bit. In truth, however, inaccurate estimates for individual tasks are usually offsetting and the total is often not far from reality.

Another objection is this: "I always schedule more than I can do so this is not surprising; I'll just do what I can get done." If you really feel that way, then go back to Step 2 above, do it right, and repeat the process. Remember, only tasks that really *must* be done in the next week should be on your list at this point.

Side Note: *If you know Outlook well you probably know there are hidden fields for entering and tracking work hours on tasks; you could use those fields instead of entering the hours as text on the subject line. But I am purposely not getting fancy here. The point is to do a very quick estimate of what work is on your plate. Jotting hours onto the subject line and doing a quick summation by eye is fine for our purposes and ensures that you may actually do this check now and then.*

Resolution

So now what? Assuming you have discovered that you are overbooked, you now know you have a problem and why. Like many problems in life, this is an important first step toward a solution. At least you now have a clear picture of the problem and can start doing something about it. And you can take some relief in the knowledge that no, you are not a bad or horribly inefficient worker who needs to work harder; rather you just really do have too much on your plate and you now need to fix that.

Clearly you have some corrections to make. Either you have to add a lot more task time, find others to delegate tasks to, or start renegotiating some of your commitments. Those next steps I leave to you. The beauty of this is, if you do this at the beginning of the week, well before tasks become due, you have time to start negotiating alternatives. You have time to seek permission rather than forgiveness.

The only thing more amazing than how simple this activity really is, is how rarely it is done. This seems so obvious and yet so few of us ever do it. The gap here is this: we fail to recognize that we usually estimate low when mentally adding up the work we have committed to. It is a part of our human nature that we need to work around, consciously, by periodically stepping back and doing this math exercise.

I cover next how to set up the view for this activity.

Setting Up Your "This Week's Tasks" View for Doing the Math

There are two approaches to creating the view needed for the Doing the Math activity. You can use one or the other, or both, according to your needs. The first approach identifies all tasks due in the next seven days. If you are doing this exercise on a Wednesday it will list all tasks scheduled through Tuesday of the following week.

Side Note: *Note that you already have a Tasks folder view delivered by default with Outlook called Next Seven Days; this view is not configured correctly for our needs, so do not use it.*

This seven-day view may or may not be what you want; many workers use Friday as a natural deadline for a week's worth of tasks. In this case, if you are doing the exercise on a Wednesday morning, you want to see only tasks for the next three days. For this you need to instead create a view that displays all tasks in a given calendar week.

Using skills you learned in chapter 3 (pages 61-67), here is how you create both these views:

Creating the Views

1 Activate your Tasks folder by clicking on the Tasks folder icon, then...

2a In Outlook 2003, from the View menu choose Arrange By, then Current View from the submenu, and then Define Views... from the next submenu.

2b In Outlook 2002, from the View menu choose Current View from the submenu, and then Define Views... from the next submenu.

3 Select from the list of views you previously created the view called All Daily Tasks; you are going to copy and modify that view.

4 Click the button labeled Copy, on the right.

5 Give the new view a name like This Week's Tasks and click OK.

6 The View Definition dialog box appears. The only thing you are going to change here is the filter. Click Filter..., and then select the Advanced tab.

7a If you wish to see all tasks due on or before this Friday, then modify the criteria so that it matches the figure below. When doing this, you need to type the word Today.

Side Note: *If needed, refer to page 65 of chapter 3 for more details of how to configure this dialog box to filter tasks.*

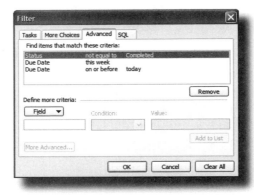

7b If however you want to list all tasks due in the next seven days, then modify the criteria so that it matches this next figure.

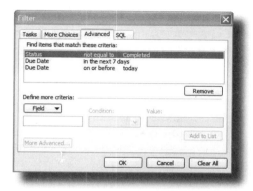

8   Then click OK, OK again, and then Apply View. From now on you can activate and use this view by selecting it from the Current View selector.

Cleaning Up Your Task Time

Inefficient Task Time

Under the category of time management I recommend one other thing: clean up your task time. Let me elaborate.

First, as mentioned many times, I recommend for most of you that you set aside dedicated time for doing your tasks. You should schedule this time on your calendar. Otherwise, if you only try to "work them in" you will be utterly disappointed; things are just not going to get done. Get this time assigned on your calendar early before others start placing appointments throughout your days. Honor those task-time appointments and do not set other appointments on top of them.

Then, if the analysis described in the section Doing the Math on Your Work-week above shows that you have enough task time, yet you are still not getting your tasks done, you have one more analysis step to do. You need to make sure you are keeping your task time "clean." What I mean by that is you need to ensure that you really work your tasks during your dedicated task period.

Relaxing into Your Task Time

Here is a common problem. Unfortunately, what people often do when the scheduled task time arrives, is they relax into that time. If that time is in the afternoon it is often the first time of the day away from intense meetings or away from a constant stream of visitors. It may be the first time sitting at the desk in a while. As a result, people as they enter the task period tend to shift gears. They unconsciously start to unwind and look for distractions. They might visit cube mates. They might take a "quick glance" at the web, make a few personal phone calls, or go get a snack. Or they may go into collection mode: reading e-mail, listening to voice messages, reconciling loose papers on the desk, and so on. Before they know it, the task time is gone and they have accomplished very little on their list.

So you need to consciously account for this requirement for taking breaks, socializing, and reading e-mail. One approach is to build in separate break and e-mail reading time into your schedule. For instance, I add about an hour a day to my tasks time to account for e-mail reading and breaks. If your task time is in the afternoon, add the delineated break time just before the start of your task time with a hard deadline on when you actually start on tasks. That way you are refreshed as you enter your focused task period. See the section titled Time Mapping on page 122 of chapter 5 for more ideas like this.

Avoiding Interruptions

Then, once you are focused on tasks, you need to avoid outside interruptions. Agree with yourself that this is the purpose of this time and that you will discourage visiting, unneeded calls, and other distractions. You may even need to decide that you will not answer the phone, not take incoming e-mails when Outlook beeps at you, and most importantly, turn away visitors. This can be difficult. The social aspect of work is one reason people don't work alone. They enjoy interacting with coworkers. It feels good to help people who stop by for assistance. It feels good to get up from your desk and chat with others. But you need to solve this problem of interruptions to make your task time effective.

You might try some sort of physical change in your environment to delineate pure task time. This could be closing the door to your office if you have an office. Or if you work in a cubicle either finding some other physical space you can escape to, or putting a do not disturb sign on the edge of your cube. Somehow you need to signal to others and yourself that this is a special time with a distinct purpose.

This is a very challenging problem and you may need to experiment to solve it. It is difficult to turn away visitors, difficult not to take phone calls. In the end, however, you need to find a way to isolate a period of pure task time in your day. You may want to brainstorm with your colleagues on agreed methods to accomplish this, so that you each respect each other's private time.

Identifying Deliverables

One more technique you may want to use to clean up your task time is to clearly identify deliverables you expect to accomplish in a given task time. Here is how this works. At the beginning of a scheduled task period, decide what tasks you intend to accomplish. If you have recently done the "do the math on your workweek" exercise, the tasks in your daily list each have durations written next to them; use those durations to determine which tasks you can get done now. Then identify a deliverable, or end product, that must be created to signal the completion of each task. This might be an Excel document, a written report, or a memorandum. Copy that deliverables list right into the subject line of your task appointment in your Outlook calendar.

This is very effective. While working at your desk during the task time, each time you glance at your calendar to see what is up next you'll see those deliverable commitments staring at you. You will know they are due during the next hours, and you will refocus on the task at hand. It's a great way to get serious if you find yourself slipping off track. It's also a good way to manage interruptions. If someone stops by your desk with a request during your task time, you have the focus you need to be able to say something like "I'd like to

The War Room

Here is something to consider for driving tasks to completion: the way large project consulting companies accomplish task efficiency with their junior and midlevel staff working on projects is just the opposite of finding privacy for everyone; rather, they seek out team group work settings and then use the peer pressure of the team to keep each other on track. This is commonly done in a "war room" approach: give a team of colleagues a common goal to reach with a challenging deadline, place them all in a single large conference room working on laptops, and have them work together to complete the tasks. Often the team members decide among themselves which tasks each team member is assigned. Through a combination of urgency, peer pressure, and teamwork, the tasks get done rapidly. In such a setting, since the team's success is measured as a whole, individual interruptions are not tolerated by peers, and staff that wander off on personal errands are met with glares upon their return. Weekly internal team assessments weed offending staff off teams, like getting voted off the island.

At the consulting company Accenture where I once worked, entry-level training consisted of several weeks of boot camp where newly hired staff were thrown into such team settings solving hypothetical problems under urgent deadlines. The consultants that came out of such training were remarkably adept at knocking off tasks quickly.

If you and your colleagues are having trouble getting project tasks done individually, and you can pull away from meetings for a few weeks, you might consider such a war room approach. This works especially well if you are all working on parts of a larger project with clear deadlines. It can be remarkably effective.

help you, but I really need to get this memo done in the next half hour; let me talk to you later."

My advice is, do this transfer of deliverable names into your calendar just as you start on the task period, not in advance. Priorities can change over time too much to have advanced assignment work well on a collection of small deliverables. More on this in the next section.

By the way, this deliverables focus is a common technique used in large project–oriented consulting companies to drive project tasks to completion. The association of a distinct deliverable with a task is an effective way of adding structure to a task and ensuring its completion.

Scheduling Tasks versus General Task Time

Given the previous discussion, you may wonder when it is appropriate to schedule tasks individually on your appointments calendar in advance as opposed to just listing them in your TaskPad. My rule of thumb is to leave them on the TaskPad as much as possible. Only if a task is coming due soon and its duration is rather large in size (two hours or more) do I actually schedule it on the calendar.

Why not schedule most tasks right on your calendar? You might think that this will prevent the accidental overbooking described above. You might think this will ensure task completion. "What gets scheduled gets done," right?

There are three reasons not to do this. First, since these are self-appointments based on rough estimates of effort, the scheduled time slot is almost certain to be changed by other priorities and time needs. Constant rescheduling is cumbersome. There is too much overhead associated with making and moving calendar entries to make these constant changes worthwhile, and so you will quickly start to ignore the appointed tasks.

Second, since we are working with next actions, they tend to be small tasks. Small tasks are more efficiently worked off a list than off individual appointments because our duration estimates for small tasks are usually off. This leads to inefficient completion, as we will tend to fill the allotted time even if less time is really needed. It is much more efficient to march down a list of small tasks and attempt to get as many done as possible within a large segment of dedicated task time.

Third, the best time to attack a given task may vary and present itself naturally to you when you least expect it. You will find opportunities to work tasks synergistically with others. You will find that throughout the day priorities change and that you postpone tasks you thought you were going to do today and reprioritize other tasks first. Trying to keep track of that with individual appointments on your calendar will be nearly impossible.

All that said, when a relatively large block of work needs to be done and its actual due date is near, scheduling on the calendar is often the best way to go. Just don't do it too often. One thing to remember: when you do make a task entry on your calendar, also leave a copy of that task in your TaskPad. That way if you have to blow off a task appointment due to time conflicts, you still have a copy of the task forwarding on from day to day to remind you that it is not yet done.

Working Your Goals and Roles

Nearly every book that I have read on time or task management starts with a discussion of goals. Usually that discussion is on how to identify and articulate goals and how to link those goals to tasks. However, I have found that the weakness of most workers today is their ability to get tasks done, not their ability to identify important goals or to link those goals to tasks. Clearly, if you work tasks that are the wrong tasks or not important tasks, you will be wasting your time. But most workers *do* generally know what their primary assignments are and what they want to accomplish. It is the ability to *complete* tasks toward those assignments that is usually lacking. Until the average worker achieves the ability to get tasks done quickly there is no sense assigning a number of additional goals or focusing excessively on existing ones; the goals will not get done.

An important additional consideration is this: unless staff are in sales or at the very top of the food chain within their organization, many if not most of the tasks that they will need to work will not be directly related to their goals.

For example, as a manager with a number of staff that work for me, I am interested in my staff learning how to get assignments done, not them discovering how to articulate and achieve their goals. Once it is clear to me that they are efficient in completing tasks, I am be happy to have them elevate their perspective on work and begin thinking broadly about work priorities and career advancement. But only after they demonstrate to me that they can get things done. This is the essential first step.

Putting Goals in Your Master List

Once your system of working tasks is firmly and successfully in place and you are getting all your assignments done quickly, all that changes. Now it really is time to start working your goals into your system; you have earned it.

Assuming you have a way to identity your goals (there are an excessive number of references on that, starting with *First Things First* by Stephen Covey), you need a system to ensure that actions from those goals get on your task list. I have found the best way for me to do this is to insert my goals as formal entries within my master list, so that I can consider them every time I plan my week. What I do to mark them distinctly in my master list is this: I enter a "G", a colon, and then the name of the goal. So for example: G:Increase Physical Fitness (see figure 9.1). This allows me to see that goal every week when I scan my master list, and I am spurred to insert daily actions into the coming week that will help achieve that goal. When I review my master list, if I sort alphabetically, my goals sort together.

Just as you do for miniprojects, you can use the text box portion of the Task dialog box to brainstorm activities associated with your goal. That way, each week during weekly planning when you open and examine the goal, you can decide which previously brainstormed activities are appropriate to move out to the daily list for that week in pursuit of achieving that goal.

In fact, Alec Mackenzie in his book *Time Trap* recommends that at least one of your must-do tasks *every day* be linked to one of your goals. Once your task system is in place and working well, this is a worthy goal in itself.

Figure 9.1
Example of a goals list in a master tasks list.

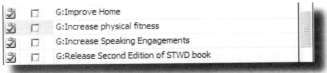

Goals list showing:
- G:Improve Home
- G:Increase physical fitness
- G:Increase Speaking Engagements
- G:Release Second Edition of STWD book

Other Planning Perspectives

Roles and Responsibilities

You can use this same approach for several other major categories of weekly planning activities. For example, Stephen Covey in *First Things First* talks about periodically reviewing the list of roles and responsibilities you have in your life and making sure tasks related to those get routinely added to your daily activities as well. Roles such as spouse, parent, committee head require more than reactions; they require proactive and thoughtful consideration of new activities you might take in the weeks ahead.

Around each of these roles, it helps to consider creative ideas, leadership needs, stakeholder expectations, and perhaps even, if the relationships are personal, random acts of kindness—all in support of that role. Proactive planning like this separates a leader from a mere doer. Without proactively placing specific activities on your daily list or appointment calendar to support these important but nonurgent roles, leadership activities toward these roles and responsibilities will likely get no attention in the heat of a busy week.

When making these entries in your master list, consider using the code "R:" for roles and responsibilities; see figure 9.2.

Then, every week when you do your master planning, think of this team leader role—think of what it means, and what extra you can do in support of that role. Immediately place those activities on the plan for the days ahead. Do the same with any other positions of responsibility you may have. Do

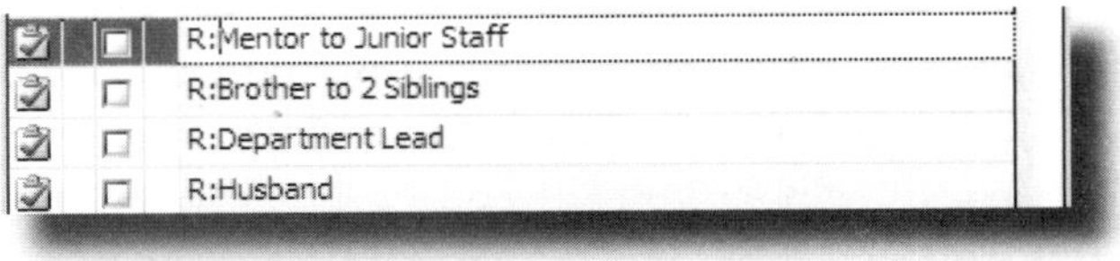

Figure 9.2
Example of a roles list in master tasks list.

Roles list showing:
- R:Mentor to Junior Staff
- R:Brother to 2 Siblings
- R:Department Lead
- R:Husband

this before the week fills up with business appointments, so that you actually get them on your schedule and have enough time to make the necessary arrangements.

Building Meeting Agendas

Another master list activity you can do is, throughout the week, prepare an agenda for regular meetings that you attend. What often happens with standing meetings is that earlier in the week you identify topics that you need to raise in that meeting, but the ideas have slipped your mind by the time the meeting arrives. So use your master list with the code "M:" and make an entry such as M:Meeting-Name. Then, throughout the week as you brainstorm items for that agenda, enter them into the text box of that "task." Later, open and examine that text box, either when you send out an agenda or just before starting the meeting.

Auto-Categorize Incoming E-Mail, Using Outlook Rules

Probably the least enjoyable part of any e-mail organization system is filing. It takes time to decide how to file e-mail and assign categories or drag to folders. Wouldn't it be great if your e-mail were categorized automatically? If e-mail arrived precategorized then all you would need to do after you read it is drag mail in bulk to the Processed Mail folder. While automatic categorization of *all* of your mail is not possible, you can do it with *much* if not *most* of your mail. You do this by creating Outlook rules. The small amount of time it takes to create these rules pays off greatly in time saved during e-mail processing.

What do I mean by Outlook rules? Outlook rules are small logical statements that you create and apply against incoming mail that will cause the mail to be processed in a variety of ways.

For instance, you can cause mail, based on its content, sender, or subject line, to automatically be filed in certain folders. Or you can use those same criteria to cause the mail to be automatically deleted, automatically forwarded, and so on. For the system in this book, the most valuable action to take is to have a category automatically assigned to incoming mail based on its contents or sender.

For example, I have an Outlook rule that assigns the category Personal to any e-mail that comes from any of my family members. I have another rule that sets an e-mail's category to a specific project name whenever I receive mail from the project manager for that project. And mail associated with a number of other projects at my work are categorized using rules that search the e-mail subject line for certain keywords that are uniquely associated with those projects. Due to a number of rules I have created, about 60 to 70 percent of my mail arrives precategorized.

These rules are never foolproof; you should expect the logic of any rule that you write to misfire periodically, assigning the wrong category. But that doesn't matter. They usually work, and even if these rules work only 80 percent of the time, they will still save you effort setting categories. Without these rules you would need to classify *all* of your mail, so needing to change a misclassified mail every so often is not a problem. You come out way ahead.

So how do you create Outlook rules? Outlook provides a simple wizard to create these rules quite easily. I will show you how to use that wizard in a way that matches our system. Use this guide to write three or four rules, and after that, you will be creating them on your own routinely without assistance.

Initiating a New Rule

Once you have thought through the logic you want to use to categorize some mail, do this:

1   Since the rules wizard is only associated with e-mail that is entering your primary Inbox, you must first open your primary Inbox view within Outlook to activate the menu choice. Note, Exchange users need to be online with your mail server to create these rules.

2   Next, from the Tools menu choose Rules and Alerts... (called Rules Wizard... in Outlook 2002) and you will then see the dialog box below.

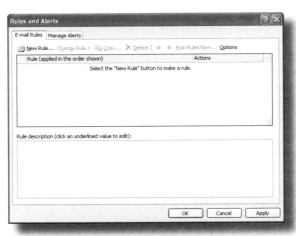

3   Next, click the New Rule button (New... button in 2002) and the following dialog box will open.

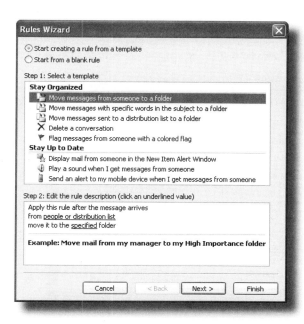

4 Click the second option button called Start from a Blank Rule and you will see the figure below.

5 Be sure that in the top subwindow of this dialog box that the phrase Check Messages When They Arrive is selected. Then click Next.

6 The following dialog box opens in which you start defining the rule.

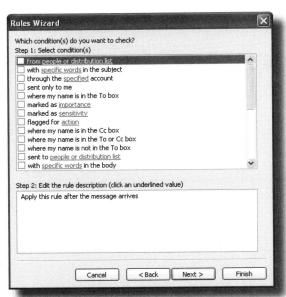

Setting the Criteria

After starting a blank rule, the first definition step is to decide the test criteria you will use to classify the incoming mail.

1 In the top part of the window above, select one of the top two check boxes (these are most likely the only two conditions that will apply to you). Once you do, this adds to the building of the rule statement in the bottom of the dialog box, which you then edit for specificity.

In this example, let's assume that the rule we are creating is a Specific Words rule for the word Legal, to be located in the subject line of the e-mail message; so select the Specific Words check box. Note that this inserts a phrase in the bottom of the dialog box, which you now need to edit.

2 Next, you are going to identify the specific keyword(s) that you wish to place in the phrase in the lower portion of this window. To do so, click on the underlined phrase: specific words. This opens the following dialog box:

3 Type the keyword or phrase (in this example Legal) into the top text box of this dialog box, and then click Add. You will see the keyword appear in the Search List box at the bottom.

If you have more than one keyword, you can add them now. After all words or phrases are added, click OK. This returns you to the Rules Wizard window.

Note that the chosen keywords have been added to the rule phrase in the bottom of the dialog box. This concludes setting the criteria.

We now need to identify the action Outlook will take on the e-mail if the criteria are met.

Setting the Action

1 In the Rules Wizard window click Next and you will see the dialog box below.

2 Select the second item down called Assign It to the <u>category</u> category. Doing this places this portion of the rule into the bottom of the Rules Wizard dialog box.

3 In that bottom portion of the window click the underlined word <u>category</u> in order to set a value for it. The following dialog box opens:

4 This dialog box should look familiar to you; it is the standard Categories selection dialog box. Select one or more categories that you want auto-assigned to e-mail that meet the earlier criteria; then click OK. In this example I chose Attorney.

You have now completely assembled the rule. Examine the rule in the lower portion of the rules wizard. You now need to take a few more steps to finalize and save the rule.

Finalizing and Saving the Rule

1 Click Next, and you will be presented with a dialog box that allows you to create an exception phrase for your rule.

I always skip past this Exception dialog box because it is usually not needed for setting categories on incoming e-mail. So click Next again, and you will see the following dialog box.

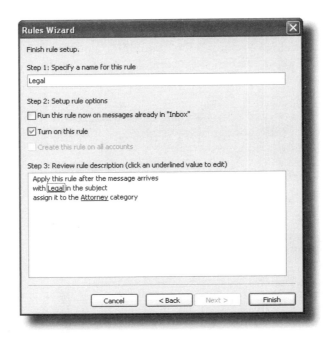

2   Now you can name the rule. The default choice is shown in the top text box of this dialog box and is usually fine.

3   Leave the check box Turn on This Rule selected.

4   If you have an Inbox full of e-mail that you would like to Auto-categorize then select the check box Run This Rule Now on Messages Already in "Inbox".

5   Outlook displays the full rule in the bottom of this window; you can edit it if you see an error; otherwise click Finish.

6   If you are in an Exchange environment, you will see a message telling you that this is a client side rule. This reminds you that rules like this are run from your Outlook client (some other types of rules are run on the Exchange Server). The significance of this message is if you use more than one computer to read, classify, and file your mail, you may need to create the rules at each computer.

Your rule creation is now complete, so click Finish; you will see your new rule listed in the Rules and Alerts dialog box. You can start another rule, or close this dialog box if you are done creating rules (be sure you click OK to close this dialog box, not Cancel, or you will lose all your newly created rules). From now on, Outlook will automatically categorize incoming mail that meets the criteria of this new rule. This will occur as you see the mail appear in your Inbox.

After a while, the above steps will become such second nature that you will not hesitate to create rules for nearly all of your categories.

Changing or Deleting Category Names

As you can see, categories are very useful in Outlook. Getting the category list right, and maintaining it, will become important. The Master Category List dialog box is where you store your category list. However it is really just a pick list from which to make category assignments; it has no influence on categories already assigned to mail. For example, if you change the name of a category within the Master Category List dialog box, filed mail with that category name will not automatically be changed. Any existing mail that has that old category assigned will retain the old assigned category. The only change is this: when you see the old category in the Show in Groups list, it will be tagged with a note: Not in the Master Category List. Otherwise it is treated as if the category fully exists. All new mail assigned to the new category name will behave correctly.

This set of behaviors is good and bad. It is good because it gives you a historical trail; you do not lose previously assigned categories in old mail. It is bad because it leaves Outlook cursed to accept and retain all categories, old and new. Usually when you change a category you want the change to be retroactive.

This acceptance of categories not on the master list also occurs in mail sent by other users. As you receive e-mail from colleagues who may also be categorizing e-mail, the mail, once in your copy of Outlook, will retain the category names from your colleagues. Outlook, in its ever-accepting mode, will treat these categories almost as though they are your own. The result is your Show in Groups list of categories will show even those imported from your colleagues (again, tagged with a note saying Not in Master Categories List).

And one more category behavior you should know: if you delete a category from your Master Category List dialog box all that happens is that the deleted category is not in the Master Category List dialog box anymore; existing mail still retains the old category.

This collection of behavior may seem complicated, but managing this behavior is actually quite easy if you follow a few steps. Let's start with changing a category name.

Changing a Category Name in Your Master List and Collection

Occasionally, an old category term needs to be refreshed. Perhaps you discover another term that fits the intention of the collection better. Your goal is that all mail collected under the old name should now be filed under the new name. If you follow a few logical steps, you can make a category name change quite smoothly.

1   Open the Master Category dialog box and add the new category; then exit that window (see chapter 7, pages 160-161).

2   Go into your Processed Mail folder and open the By Category view.

3   Select (highlight) all of the mail under the category you want to change.

4   Open the category selection dialog box with that mail selected and clear the check box next to the old category. Then select the check box next to the new category.

5   Open the Master Category dialog box and delete the old category. Exit the dialog boxes. That's it, all mail has been reassigned to the new name.

Dealing with Categories in Mail Sent to You

If your colleagues are using a system similar to this, you may start to receive mail that has categories already assigned before it arrives in your mailbox. This will cause Outlook to group your mail in your Show in Groups folder under categories that are not of your invention. These will stand out with a Not in Master Categories List phrase appended to them.

How should you deal with these? The best way to treat this is to agree with your colleagues on a consistent naming convention for categorizing mail. That way as e-mail arrives it will be precategorized in a category that is already in your list.

If you cannot get colleagues to align their category names with yours, then all is not lost; you merely need to recategorize the e-mail as you set your categories in your Inbox. The Category dialog box will allow you to clear the check box next to those unwanted categories. Then just continue by selecting the categories you do want. It is a bit annoying; you need to consciously clear the check box on the old or wrong category when assigning a new category, but it really only takes a split second of extra work. The imported category disappears once all references to it are removed.

Deleting a Category Name

Deleting a category is easy, but first consider carefully why you want to do this. Do you really want to leave all mail messages assigned to that category without any assignment? If the intention of deleting the category is rather to reassign them to a new category name, follow the steps above under Changing a Category Name in Your Master List.

If you really do intend to convert all mail previously assigned to the category to an unassigned status, or perhaps the mail already has other categories assigned, the steps are these:

1   Go into your Processed Mail folder and open the By Category view.

2 Under the category you want to delete, select all of the mail.

3 Open the category selection dialog box with that mail selected (right-click and choose Categories... from the shortcut menu) and clear the check box next to the category you wish to delete.

4 Open the Master Category dialog box and delete the category.

Managing Your TaskPad

Managing the Sort Order of Your Outlook TaskPad

The Unstable Sort Order

After using the TaskPad for a while, you will probably find that the sort order of the tasks in the TaskPad sometimes changes when you do not want it to. The primary way this happens is by inadvertently clicking the header of any column; this causes the TaskPad to re-sort on the data beneath that column. This is a standard feature of most Outlook table views, but unfortunately you cannot turn the feature off.

The TaskPad sort order configured in chapter 3 is ideal for our system. This is actually a double-level sort order: it sorts first on Priority and then, within any given Priority, on Due Date. This is optimal because it places must-do-today priority tasks at the very top and medium priority tasks with more recent due dates just below that (see page 97 for more discussion of why this design is especially useful). Losing this sort order so easily can be disruptive.

Configuring the TaskPad Sort Order

If you lose this sort order by clicking on a column title you *can* regain the double-level sort order by clicking on column titles, but only if you use a trick: click first on the Priority column heading to set its sort. Then, for the second level sort on Due Date, hold down the Shift key and click on the Due Date column title.

That will do it.

So in summary, do a regular click on the Priority column first, then do a Shift-click on the Due Date column next. Some points to remember when doing this:

■ Do not forget that each click on the same column inverts the sort direction (ascending versus descending).

■ Also note that if you click on another column while still holding down the Shift key (say because you clicked the wrong column first), you will get a third-level sort added to the second; this triple sort is probably not what you intended. So if you change your mind on which column you want to sort second on, click a column head once *without* the Shift key held down (to clear the sort), and then try again.

▦ Remember that a little triangle forms in the column heading when you sort a list on that column. When you inadvertently create a triple sort as described above you will see a triangle in *three* columns; use this as a clue to what's going on.

Manual Sorting

Using the Due Date to Control Sort Order

One reason the sort configuration described above is so useful is that with it you can force medium (normal) level tasks to the top of that section by simply setting the Due Date of a task to today. This is discussed extensively in chapter 5, pages 115-116, in the section Prioritizing within Your Medium (Normal) Level Tasks. Since I always work from the top of my task list, I routinely take advantage of this to ensure I work on a particular task more quickly.

Dragging Tasks into Order

There is another way to take control of TaskPad sort order. Outlook comes with a little-used feature that allows you to drag tasks manually into any order you wish.

The key to enabling this is that you first need to *remove all sorting* from the TaskPad. Once you do that, you can drag TaskPad items up and down into any order you wish. The advantage to this is that you no longer need to "trick" tasks into a certain order by resetting their due date. You gain full control of the display order of your tasks, regardless of their set priority or due date. But there is a catch.

The catch is that you lose all automatic sorting. So if a new high priority task appears on your TaskPad because its due date has arrived, it may appear at the bottom of the list, out of sight.

For this reason, I recommend you do *not* use this manual drag-to-position technique, but rather rely on the configured sort orders based on priority and date, to maintain your task sort order.

That said, should you wish to try this, here is how you completely remove the sort order from the TaskPad:

1   Right-click anywhere on the TaskPad heading bar (the bar with the word TaskPad on it).

2   Choose Customize Current View... from the shortcut menu.

3   Click Sort..., and on the right side of the dialog box that opens click Clear All. Then check OK, and OK again.

Now, when you return to the TaskPad, you can click and drag tasks up and down into any position you want. Note the red line that forms as you do this, which indicates where the task will land when you drop it. For easiest dragging, click on the icon at the left edge of the task.

If you decide you want to return to the previous approach, all you need to do is re-sort to TaskPad following the steps in the section above called Configuring the TaskPad Sort Order (page 221).

How to Set Priorities on Tasks with Hard Due Dates

The special meaning of the high priority designation requires a bit of special handling when assigning task dates for tasks that have a true hard due date. In chapter 4 we discussed the concept of a hard due date as being the date a task absolutely must be completed because of a hard constraint in your schedule. I mentioned that the best way to label them is to write the hard due date right into the subject line of the task.

So clearly these tasks are must-do-today tasks on the day that they are due. There is some subtlety though. Assuming you create this task in advance of its hard due date, at what priority should you set this task when you first create it? That depends. If you decide that you want that task to appear on your next action list (the TaskPad) a few days before the hard due date, say to ensure that you find time to work it, then initially set the task to medium. Why? Well, think about it: the task will first appear on your TaskPad before the day it is actually due. And since the meaning of high priority is "must do today" this task has no business being labeled that way when it first appears.

When the hard due date for that task does arrive and you confirm from its subject that it is due today, you should immediately raise the priority of that task to high. It really is a must-do-today task on that day.

If you decide the opposite—that when you create the task you will not need extra days to work the task—then the situation is simpler. In this case you do not mind the task first appearing on your daily list the same day that it is actually due, and so you can feel free to mark it with a high priority when you first create it, even if weeks in advance. In this case the first day you will see that task on the TaskPad is the day it is actually due, and a must-do-today priority can be safely set early.

Viewing Recently Completed Tasks

You may recall that we have configured all of our task views not to display completed tasks; completed tasks clutter the views. As a result, when you check a task as completed in your TaskPad, it disappears. You probably know that it is not deleted; rather the task merely takes on the status of *Completed* and is retained in the database.

Why not just delete tasks when they are completed rather than simply change their status? For a couple of reasons. First, you may decide a moment later that you marked the wrong task complete and need to resurrect it; this happens occasionally to me. I merely go in to the Simple List view within the Tasks folder, find the completed task, and change its status back to Not Started (and using the new view you are about to create below makes this even easier).

Status Reports

Second, if you do weekly status reports, it is convenient to be able to look through your recently completed tasks and find those that are worthy of reporting on.

If you wish to view recently completed tasks, an additional Tasks folder view that you can create easily will help you with this. It allows you to see all your completed tasks with the most recently completed ones at the top of the list. This view takes advantage of a normally hidden Outlook field called Date Completed. Outlook automatically populates that field with today's date when you check the Completed box on a task.

Note that a view relatively close to what we want already exists by default within Outlook. It is called Completed Tasks. However, it is not quite right, the main reason being that it sorts by Due Date rather than by Date Completed. So rather than modify it and possibly confuse other references to this view, let's create a new view with a new name. We are going to call this new view the Recently Completed Tasks view, because it sorts by Date Completed with the most recently completed tasks at the top.

Creating the Recently Completed Tasks View

Configuration Steps

1   In both versions of Outlook you should first make one of the Tasks folder views active. To do this, click the Tasks folder in the Outlook Bar (in 2002) or click the Tasks banner button on the Navigation Pane (in 2003). This step is required because custom views are always created within the currently open folder.

2   Open the View menu.

3   Recall that when defining new views, the only significant difference between Outlook 2002 and 2003 is the menu choices you use to get to the Current View window.

In Outlook 2002, choose Current View.

In Outlook 2003 choose Arrange By, and at the bottom of its submenu choose Current View.

From here on the steps for Outlook 2003 and Outlook 2002 are nearly identical; only minor differences in dialog box layout and names exists.

4 Select "Define Views..." from the Current View submenu. The Custom View Organizer dialog box opens (called Define Views in Outlook 2002).

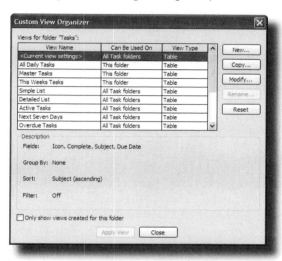

5 Then click the New... button in the upper right corner.

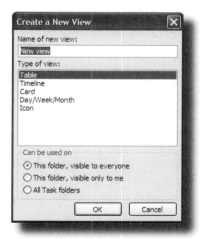

6 Over-type the phrase "New View" with "Recently Completed Tasks." Leave other default settings. Click OK and the dialog box called Customize View: opens (in Outlook 2002 this dialog box is called View Summary).

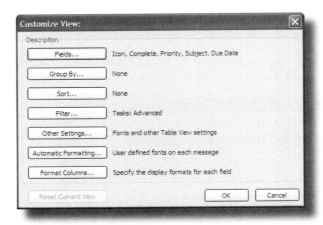

Setting the Displayed Fields

1 Select the columns to display by clicking Fields…, which opens the following Show Fields dialog box (this dialog box looks slightly different in Outlook 2002, but all the controls we need to use are the same in both versions).

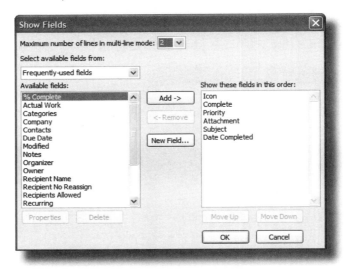

2 Use the Add and Remove buttons to create the following field list on the right side: Icon, Complete, Priority, Attachment, Subject, Date Completed.

This probably means adding the Complete field and the Date Completed field and removing the Status, Due Date, and %Complete fields. Other changes may be necessary.

If you have any trouble finding any of the field names above in the list on the left, try selecting All Task Fields in the selection box titled Select Available Fields From:, and then look again at the scrolling field list. That should display the fields you need.

3 Note that the order of fields in this list on the right side of the window is the order that the fields are displayed left to right in the new view. Adding new fields to this list will usually add the fields to the bottom of the list, which means they will be displayed at the far right in the view. We want these fields displayed left to right to consist of the following fields in the following order:

Icon, Complete, Priority, Attachment, Subject, Date Completed

So if your order of fields does not match above, then the next step is to use the Move Up and Move Down buttons below the right side of the window to adjust the positions of the fields. Or simply click the field name and drag it to the desired position.

4 Click OK..., which returns you to the dialog box shown in the previous Step 6.

Setting the Filter

1 On the dialog box that is now open, click Filter... and the Filter dialog box opens.

2 Click the Advanced tab. You are going to use this dialog box to build a query-like filter, to show only completed tasks.

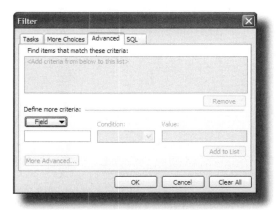

3 Click Field, and under the Info/Status category, choose Status (you might have to look under the All Tasks category to find this field).

4 Working to the right, choose a Condition of Equals, and then from the Value list at right, choose a value of Completed.

5   Then click Add to List to place this condition in the criteria list at the top middle of the dialog box (see next figure).

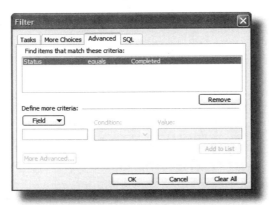

6   Click OK to close the Filter dialog box, but leave the Customize View dialog box open (View Summary in 2002).

7   Click Sort... and a Sort dialog box opens; from the Sort Items By list at the top, select Date Completed, and then click the Descending option. Click OK to close this dialog box.

8   Click Automatic Formatting... and clear the top three check boxes as shown in the next figure. This removes the strike-through formatting on your completed tasks so that they are easier to read. Click OK to close this dialog box, and then OK again to return to the list of views.

9   Confirm that the new Recently Completed Tasks view has been added to
your list of views in the Custom View Organizer dialog box (called Define
Views in Outlook 2002), then click Apply View to view it.

Your new Recently Completed Tasks is shown in figure 9.3.

You can now use the Advanced toolbar Current View selector control (added
on pages 51-52) to pick this view within the Tasks folder whenever you want.
And in Outlook 2003 you can pick this view from the Navigation Pane (again,
from within the Tasks folder).

Figure 9.3
Recently Completed Tasks
view

Tasks		(Filter Applied)
Subject	Date Completed	
Click here to add a new Task		
IUP Status	Sun 1/9/2005	
Write repsonse: Spotlighting your talents	Sun 1/9/2005	
Ask Deborah to find 49r rollout time	Thu 1/6/2005	
PMO Status	Thu 1/6/2005	
Drop book off to Jon	Thu 1/6/2005	
F: Steve Rawles Div Capital	Thu 1/6/2005	
Complete Project Close Sheets	Thu 1/6/2005	
PMO Status - Helen Vu Meeting	Thu 1/6/2005	
F: Helen eTransformation Room next steps	Wed 1/5/2005	
send reminder on status to Shannon	Wed 1/5/2005	
Marty Meeting: show list of PM's	Wed 1/5/2005	
Schedule time with Dom: BR Simplification	Tue 1/4/2005	
Call AP Hair - Fri appt plans	Tue 1/4/2005	
RE: EOCA 2005 Supply Worksheet v3.xls	Tue 1/4/2005	
Program Carryover Procedures 2004 ==> 2005 for IUP	Tue 1/4/2005	
Remind Shannon: RE: Program Carryover Procedures 2004 ==> 2005	Tue 1/4/2005	
finish Standing Meeting list	Tue 1/4/2005	
Note to Mark C: Portfolio Project assignment	Mon 1/3/2005	
Set time with Jon to review EPMO Asset Series - BR	Mon 1/3/2005	

Purging Completed Tasks from Your Task Collection

After months of using the Outlook task system, you can build up quite an extensive list of completed tasks. While they are generally out of view, if you are in an Exchange environment (see Appendix A to determine that) these tasks will contribute to your total exchange storage and eventually impact your ability to hold mail in your Exchange Inbox. So periodically you should clear out or purge these old tasks. Unlike old mail, there is almost no reason to store old completed tasks past the length of time needed for status reports. You may as well clean your old tasks out almost completely.

Manually Purging Tasks

To do this you first need a way to view your complete tasks sorted together chronologically with most recently completed tasks at the top. You then should start deleting from the bottom of that list. The view we created immediately above for your status reports is ideal for this purpose. Simply open this view, take a point in time beyond which you don't mind deleting completed tasks, Shift-select all tasks below that, and tap the Delete key. Don't forget to empty your Deleted Items folder after that to free up your server space.

Automatically Purging Tasks

Tasks do not take very much storage so you don't need to do this often. Regardless, you may feel that you want to automate this operation by using Outlook AutoArchiving to delete your old tasks automatically. Conveniently, when applied to tasks, AutoArchive deletes based on Completion Date and does not delete uncompleted tasks, no matter how old they are. This is exactly the behavior you want; for example, master tasks that we may wish to save for years will still be retained. Study Appendix B, specifically page 273, to learn how to do this.

Add-In Tools for Outlook

Because Outlook is such a ubiquitous and popular tool it has been the target of many add-in pieces of software. Many software packages extend the task management power of Outlook. Two in particular are worth mentioning: FranklinCovey PlanPlus for Outlook and David Allen's Outlook Add-In.

FranklinCovey PlanPlus

There are two versions of FranklinCovey PlanPlus: PlanPlus for Windows XP and PlanPlus for Microsoft Outlook.

PlanPlus for Windows XP is software that was originally written for the Tablet PC (known as FranklinCovey TabletPlanner at that time) and has since been expanded to run on desktop computers. It uses its own calendar and task management system that implements the FranklinCovey methodologies for task and appointment management. It has no built-in e-mail.

FranklinCovey PlanPlus 3.0 for Microsoft Outlook is an add-in software package for Microsoft Outlook. It modifies and runs on top of your already installed Outlook software. It leaves Outlook appointments, contacts, and e-mail functionality essentially unchanged, though it does integrate with them. It enhances Outlook's task management capability so that it follows the FranklinCovey approach. And it adds to Outlook these capabilities: note taking, document management, and goal setting.

Netcentric's Getting Things Done Add-In for Outlook

David Allen on his web site sells an add-on package called Getting Things Done Add-In for Outlook. It inserts functionality into Outlook that automates much of the Getting Things Done methodology.

Einstein Technologies Tablet Enhancements for Outlook

If you use a Tablet PC, this software makes entering tasks in Outlook, using digital ink, easier to do.

Other Task Management Software Besides Outlook?

There is no doubt that other automated systems for task management also exist. If your work function is primarily sales, you may find the ACT system to be useful to you.

If you use a Tablet PC, other Tablet PC specific applications, like PlanPlus for Windows XP, and GoBinder, provide task management capabilities.

However, even for those who use the Tablet PC, I still primarily recommend Outlook. There are just too many well-designed and well-implemented features in Outlook to consider using any other software. And with the fact that it is probably already installed on your work computer and probably the standard at your office, there is little reason to consider any of the alternatives. So the only other software I would recommend is software that is added on to Outlook such as PlanPlus for Microsoft Outlook, the David Allen Getting Things Done Outlook Add-In, and Tablet Enhancements (all listed above).

Add-In Software Not Needed

In reality, you don't need add-in software; all the best practices I recommend can be implemented in Outlook directly. Add-in software often tends to slow Outlook down. It can complicate reinstall and updating of Outlook, it sometimes introduces buggy behavior, and if you work in a corporate environment where only preapproved software can be used, you may not be able to install it.

So, in general, Outlook without add-ins is the software of choice for this system and the one I recommend for most users. My one exception to this: if you use a Tablet PC, do consider the FranklinCovey PlanPlus for Microsoft Outlook add-in software. It adds features useful for users of a Tablet PC.

Wrapping Up

The journey is now complete. You have learned the best task management system available, one based on the most effective best practices in the industry. You have learned how to move tasks out of your e-mail and into your task system, thus removing the most common source of out-of-control e-mail. You know how to file your mail, helping to keep your Inbox clear. You have worked through all the principles, and applied them in Outlook.

Next is only practice. Follow the e-mail workflow presented at the end of chapter 6. That workflow is copied at the end of Appendix C so you can tear it out and place it next to your computer.

Use this workflow, and all teachings in this book, only as a starting point, and then adapt them to fit your work style.

Be sure however to do the daily planning routine discussed in chapter 5. Do weekly planning. If you keep up with this, if you continue to apply what you have learned, you will see dramatic results.

Plan, a few months from now, to skim through the book again, rereading select chapters. The book is packed with suggestions, many of which may not sink in until you have used the system for a while. Your use of the system will evolve over time. Rereading will re-raise suggestions of usage, at a time when they are more applicable and more useful. In particular, chapters 5 through 9 contain much rich information that you will benefit from on subsequent reads.

But most of all, use the extra time you achieve from this system wisely. You have now mastered something few are able to do: getting everything important done; keeping easy pace with your e-mail; being in control of your workday. This is important stuff. Go home from work on time for a change. Do some strategic thinking and planning. Think big. You are ready for the next level, so start planning to be there.

One last thing. If you find this system is as powerful as others find it at getting your workday under control, consider introducing these concepts to your colleagues. Raising the efficiency of your whole organization is a worthy goal. Note however this: while you may be proficient at learning from a book, many people are not. So consider the many CD-based and in-person training options you can find at the author's web site: www.workdaycontrol.com. Take a look, and then consider next steps.

Appendix A
Understanding Outlook Folders

Most Outlook users work for years in Outlook without ever really understanding the folder system built into Outlook. For example, most Outlook 2002 users never even open the Folder List pane but rather work exclusively from the Outlook Bar when navigating through the primary Outlook folders. Even in Outlook 2003 where mail folders are viewed by default, few users really understand the file setup behind the mail folders or realize that an expanded Folder List pane is available. And a majority of users do not know the difference between an Exchange-based Outlook configuration and a local file–based one. This level of understanding, while limited, is acceptable and sufficient for simple Outlook usage. And for the purposes of this book, the importance of fully understanding folder configurations is also relatively minor.

A deeper understanding of folders *will* help you to get the most from this book, however. For example, you will be setting up and using a personal folder as part of your daily system, and while I briefly walk you through this operation in the body of this book (chapter 7, page 156), learning what the steps actually mean is useful. It is also worth figuring out whether you are using an Exchange Server or not, because this drives a number of differences in what you can do with Outlook. And if you save a lot of e-mail, you'll need to understand folders to set up an effective archive system. Let's explore this topic of folders and their underlying data sources to create the groundwork for deeper understanding of Outlook.

Folders Explained

By Outlook folders, I am referring to the hierarchical structure of Outlook data optionally displayed on the left side of the Outlook screen. This structure is sometimes labeled at its top Folder List, but in Outlook 2003, it may have other labels at the top (see figures A.1 and A.2).

Viewing All Folders

Outlook 2002 users need to enable the Folder List pane to see all folders. Do this by going to the View menu and choosing Folder List, which displays the folder structure (shown in figure A.1) on the left side of the Outlook Window.

Outlook 2003 users will most likely see some form of a folder list by default. In Outlook 2003 the entire left side of the screen holding Outlook folders and

Figure A.1
The Folder List in Outlook 2002.

Figure A.2
The Navigation Pane in Outlook 2003.

Figure A.3
The full Folder List in Outlook 2003.

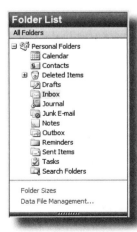

banners is called the Navigation Pane. Figure A.2 (previous page) shows an example of the Navigation Pane with the mail folders open.

If for some reason you do not see this structure, open the View menu and click Navigation Pane to activate it. To see the list of mail folders, click on the Mail banner button near the bottom of the Navigation Pane.

To see a full list of Outlook folders in Outlook 2003, click the Folder icon at the very bottom of the Navigation Pane, which displays the folder structure shown in figure A.3 (previous page).

Chapter 3, pages 43-55, and chapter 7, pages 153-158, provide more discussion of the Outlook window layout including folders, along with details on how to manipulate the folder views.

Similar to Windows Folders, But Not the Same

This folder collection may remind you somewhat of your computer's folder and file list as displayed in older versions of Microsoft Windows (and which by the way can also be optionally displayed in Windows XP). The reason they are called folders is because if you open any one of them you are likely to see a collection of individual matching items contained within. For example, the Inbox folder contains a list of e-mail, the Contacts folder contains a list of contacts, and so on. Like folders, you can drag items from inside one folder into another (if they hold similar types of information) to organize them better. The actual graphics for these folder icons do not look like traditional folder graphics, however; rather the artwork represents some reference to the type of data contained within. Nonetheless, they act like the hierarchical folders you have become accustomed to in the Microsoft Windows file interface.

These Outlook folders are not really Microsoft Windows folders. They do not correspond to actual folders in your computer's file system. They are *virtual* folder structures visible only from within Outlook. In fact, other than the folders in your Mailbox group (Exchange users only), a given group of Outlook folders are usually stored together, invisibly, within a single Microsoft Windows file; knowing about this file and its name will be helpful to you later in this discussion when I show you how to create additional folders. It will also be useful when you learn how to archive your mail. Since these folders are solely owned by Outlook, all your folder creation and manipulation activities must take place from within Outlook's menu system.

Four Major "Buckets" in Outlook

The folder list within your copy of Outlook may have just one group of folders as in figure A.2, or it may have multiple groups of folders as in figure A.1. Each group represents a different "bucket" of information and in fact corresponds to different Outlook data files. The groups each might have similar-looking items inside them (there may be an Inbox within each group, for instance), but each group or bucket of information has a distinct and different functional purpose within your usage of Outlook. Furthermore, the files corresponding to these buckets may be stored in different locations: some on a server, some on your local hard drive.

In fact, there can be up to four different buckets or types of information that Outlook may use which correspond to these groups of folders. If you look again at figure A.1, you will see these four distinct types:

- Mailbox (Exchange Server, probably labeled Outlook Today)
- Personal folders
- Archive folders
- Public folders

Mailbox (Exchange Server, Probably Labeled Outlook Today)

The first type, the Exchange Server mailbox, is the most common data type in large companies. The folders displayed in this group represent data stored on a central Microsoft Exchange Server. Server-based data like this enables powerful collaboration capabilities but has a few disadvantages; more discussion on this ahead.

Personal Folders

Personal folders are locally stored files that act similarly to data stored on the Exchange Server, but they are somewhat limited in their capabilities. If you are using Outlook at home, or in a small business without an Exchange Server, this will be your only choice for storing Outlook data. Even if you are working in a company with an Exchange Server, adding personal folders is a good way to store local copies of your Exchange Server–based data. I cover this topic extensively below.

Archive Folders

The third type of data folder you may have is the Archive folder. The Archive folder is really just another personal folder, with the added feature of having automatic copying of data into it. See Appendix B for a full discussion of the Archive folder and how to archive with Outlook.

Public Folders

The last of the major data buckets within Outlook, which you may see in your folder list, is Public Folders. You will see these only if you are working within an Exchange environment. They are usually configured by your Exchange administrators and if created will show up automatically within your folder list. These are shared Outlook accounts that multiple users can read and in some cases contribute to. The common use of public folders, in the companies where I have worked, is to display public calendars containing the schedules of shared resources in the company (e.g., conference rooms, equipment, and so on).

Each one of these four types or buckets of folders can hold a full set of all of Outlook's functions: e-mail, calendar, contacts, tasks, notes, and so on. While a single bucket is really all you need, you may want to use more than one bucket to help organize your information; the additional groups of folders allow you to create alternate structures to separate your information logically. They also provide optional data backup structures. And depending on your work environment, you will actually be forced to use certain types of these folder sets; you will have no choice. Let's explore these concepts.

Mailbox (Exchange Server)

Determining If Your Outlook Uses an Exchange Server

The most important thing to understand about these groups of folders is to determine whether your copy of Outlook is set up as part of a Microsoft Exchange Server or not. Many large corporations (and even many medium and small businesses) use an Exchange Server as part of their Outlook deployment. In contrast, if you work with Outlook from a home business, you most likely do *not* use an Exchange Server (there are exceptions).

If you are uncertain which one you have, you can settle this question by looking at the folder list on the left side of the Outlook window. Open your folder list now using the instructions above. If you see at the top of the folder list an entry like "Mailbox – Linenberger, Michael" (substitute your own name or user name), then you are working from an Exchange Server. This may be preceded by the words "Outlook Today," and the word "Mailbox" may be absent. The top portion of the folder list in figure A.1 is an example of how your folder list might look if you are working from an Exchange Server.

If, however, at the very top of your folder list you see a label with the words: "Personal Folders" in it, or perhaps "Main Folders," then no Exchange Server is being used. The folder list in figure A.2 is an example of this.

Note that even when using an Exchange Server you may still have a separate personal folders section, but it will probably not be at the very top of your list; that is how you make the distinction.

If you are in an Exchange environment then your primary e-mail, appointments, contacts, and tasks folders are stored on a central mail server shared by others in your company. If you are not in an Exchange environment but rather are solely using personal folders, then your primary folders are instead stored within a simple file structure, probably on your computer. Their content is periodically updated, most likely by accessing an Internet mail service.

Why Use an Exchange Server?

You may wonder: Why do large corporations often use Exchange? What does an Outlook user gain by an Exchange Server over just personal folders?

There are two main advantages. One is cost to the business. The alternative to an Exchange Server is using Internet-based e-mail; at high user counts, Exchange may be cheaper. Why? With an Exchange Server, your company hosts the e-mail accounts "internally." The mail is stored on *your* Exchange Server and the costs for all users can be spread across your internal server investment. This cost advantage does not always exist, though, and so it is the next reason that usually drives the decision to use Exchange.

Hosted Exchange Accounts

By the way, even if you work from a home office or a small business that has not installed an Exchange Server, you can gain the extra benefits of Exchange by signing up with a hosted Exchange service. This in an Exchange mail service you reach over the Internet that provides an experience nearly identical to having Exchange in your organization, without any of the server maintenance headaches. Most companies that provide such hosting allow you to purchase either an individual account (if say you work alone at home) or a set of accounts (if you own a small business with multiple employees). While you reach these servers over the Internet, this is not your typical Internet e-mail account (usually called a POP mail account), but a full Exchange account with all of its benefits. Search the Internet on the term Exchange Hosting to find such a provider.

The primary advantage of using Exchange is the wide set of additional features that Exchange offers to Outlook users — features like intelligent meeting scheduling, shared e-mail distribution lists, ability to recall messages, Out of Office Assistant, and so on. Many of these features are particularly useful for collaboration within team environments. Because of these extra capabilities, many companies that are large enough to afford the costs opt for an Exchange Server. Most of these feature-gains are not pertinent to this book, and so in general this book applies equally to Outlook used in either environment (Exchange or Internet mail).

Personal Folders

Personal Folders Explained

If you see at the very top of your folder list some version of the label: Personal Folders, then you know that you are probably *not* working in an Exchange Server environment but rather are storing your primary e-mail, appointment, contacts, and tasks folders in a personal folders file. What does this mean?

It means that your primary Outlook data is stored on your local computer. When you open your Inbox, for example, you are looking at a list of mail stored within a file on your computer. You must periodically synchronize that file with your Internet e-mail provider to keep it up to date (this is probably set to happen automatically). With an Internet mail account and Outlook, downloading your mail into your personal folders is the *only* way you can view and read your mail; you cannot look directly at your Internet mail server (at least not with Outlook; there are exceptions to this, such as if you have an IMAP account at your Internet mail provider). Personal folder mail has the advantage of always being readable, even when disconnected from your network.

The other types of data visible in Outlook—sent mail, appointments, contacts, tasks, and so on—are also only on your local personal folders file. In fact, these other data types have nothing to do with your Internet mail provider; they are concepts known only to Outlook and only stored locally when not using an Exchange Server.

In contrast to the local storage of personal folders described above, when using *Exchange* you are essentially looking at the live contents of a server, probably located somewhere in your organization. Using server-based data like this enables powerful collaboration features of Exchange. Server-based data also have a major disadvantage compared to personal folders in that if you disconnect from your network or Exchange Server you lose the ability to read your mail, appointments, contacts, and tasks. So if you take your laptop on the road, unless you have some sort of remote access to your corporate network, or have configured other solutions (such as Cached Exchange Mode, or Offline folders, described ahead), with Exchange-based mail your data is inaccessible. More on this below.

Mixing Personal Folders with Exchange Folders

While personal folders are *required* if all you have is an Internet e-mail account, personal folders can be *optionally* added if you have an Exchange account. If added, they exist in addition to the Exchange mailbox set of folders. Figure A.4 shows such a situation. The top group of folders represents the Exchange folders, and the middle expanded group represents a local set of personal folders.

Personal Folders Enable Offline Access

Why would you add personal folders to an existing set of Exchange folders? One (relatively weak) reason is the one described above; personal folders can serve as a partial solution to enabling offline visibility of your (old) Exchange data. Since personal folders are usually stored locally, you can see their contents whether connected to a network or not. So if you periodically copy your mail from your Exchange Inbox into your locally stored personal folders Inbox then that copied mail will be visible no matter where you are; this is

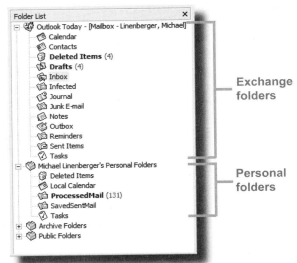

Figure A.4
Personal fold-
ers added to a
set of Exchange
folders.

true of the other data types as well (contacts, calendar, and tasks). The trouble
with relying on this solution is you need to remember to copy your Outlook
data from the Exchange Server to your personal folders before you leave the
network. Most people will not remember to do that and it is a little cumbersome. Of course you cannot see new mail received into your account since
disconnecting. For these reasons, solutions other than personal folders are
usually a better way to enable offline access to the mail (these other solutions
are described in the section Offline Access to Outlook Data, page 247).

Personal Folders as Locally Saved Mail

A more significant reason for adding a set of personal folders to an Exchange
Outlook configuration is this: the mailbox on the Exchange Server tends to
fill up quickly and, in companies with hundreds or thousands of users, these
mailboxes consume considerable central server storage. Excess Exchange
Server storage leads to slow mail performance. Your IT staff does not like
this and so they will put size limits on the amount of mail you are allowed to
store on the Exchange Server; it is likely that you will reach those limits well
before your interest in the old mail stored there has passed. So you need to
find a place to store your old mail, a place where, once stored, you can get
at it quickly. Personal folders created on your local computer are perfect for
this. They allow you to set up an Inbox that looks just like the Inbox on your
Exchange Server but that is stored locally on your computer. Therefore, as
your mail ages, you can manually drag it from your Exchange mailbox to
your local Inbox, thus freeing up the Exchange Inbox space and providing
long-term storage of your older mail.

Side Note: *This by the way is one advantage of having an Internet account over an Exchange*
account. With an Internet account and a personal folders–based Inbox, you have

complete control over your primary Inbox and can let it fill up with much more mail before needing to invoke space management techniques (but don't forget to add a backup capability).

Personal Folders as Filing Systems

Another reason for using personal folders is this: within a personal folders group you can create multiple folders with names that match filing classifications. So as you finish reading mail in your primary Inbox you can move that mail to a variety of intelligently named folders where it will be easier to find later if needed. This is a very common technique used by many Outlook users to help organize their massive amounts of mail. Creating multiple personal folders for filing works either in an Exchange environment or in an Internet mail environment. You can add as many additional folders as you would like to your Internet-based personal folder group. You can even nest folders within other folders to create as deep a folder hierarchy as you like. Using a personal folders–based filing system in the Exchange environment has the side benefit of keeping the Exchange Server–based Inbox relatively empty; this will make your mail administrators very happy.

Side Note: *You could also create these multiple filing folders within your Exchange Server group of folders. Doing so would still contribute to the total Exchange account storage and be subject to the same storage limitations as your primary Inbox. Since little advantage is gained by this, it is nearly always better to create your filing folders within your personal folders group (again, assuming backup capability is in place).*

Note, however, after all this said about the advantages of filing into personal folders, I do not like or recommend this creation of *multiple* named personal folders for filing purposes, and I have described in detail in chapter 7, page 149, why that is. Instead, I recommend the creation of only *one* additional personal folder to empty your Inbox into as you process it, and the assignment of Outlook *Categories* to e-mail stored there for filing purposes.

How to Set Up Personal Folders

Now that we have reviewed all the major folder group types, let's go over how to create the primary type you are likely to be manipulating: personal folders (also go to www.workdaycontrol.com for other folder options).

Each group of personal folders in your folder list corresponds to one local data file within Outlook. This file is by default either called Outlook.pst, or PersonalFolders(n).pst where n is an incremented number that starts at 1 and gets larger as you add additional personal folders files. If you work in an Exchange environment and currently have no personal folders, adding a personal folders group is a two-step process: you will first need to create that local data file, and then you will need to add logical folders to it. And if you already have a group of personal folders, a personal folders file already exists and adding additional logical folders within that file is a single simple step.

Considerations When Adding a Personal Folders Group

The first step when adding a new personal folder group is to consider *where* to store the personal folders file. Usually, the default location proposed by Outlook as you start to create the file is the correct location. The default location that Outlook chooses is usually on your local hard drive.

If Your Company Uses File Servers for Local Files

However, some companies require the use of central file servers for all "local" files; this is to enable easier automatic backups and easier movement of each employee between multiple computers. In this case, you may want to store the personal folder file on that central file server instead of locally. For instance, a company I worked at recently had such a central file server available and encouraged its staff to store their local files there. It issued personal file server space to all of its employees and mapped that space to a logical drive called the "P drive" ("P" stands for "Personal"). In their standard configuration, the Windows My Documents folder was also mapped to this server space; so all "locally" saved files were actually saved to this file server, which was backed up nightly.

If you work in a company with a similar arrangement, this automatic backup service is quite valuable and something you will probably want to take advantage of when deciding where to store your Outlook personal folders file. Storing your personal folders on the file server also enables you to get at your personal folder stored mail if you are working remotely over a wide area network connection. If your company uses file servers for local files I recommend you store the personal folders file there.

Do You Need More Than One Personal Folders File?

The next consideration is to decide if you need more than one personal folders file (group). The only reason you might need more than one in this system is if your personal folders are filling up rapidly (reaching 300 to 500 MB in size using the older personal folders file structure) and you are not ready to delete the mail in the Processed Mail and Sent Items folders contained within. If this is the case, then you should either take advantage of the archiving feature of Outlook (the subject of Appendix B) or create additional personal folder groups. Also go to www.workdaycontrol.com for other folder options.

In the latter case, you would periodically manually drag older e-mail out of the primary personal folder group into a secondary folder group, creating additional secondary folder groups as they fill up. If you take this approach, I recommend you name the secondary personal folder groups by the date range of mail that they hold. Figure A.5 shows one example of this method. Again, this is only necessary if you are using the older Outlook 2002 file structure, which at the time of this writing is still the most common file structure even among many Outlook 2003 users.

Figure A.5
Multiple dated
personal folders
groups.

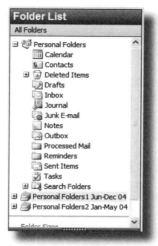

I also know of some users who create multiple personal folder groups for purposes of classifying filed mail; each folder group received a particular category of mail. However, with our system of filing in only one personal folder at a time, this method is not recommended.

Creating the Personal Folders File: The New Personal Folders Group

If you do not already have a personal folders group in your folder list, or want to create another, here are the steps to create a new personal folders file.

1 Open the File menu and choose Data File Management... (you will probably need to expand the File menu choices to see it). The following dialog box will open:

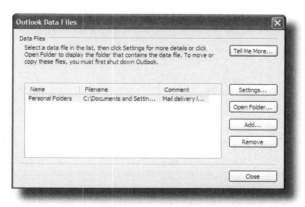

2 Click Add... and the following dialog box opens:

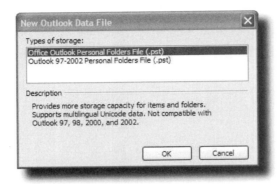

This example is what you'll see if you are using Outlook 2003. The only real difference from Outlook 2002 is that you have a choice of file types; as mentioned above Outlook 2003 added a new personal folders file type with a nearly unlimited storage capacity. It is labeled in this window as Office Outlook Personal Folders File (.pst). The only reason not to choose this new data type is if you are upgrading from a previous version of Outlook and you intend to copy saved mail from your previous installation into the new personal folders. If this is the case, then choose the older data type: Outlook 97-2002 Personal Folders File (.pst). In Outlook 2002, you only have one data type choice.

3 Select the data type per the discussion above and click OK, and the following Save dialog box appears.

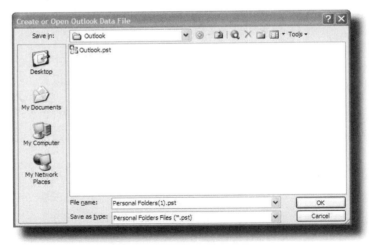

4 Normally, you would simply click OK on this dialog box, thus accepting the default filename and default filed location.

5   However, if you are in an organization that uses file server–based local files as described above, and you wish to store your personal folders on those file servers for backup and remote access purposes, then you are going to need to select a different storage location. You do this by clicking the arrow next to the Outlook folder at the top of the dialog box. This will open a list that displays the full nested folders path for where Outlook originally intended to save your personal folders file by default, as below:

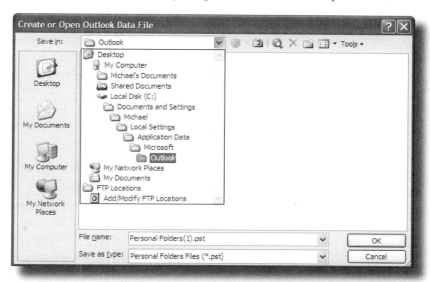

Your job now is to find the file server location where you are going to save your new personal folders file. It may be under My Computer (if the new location has been mapped to a drive), or it may be under My Network Places. If you have no idea where to find this, ask a knowledgeable colleague or your IT department for advice. Once you have navigated to the correct location click OK on this dialog box.

6   Whether you use step 4 or 5 above, the following dialog box opens, where you are able to choose the file encryption type and assign a password to the file. I recommend the default choice — Compressible Encryption with no password — in other words simply click OK (you might consider using a password if this file is stored in a location accessible to others).

7   This returns you to the Outlook Data File dialog box where you will see that another data file has been added. Click Close.

If you look at the folder list in your Outlook window, you will see that a new personal folders group has been added. By now it should be clear to you that each personal folders group in your folder list corresponds to a separate personal folders file.

8   If you have more than one personal folders group, I recommend that you rename the new group name something other than personal folders. Otherwise, you may get confused as to your intended purpose for each group. To rename a personal folders group simply right-click the top level of the group in the folder list, choose Properties from the shortcut menu, click Advanced..., and edit the name in the Name box.

Adding Folders within the Personal Folders Groups

After creating a personal folders file you now need to take a few steps to create the folders themselves within the new group. These steps are quite easy.

1   First, open the File menu and choose New. From the submenu choose Folder... and the following dialog box appears:

2 Type the name of the new folder in the Name box.

3 From the second box down choose the type of folder you are creating; for example, choose Mail and Post Items if you are creating an e-mail folder.

4 In the folder structure frame in the bottom, select the folder group that you wish the new folder to be created within. Normally this means choosing one of the top-level personal folder groups. But occasionally you may wish to create a folder nested within one of the other folders within a folder group, to create a hierarchical structure.

5 Click OK, and you should see the new folder appear within your Outlook folder list, ready for immediate use.

Offline Access to Outlook Data

Offline access refers to access of your Outlook data when you are not connected to your corporate network or to the Internet and not dialing in remotely. This is not to be confused with *remote access,* which refers to accessing your *live* data via an Internet connection or phone dial-up connection.

Offline access gives you access to data stored on your local copy of Outlook, data left from the last time you were connected live. It should be obvious that offline access only allows you to see server-based data that were current up to the time that you disconnected.

Offline Access for Internet Mail Users

Figuring out how to configure for offline access is important only to users in an Exchange environment. In contrast, Outlook users not in an Exchange environment (and so accessing their mail from an Internet mail service) have no need for special offline access configuration because such users never lose sight of their data, even when not connected to the Internet. Since such data is stored in personal folders (usually locally in such settings), Outlook automatically provides offline access in these configurations. In this setting, only e-mail data might lack currency when disconnected from the Internet since all other Outlook data (calendar, contacts, tasks, and so on) are *only* stored and manipulated in local files. So such users need to do nothing special when they disconnect from the Internet; they can just continue using Outlook as before.

Side Note: *If however your Internet-accessed data is actually stored on a hosted Exchange Server then the automatic access to offline data, described above, will not be possible; you will need to treat this setup as an Exchange Server environment, discussed next.*

Offline Access for Exchange Users

Without custom configuration, Exchange users lose access to their Exchange Server data when they are not connected to their corporate network or if their corporate network is down. For instance, if you disconnect from your wired network and carry your laptop or Tablet PC into a conference room meeting, you will not be able to see any of your Exchange-based Outlook data (your schedule, old e-mails, and so on). Because of this, it makes sense to do configuration steps that enable automatic offline access.

What are these configuration steps? In the sections above I mentioned that one possible use of added personal folders was to enable offline access to data copied from the Exchange Server. However I also mentioned that using personal folders for this purpose is a relatively weak way of accomplishing offline access for Exchange users. This is because, for this to be useful, users would consistently need to remember to copy their Exchange data into their personal folders. So personal folders is not a good way to gain offline access. There are better ways, using custom Outlook configurations, to enable offline access to Exchange data.

Outlook Offline Folders (.ost)

The only better way for Outlook 2002 users is to create what Microsoft calls Outlook offline folders. These are hidden Outlook folders which when configured are stored in a file with an ".ost" extension. This file is very similar to your .pst file, except that it does not display separately in your Outlook folder hierarchy but rather exists hidden within the Outlook file system and is only accessible automatically by Outlook. These folders automatically mirror the contents of your Exchange folders onto your hard drive. When you disconnect from your network, they invisibly replace the data behind your Exchange folders in your folder list with the local mirror copy. The result: one moment the Inbox in your Mailbox folder group is pointed at the Exchange Server, the next moment it is pointed at the local mirrored data file. So when you disconnect from your network you still have access to all your Exchange data current at the time that you disconnected, and you get to it as if you were opening your regular Exchange Inbox. And this works in the same way for all the other data types as well (calendar, tasks, contacts, and so on). This behind-the-scenes mirrored data swapping is actually quite remarkable. And the supporting synchronization can be scheduled to occur automatically, all invisible to the user. The .ost offline folders feature is available in both Outlook 2002 and Outlook 2003. I cover how to configure this below.

But Outlook offline folders are not the perfect solution. The downside is that every time your network status changes you will need to quit Outlook and restart it. For instance, when you disconnect your network cable as you run with your laptop or Tablet PC to a meeting, an Outlook restart is needed in the meeting. And when you return from your meeting and plug back into the network, another Outlook restart is needed at your desk. This is the only way to reaccess the up-to-date server data. While this takes only a few seconds, it is annoying to have to do, and more importantly, you will often forget to do it. I have worked for hours at my desk not realizing I was not getting e-mail due to forgetting to restart Outlook after returning from an earlier meeting. You'd think there would be a better solution, and there is: Exchange 2003 and Outlook 2003.

Cached Exchange Mode for Exchange 2003 and Outlook 2003

If you are lucky enough to be using *both* Exchange 2003 and Outlook 2003 then you can take advantage of a third mode called Cached Exchange Mode. It is much better than configuring offline folders in the 2002 version. The reason it is better is Cached Exchange Mode does not require you to quit and restart Outlook when you switch from working online to offline and back. Rather it works transparently and automatically, behind the scenes, as your network status changes. Online and offline functionality kick in automatically, and when back online, subsequent synchronization happens automatically.

To configure this setting, first check with your IT department to confirm they are using Exchange 2003 and that Cached Exchange Mode has been activated. If so, you still need to activate this within your copy of Outlook 2003. To do this, from within your Outlook 2003 client, choose Tools, E-mail Accounts, View or Change Existing E-mail Accounts, then select your Exchange account and click Change, and then check the box marked Use Cached Exchange Mode. Note that the first time you do that, if your mailbox is large, a lengthy synchronization period will occur; so start this and go get some coffee. After the initial sync, the process is quick for updates.

This is by far the easiest method to enable offline access, and it's a reason to encourage your IT department to upgrade to Exchange 2003 if they have not done so.

Configuring Outlook Offline Folders (.ost)

At the time of this writing, most readers are still in an organization using Outlook 2002 or earlier and so will need to use the .ost approach mentioned above. Here's a high level summary of how this is configured and used for Outlook 2002, followed by detailed instructions; the approach is similar in other Outlook versions.

A First you must tell Outlook and Exchange that you want to create the .ost file and where on your hard drive to store it.

B Once the file is created, you then need to set up synchronization of your Exchange folders with your local .ost file. You could synchronize manually; but better is to schedule automatic synchronization events. I configure Outlook on my PC so that synchronization occurs every 15 minutes and whenever I quit Outlook.

C And finally, you need to access this offline data when you are in fact offline.

Detailed Offline Folders Configuration Steps

Here are the details to the three general steps described above.

A Create an Offline Folder (.ost) File

1 On the Tools menu, click E-mail Accounts, click View or Change Existing E-mail Accounts, and then click Next.

2 In the list titled: Outlook Processes E-mail for These Accounts in the Following Order, click Microsoft Exchange Server, and then click Change.

3 Click More Settings.

4 Click the Advanced tab, and then click Offline Folder File Settings... in the lower right corner. You will see the following dialog box:

5   In the File box of this dialog box, you should see a file path with a file-name outlook.ost at the right end. If so, click OK. Note: all users should use this default .ost location including those who use file servers for personal files. This default places the .ost file on your local hard drive, which is essential for offline folders to work properly.

6   Assuming you have not used offline folders before, you will see a message that this file cannot be found and asking permission to create it. You should click Yes.

7   Click Next and then Finish to close the Accounts dialog box.

B   Setup Synchronization

1   From the Tools menu, select Send/Receive Settings, and then click Define Send/Receive Groups.

2   In the list, click the All Accounts group.

3   To automatically synchronize all folders at specified intervals while you're online, select the Schedule an Automatic Send/Receive Every [x] Minutes check box, and then enter a number between 1 and 1440 (I set mine for 15 minutes).

4   To synchronize all folders after every online Outlook session, select the Perform an Automatic Send/Receive When Exiting check box (recommended).

C   Using Offline Folders

Once configured, when you launch Outlook and you are unplugged from the network, Outlook will go into offline mode, and your standard views of Inbox, calendar, and contacts will all automatically point to the .ost offline data on your hard drive. If you write and "send" e-mails while in offline mode, those e-mails will be temporarily stored in the Outbox folder. Once back on your network and in online mode they will be sent upon synchronization. Note again that you will need to restart Outlook in order to switch back to online mode.

Appendix B
Using Outlook AutoArchive

The Outlook Archive Capability

You may periodically get messages from Outlook offering to archive your old mail. New installations of Outlook are configured to display these messages automatically. If you were like I once was, you quickly canceled out of those messages and perhaps scratched your head wondering what they really meant. You probably wondered where e-mails went after you archived them and if you would be able to see old messages again easily. Or perhaps you actively accepted those messages and are using the AutoArchive features of Outlook, but you don't really understand the process. Few people take the time to figure out what is going on.

Should You Use Outlook AutoArchive?

Here is a quick answer: if you are using Outlook 2003 and its new personal folders file format and using the system in this book, you probably do not *need* to use AutoArchive. There are no significant system limits you may reach that could be avoided by cleaning out old e-mail messages automatically. That said, you might wish to use AutoArchive to remove clutter from your primary Processed Mail folder.

Outlook 2002 users *can* have their life greatly simplified if they use AutoArchive. But even for Outlook 2002 users, there are manual ways to accomplish nearly everything AutoArchive does. So you should study the moderately challenging steps ahead and see if you conclude configuring Outlook AutoArchive is worth the effort. At a minimum, you may want to study this appendix so you know how to turn off any default archiving settings and stop those pesky messages that you may be getting every couple weeks.

One Reason to Use AutoArchive: Avoiding Size Limit Infractions on Your Exchange Folders

First, why use Outlook's AutoArchive capability? It's useful primarily for its automatic mail-moving feature, which you can apply in a variety of ways.

If you use an Exchange Server Inbox and are not in the habit of manually moving old mail out of your primary Inbox into some other storage location, then the automatic archive features of Outlook AutoArchive can be a good way to keep the "Your mailbox is over its size limit" messages at bay. For the majority of Exchange users, this is the primary benefit of using AutoArchive and a very good reason to do so.

However, this need is generally not applicable to readers of this book since, as part of this system, we *do* manually move mail out of our Exchange folders into the Processed Mail folder. Still, AutoArchive can be useful to us.

Keeping Your Processed Mail Folder Small

Another way to apply the automatic move feature, and more applicable to us, is this: your personal folders file has space limitations. Granted these limits are much larger than those imposed on the Inbox of the typical corporate implementation of Exchange, but still, I have seen personal folders in Outlook 2002 fill up quite often. The absolute limit of a personal folder in Outlook 2002 is 2 GB (see size discussion about Outlook 2003 below). It is my experience though that as you exceed 300 to 500 MB the performance of personal folders in Outlook 2002 can slow down or become unreliable (particularly when the file is located on a file server). I have seen colleagues lose mail as a result. Since we are dragging all of our mail out of the Exchange Inbox and into the Processed Mail folder, which is of course stored in a personal folders file, that file could get very large, and this should be of concern to us.

If you are using the old 2002 personal folders file format, eventually you'll want to move old mail out of a single personal folder set as it fills up, and Outlook AutoArchive may be for you.

Side Note: *I have seen many Outlook 2002 users extend the file size of their personal folders file quite close to the 2 GB absolute limit. This recommendation to keep the file size less than 500 MB is purely for risk mitigation purposes.*

Alternatives to Using AutoArchive

You do not *need* to use AutoArchive to keep your primary personal folder at a safe size though; there are other approaches to saving your old mail as it fills up.

One common solution is to periodically move the old mail manually (select and drag the mail) to another personal folders file. This is a perfectly legitimate approach and a good way to manage your folder size, particularly if you want to avoid the complex steps in this appendix for configuring AutoArchive. To use this method you'll need to create an additional personal folders file and folders group (see Appendix A), and then drag mail to it regularly. Specifically, you would monitor the size of your primary personal folders file and if you see it starting to drift above 300 MB, open your Processed Mail folder, select say the oldest one third of your mail, and drag those items to the new personal folders location. You would repeat this operation with Saved Sent mail. You would then compact the personal folders file using the instructions on page 268 of this appendix, check the file size, and repeat if needed.

If you do not care about saving your old mail, this method is even easier; after selecting the oldest one third of your mail you merely press the Delete key. There is no need to create additional personal folders when you do this.

Advantages to Using AutoArchive

However, there are advantages to using the AutoArchive capability in Outlook to do this transfer automatically. The primary advantage of Outlook AutoArchive is that you do not need to *remember* to move (or delete) your mail; every week or so your oldest mail is automatically moved to another folder set. Furthermore, in our system where the Processed Mail folder collects all our read mail and could fill up quickly, automatically running AutoArchive frequently keeps your Processed Mail folder at a fairly constant size and "aged" status, which makes that folder more useful. If you are using the Outlook 2002 or older file formats, you really should consider doing this.

Not for the Faint of Heart

Setting up and using the archive in Outlook 2002 is not for the faint of heart. AutoArchive, if you choose to apply it just right, can get a little complicated; the steps ahead are a bit extensive and require periodic maintenance. You probably should set aside a couple hours to work through the configuration steps. If you feel overly challenged by these steps and yet feel strongly about saving old mail, stick with the alternative method described immediately above. In the long run, the manual methods take more work and are inherently more risky, but they require less up-front configuration and understanding.

Because it is the Outlook 2002 personal folders file size limitations that are driving this need to use AutoArchive, if you save lots of old e-mail, upgrading to Outlook 2003 is worth the price.

Outlook 2003 and Your Processed Mail Folder

Outlook 2003 has an optional new file format that allows a nearly unlimited personal folders file size. If you use this format when you create your Processed Mail personal folders group, archiving in our system is virtually unneeded. You can let your single personal folders group get as large as you like. This is a great feature of Outlook 2003 and one of the many reasons to upgrade (but do not forget to back up your mail stores).

The only slight disadvantage is that this new file format is not backward compatible with Outlook 2002 or older mail you may have stored prior to upgrading; you need to keep these two data types separate. If you have just upgraded to 2003 and are trying to mix in your older mail, you cannot opt for the newer format. Rather you will either stay completely with the old format or use the new file format only for new mail.

While with the Outlook 2003 new file format you will not hit a system limit on your personal folders, you may decide you do not need to see mail older than, say, one year. If so, AutoArchive could be of use to you to help remove clutter from your mail views.

So as you can see, using the AutoArchive feature of Outlook is purely optional; but in our system if you are using Outlook 2002 it has its value. And even if you are starting fresh with Outlook 2003 and can use the new unlimited file format for your Processed Mail folder, you may want to use AutoArchive only to remove very old mail.

What Is an Archive Folder?

If after studying why you might want to AutoArchive you decide to do it, the second important lesson of archiving is learning what an archive folder is and where your mail goes once archived. An archive folder is effectively just another personal folders file, like the ones that we have described in Appendix A. Like the personal folders file, it's a "local" file that accepts and stores e-mail and other Outlook data types. There are only two things that really make it different:

- It may not be visible in your Outlook folder list (but you can easily make it visible).

- It is supported by a powerful automatic system of moving mail based on how old the mail is.

Other than this, think of your archive file as just another personal folders group. If you make it visible you can easily open and read your archived mail and you can move mail in and out of it like with any other personal folder. The file itself even has an identical file extension as your personal folders file: .pst.

Turning Off Outlook AutoArchive Completely

If your sole reason for coming to this appendix is to learn how to turn off Outlook AutoArchive completely, to eliminate those annoying "would you like to archive your mail" requests every couple weeks, here is how to do that.

Out of the box, Outlook ships with some folders configured for AutoArchive and some not. You could go to each folder and turn AutoArchive off if it is on. An easier method is this:

1 Right-click your Processed Mail folder, choose Properties, and choose the
AutoArchive tab; you will see the dialog box below.

2 Click the second option button: Archive Items in This Folder Using the
Default Settings.

3 Click Default Archive Settings….

4 In the dialog box that opens select the first check box at the very top
labeled Run Archive Every. Ignore the duration box to the right.

5 In that same window, about two thirds of the way down, click the button
labeled Apply These Settings to All Folders Now.

6 Now, go back to the check box in step 4 above, and clear it. By this set
of actions, you have forced all folders to follow a default setting of no
archives.

7 This setting applies to all the folders in the currently selected folder
group. If you have any other folder groups (Exchange uses have the
Exchange group of folders still to do), repeat steps 1 through 6 on one
folder in each group to clear archive in those groups as well.

That's it; that will turn off AutoArchive for all your folders and prevent
the periodic messages asking for permission to archive.

Checking Outlook Folder Sizes

Before configuring and using AutoArchive, you should learn how to check
the folder size of your Exchange mailbox or personal folders file so you can
tell whether you have space problems yet. And even if you are not using

AutoArchive, to use the alternate techniques to keep your file size under control, you need to know how to see your mail file size. These steps will show you how.

Always Check at the Folder Group Level

Since it is the Exchange mailbox or personal folders file that has the size limit (and not individual folders within a given folders group) you will always check the size of a group as a whole. So the first step is deciding which folder group you want to check. The Exchange mailbox is worthy of checking to see if you are about to exceed your corporate limits (these limits are often are as small as 40 MB). And if using the older Outlook personal folders file structure, you should check each of your personal folders groups (if you have more than one) to see that they do not exceed 300 to 500 MB each.

Steps to Check Folder Size

1   Right-click the top-level Exchange icon (probably called "Outlook Today–Mailbox…") in the folder list (or a top-level personal folders icon if checking that folder group).

2   Choose Properties.

3   In the window that opens, click the button in the lower left titled Folder Size. The following dialog box opens.

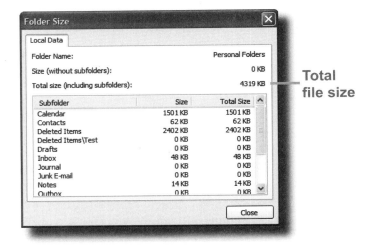

Note the third line down titled Total Size, and to the far right of that label a number in KB. This is the number you are looking for. Of course, you should divide by a thousand to get MB. In the example above this file contains only 4.3 MB, which is way under the limit for Outlook 2002. If your personal folders file is above 300 MB and you want to save your old mail, then you should proceed with the rest of this appendix and set up an archiving system.

You can also examine the sizes of individual folders within the folder group by studying the scrolling list at the bottom of this window. This is useful if you are getting messages from your Mail Administrator that your Exchange mailbox is too big. You can use this to identify which folder you need to drag files out of. For users of this system it is usually your Sent Items folder that gets too big (see the last section of this appendix for more discussion).

Setting Up AutoArchive Intelligently

So if you decide that your folders are getting too large and that Outlook Auto-Archive is for you, you will need to dig into the configuration screens and set AutoArchive up intelligently. Rather than just turning it on, it is worth taking the time to set it up right, so that you can work with it for months and years ahead.

Realize that there are a number of different ways you can set up archiving, dependent upon your goals (go to www.workdaycontrol.com for other options). The goals of the steps ahead are to keep both your Processed Mail folder and your Saved Sent Mail folder at a safe but reasonably large size, without the periodic need to empty them manually. And the steps assume that you will be manually dragging mail out of the Inbox and Sent Mail folders, and so will not need to activate AutoArchive on those.

For this system, you need to set up four main operations to use Outlook Auto-Archive:

A   Calculate or decide on the "Older Than" setting.

B   Set up and configure AutoArchive.

C   Run your first archive and fine-tune your setup.

D   Periodically swap out the old Archive folder and insert a new one.

Here are detailed steps for these operations for setting up and using AutoArchive:

Side Note: *I recommend you read Appendix A before embarking on Outlook AutoArchive; it will give you the understanding of Outlook folders that you need to be successful.*

A: Determine the "Older Than" Setting

AutoArchive works like this: when it runs, all mail older than a certain number of months from today (the "Older Than" setting) is removed from the folder and placed in an archive folder (or deleted if that setting is chosen). All mail younger than that setting is retained in the original folder. So the Older Than setting is the maximum age of mail you would like to retain in your folder being archived. The Older Than setting is a value that you enter in the AutoArchive configuration screens (described below). How do you choose the correct value?

Outlook 2002 Users (and Outlook 2003 Users Using Old File Format)

With Outlook 2002 (and Outlook 2003 users with the old file format), a limiting factor is the 300 to 500 MB file size (my recommended limit for Outlook 2002). I like using as long an Older Than setting as possible while not reaching that limit, because I'd prefer to look in only one location (the Processed Mail folder) when browsing for old mail. I assume most people have that same goal: maximum amount of mail stored together, safely.

So with Outlook 2002 you need to do a simple calculation to see how that file size limit translates into an Older Than setting. For example, after some calculation, I chose six months as my Outlook 2002 Older Than setting. At that setting, I was able to keep my personal folders file at about 300 MB. But this is controlled by the rate at which I receive and send new mail. Your rate may be different, so you should do your *own* simple calculation to determine the best Older Than setting to keep your file at about 300 MB.

Calculating the Setting

To calculate the setting, do the following. First, look at the oldest date in your Processed Mail folder and figure out how many months' worth of mail is in there. Next, check the size of your personal folders file that contains the Processed Mail folder (see Checking the Folder Size earlier in this appendix). Divide this and figure out about how many months of mail activity it takes for you to reach 300 MB. For example, if your personal folder size is currently 600 MB and you have eight months' worth of mail in there, your Older Than setting should be four months. You can think this through logically or apply the following formula:

Older Than setting (months) = (current months old mail X 300) / current Personal Folders file size in MB

Use this to calculate your capacity, in months, given the average rate you are currently receiving and sending mail. This is the value you will use in your Older Than setting in the configuration steps ahead. If you use anything much larger than this then you are likely to exceed the 300 to 500 MB recommended file size.

Side Note: This calculation is not exact because it ignores the impact of the contents of other folders within that personal folders group. No worries, however; the calculation will still provide a good starting point, and I will show you how to fine-tune the settings later to adjust for experience.

Setting Smaller Than the Calculated Value

If you receive little mail and so your calculated Older Than setting is quite large (well over a year), you may decide to set your Older Than setting smaller than the calculated value, opting to reduce your folder clutter. For example, you may wish not to see two-year-old mail every time you sort your Processed Mail folder by sender or category. If this is the case, then decide what your reduced Older Than setting is based on your age-of-mail tolerance, and use that instead in the steps below.

Outlook 2003 Users Using the New File Format

If you are in Outlook 2003 using the new unlimited file format and considering using AutoArchive, it can only be because you want to reduce clutter. In that case, decide what your desired Older Than setting is based on your age-of-mail tolerance, and use that in the steps below.

B: Set Up and Configure AutoArchive

There are many different ways to configure AutoArchive. The easiest way is to set the default settings (while configuring the first folder) and subsequently apply those to multiple folders.

Here is how you configure your first folder and create the default AutoArchive settings:

1   Right-click your Processed Mail folder, choose Properties, and choose the AutoArchive tab; you will see the dialog box below:

2   Click the second option button: Archive Items in This Folder Using the Default Settings.

3   Click Default Archive Settings...; this will open the dialog box below:

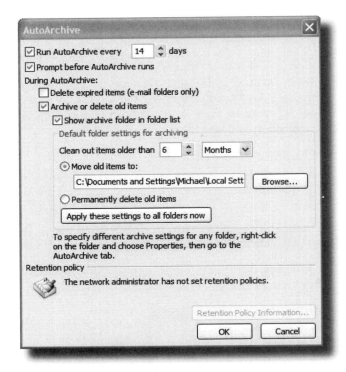

Configuring Default Archive Settings

To configure this dialog box:

1   Set all the check boxes as shown.

2   The 14-day interval default should be adequate for most users; 7 days is even better as this will keep your folder size a little more consistent.

3   After you are comfortable using AutoArchive for a few weeks and confident your settings are correct, you may want to come back to this window and clear the second check box (Prompt Before AutoArchive Runs) so that you are not interrupted by the operation. But leave it checked for now.

4   Set the Clean Out Items Older Than setting to the value determined in part A above (this is your Older Than setting).

5   Next, assuming you intend to save your old mail (if you do not wish to save your old mail see the next section), click the option button labeled Move Old Items to. This tells Outlook where to place the Archive.pst file, which is the file that holds all your archived items. Usually the default location is adequate (in your Documents and Settings folder).

6 If you wish to change the Archive.pst file location, use the Browse... button. If you are working in an organization that uses file servers for all personal files, I recommend you *do* change the location and store it on your mapped server file (that way it is backed up). You may have a folder in that location already devoted to Outlook or Exchange files; if so, use that as your storage place.

7 Click OK, and then OK again.

You have completed settings for your first folder and the AutoArchive default settings have been created. Note that the Archive folder group will not show up in your folder list until after the first AutoArchive session is run (as described below).

If You Don't Save Your Old Mail

If your purpose for running AutoArchive is just to clean out old mail but not save it, then in step 5 above don't click the option button labeled Move Old Items To.

Rather, click the option button labeled Permanently Delete Old Items, and then skip step 6 above. No Archive folder will be created and mail older than your clean-out setting will simply be discarded. Continue to follow the instructions below.

Configuring Saved Sent Mail AutoArchive Settings

Next, you want to configure your Saved Sent Mail folder to be archived as well (this folder was optionally created in chapter 7, page 158):

1 Right-click your Saved Sent Mail folder (just below the Processed Mail folder) and choose Properties, then click the AutoArchive tab.

2 Click the second option button Archive Items in This Folder Using the Default Settings, then click OK, and OK. See figure below.

Note that since we have already set the default AutoArchive settings, there is no need to define them again for this folder; no other configuration is needed.

Clear Your Exchange Mailbox AutoArchive Settings

Next, you need to remove archiving from all your Exchange mailbox folders. Since you manually drag your Inbox mail to your Processed Mail folder (and periodically drag older items in your Sent Items folder to your Saved Sent Items folder), archiving these folders is not needed or desired. However, many of your Exchange mailbox folders come with AutoArchive turned on by default, so you need to turn that off. Here is how to do that.

1   Right-click the Inbox and choose Properties, then click the AutoArchive tab.

2   Click the first option button: Do Not Archive Items in This Folder.

3   Repeat above steps for Sent Items folder.

4   Repeat the above steps for the Tasks folder (assuming you clean out your completed tasks periodically by hand; see chapter 9, page 230). Also, see the very last section of this appendix, in the subsection titled Purging Old Completed Tasks, for another approach to archiving tasks.

5   If you decide you do not want to use AutoArchive on any other folders you may have in this group, follow the same steps on those folders.

Clear AutoArchive Settings for Any Other Personal Folders Groups You May Have

Repeat the above steps for any other personal folder groups you may have. If you are now following the system completely, you should not be saving mail into any other personal folder groups (these may have been left over from your previous mail-saving systems), and so there is no reason to archive those folders.

Side Note: *If you are actively filing in multiple hierarchical folders, note this: settings made to a parent folder are not inherited by child folders. You need to apply AutoArchive settings to all the folders individually. This is another reason a complex set of multiple Outlook folders is hard to use.*

C: Do the First Archive and Fine-Tune Your Settings

You next need to run a first archive to create the new Archive folder group and to fine tune and confirm the settings of your AutoArchive configuration. Normally archive is an automatic process and you would not run it manually. However, while configuring your settings for the first time you *do* want to run it manually once so that you can see the effects of your settings and confirm they were correct. Here's how:

1   Check to see if you already have an archive file in use. Have you been accepting Outlook's periodic archive requests in the past? If so, then you have an archive file created. Look for a folder group with the name Archive. You'll need to rename the file behind that group so that you can start fresh. Follow steps 1 through 4 in the section titled How to Swap Your Archive Files, starting on page 269 of this appendix, to rename the underlying archive file.

Side Note: *This file might not be visible as a folder group, so to accurately determine if an archive file exists, do this: from the File menu choose Data File Management... and a dialog box will open. If you see the word Archive in the file list within that dialog box, then you currently have an archive file in use. If so, you will need to rename it using the steps referenced above.*

2   Before running Archive for the first time, do two things: check the size of your personal folders file that holds the Processed Mail folder, and write it down. Also, open your Processed Mail folder, sort by date, and write down the date of the oldest mail in that folder. You will need these figures in a moment.

3   You are now ready to start the test archive. From the File menu choose Archive… (you may need to expand your menu to see this choice) and you will see the following dialog box open:

4 Select the first option button at top, as shown above.

5 Click OK. This starts Archive.

6 You will see a message in the lower right corner of your main Outlook window stating that Archive is in progress.

7 This can run in the background while you do other work; if you have a lot of aged mail, it may take 5 to 10 minutes or more.

8 When it is complete, you will see a folder group appear in your Folder List named Archive (unless you are simply deleting your old e-mail).

Side Note: *If you are saving mail and yet you do not see the Archive folder group appear in your folder list, then go back to Configuring Default Archive Settings, on page 262 of this appendix, and confirm that you selected the Show Archive Folder in Folder List check box in the AutoArchive dialog box.*

Examine Archive Folders

The first thing you should confirm is that mail was in fact moved from your Processed Mail folder into the new Archive folders. Open the new Archive folder group and find the Processed Mail folder; is there mail in there now? If yes skip to the subsection below titled Mail in Archive folder.

If you are simply deleting old mail (and so no Archive folder group was created), open the Processed Mail folder in your main personal folders group and confirm that mail older than your Older Than setting has been removed.

Side Note: *You may need to add the Modified field to the Processed Mail folder view to confirm this because AutoArchive actually uses the modified date rather than the received date when deciding whether to archive an individual piece of mail.*

If No Mail in Archive Folder

If there is no mail in the Archive folder, the first thing to check is the age of the oldest mail in your Processed Mail folder, the one that you wrote down a moment ago before you ran Archive. Was your oldest mail younger than the Older Than setting you used when you setup AutoArchive? If yes, then no mail *should* have moved and everything is fine. In fact, you probably should not have bothered setting up AutoArchive yet.

In this case, there is not much to confirm yet, so figure out how many weeks or months before your oldest mail will reach that Older Than setting and then come back to this section at or beyond that time to do the rest of the confirmation steps.

If on the other hand your oldest mail *was* older than the Older Than setting, mail should have been moved to the Archive folder and something is wrong. Go through the configuration steps again.

Mail in Archive Folder

If there *is* mail in the Archive folder, check the date of the youngest mail there. Compare that to the Older Than setting. It should roughly correspond. If so, so far so good.

Examine the Size of the Personal Folders File

As stated earlier, the reason you are using AutoArchive is (most likely) to ensure that your personal folder file size is maintained around 300 to 500 MB. So the next logical confirmation step, now that you have run archive once and moved mail to your Archive folder, is to examine that file size and see if it was reduced to your target size. If so, this will confirm that the settings you roughly calculated were correct. If far off from the target, you will need to adjust your settings.

There is one catch here. Immediately after running Archive, Outlook may not have yet cleaned out the old file space occupied by old mail. Outlook does this clearing automatically in the background, but it waits for a period of inactivity before doing so and it may take a while before it is complete. Let's check this.

Check the file size, now, of your personal folders file. Compare that to the number that you wrote down a moment ago before running Archive. If they are the same number, but in fact you confirmed that mail did get moved out of the personal folders file during archiving, then Outlook has not cleared the old file space yet. Let's do that cleaning (compacting) now, manually. Here is how you do that.

Side Note: *If you had a lot of old mail that was moved, the compact operation ahead could be very slow and so could prevent you from using mail for up to 60 minutes.*

Compact Your Personal Folders File

1 Right-click the top-level personal folders group icon and choose Properties.

2 Click Advanced….

3 Then click Compact Now.

4 You will see a very small window with the message Compacting….

5 When that message is gone (up to 60 minutes or more), click OK, then OK.

Examine the New File Size

Once compacting is complete, check the file size on your personal folders file again. Compare this new number to the number you wrote down just before running Archive. Is the new number smaller? If mail moved during archiving into the Archive folder, it should be. I have not seen a case where it wasn't.

If it is still a lot larger than 300 MB (say 500 MB or more), then you will need to adjust your Older Than setting to some value smaller than your initial setting, and then repeat the archiving and compact operations.

If on the other hand the new file size is a lot *smaller* than 300 MB you may want to increase your Older Than setting (unless you purposely set your Older Than setting small to remove mail clutter).

Once an approximately correct Older Than setting is found, you should not need to change this setting for a while unless your work habits change dramatically.

Side Note: *Whatever Older Than setting you choose you probably should revisit the effects of that setting later. For example, if months later you find that your personal folders file is larger than 400 to 500 MB, then your mailbox is filing too fast and you should set the Older Than setting to a smaller number of months. On the other hand, if you find your personal folders file is less than about 100 MB, then you can set the Older Than setting to a larger number of months.*

Setting the Order in Your Folder List

Next, if you are using Outlook 2002, you may need to change the placement of the Archive folder group within your folder list. The reason for this is that by default in Outlook 2002 the Archive folder tends to sort, alphabetically, to the top of your folder list. This top position is not an ideal location given the relatively low priority of the Archive folder. If you are using Outlook 2002 and you find that this occurs, you will need to rename the folder in order to reposition this folder to the bottom of your folder list. And even with Outlook 2003, over time, if you collect multiple Archive folders, you will want to rename them to distinguish their date ranges. Here is how to rename the Archive folder groups in both 2002 and 2003:

1 Right-click the top level (the group level) of the new Archive folder.

2 Choose Properties.

3 Click Advanced….

4 In the Name box, type "Z - " in front of the words "Archive Folder" (or some other letter or word that will drive it to the bottom alphabetically).

5 After you click OK and OK, you should see the Z - Archive Folder sort down in your list.

D: Periodic Archive File Swap

Why You Need to Swap Archive Files

Since the Archive.pst file is a personal folders file, it too has space limitations if you are using Outlook 2002 (or using the old personal folders file format in Outlook 2003). Once it reaches 300 to 500 MB in size, you will want to swap it out and create a new empty archive file. This is to avoid possible problems with an oversized file.

Side Note: *Again, I have seen many Outlook 2002 users extend the file size of their personal folders file quite close to the 2 GB absolute limit. This recommendation to keep the file size less than 500 MB is purely for safety reasons.*

If you calculated your Older Than setting correctly, this file size will be reached after a period equal to your Older Than setting has passed. So do this: when you first start archiving, set yourself a task with a due date in the future for that day. When that task appears, examine your Archive.pst file and check its size. If it is larger than 300 MB, do the file swap as instructed below.

Side Note: *If at this time you find that the file size is significantly different from 300 MB (+/- 100 MB) you probably need to adjust your Older Than setting.*

How to Swap Your Archive Files

Swapping archive files is a two-step process. First, you need to rename the current active archive file and corresponding folder group to something else, which removes it from the current archive process. Doing this also makes the Archive.pst name available for use in a new archive file, which will be created next.

Then run Archive manually. When Archive runs, if no Archive.pst file exists, it will create a new blank Archive file and folder group. This becomes your new target archive store. You now are left with your retired archive file (which you can view your old mail in), and a new near-empty archive file ready for your continuing batch of archived mail.

Renaming your Active Archive

The AutoArchive process we have defined always writes to a data file called Archive.pst. This file is linked to the current archive folder group displayed in your folder list. The file and group start out named the same (Archive), but you can name them separately. To swap archive files you must find that data file, and rename it to something else. You then need to rename the corresponding archive folder group to something else. Preferably you name both with names representing the date range of the retired archive group. And finally, since renaming a data file breaks the link to the folder group, you need to relink the two. Here are those steps:

1   Find the Archive.pst file wherever you stored it during the initial configuration. To do this, open the File menu and choose Data File Management... Select the Archive entry in the dialog box that opens, and click Open Folder. This opens the containing Windows folder for that file, with the file selected.

2   With that Windows folder open, but without yet renaming anything, go back and Quit Outlook (you cannot rename a data file while Outlook is running).

3   In the open Windows folder, which will still be present after quitting Outlook, rename the Archive.pst file to something like Archive-Jan-Jun05.pst (using dates as appropriate for the range it represents). Keep that window open because you may need to refer to the file path in step 4 below.

4   This renaming will break the link to the original folder group, so you must recreate that link. To do this in Outlook 2003, when you restart, accept the file not found error message you will see (you may need to click the folder group to see it), and a file dialog box will open showing the contents of the folder where the archive files are stored. In that dialog box select the newly named file and click Open. This will relink the folder group to the file. In Outlook 2002 you'll need to go to the File Menu, choose Data File Management... start to create a new personal folders file by clicking the Add button, but instead of naming a new file, select in the file list the one you renamed above; you may need to hunt for it. Then in the next window name the new folder group accordingly. Then exit those dialogs, and immediately reenter File, Data File Management... and this time remove the old archive group name from the list of data files.

5   Quit and restart Outlook one more time to test that you did all this right. Open the folder group corresponding to the file that you just renamed, to confirm that you have relinked it correctly (it should open without error).

6   Outlook 2003 users should now rename that archive folder group using the renaming technique in the section titled Setting the Order in Your Folder List on page 268. Rename this to something similar to the file name you just used, like Archive-Jan-Jun05. It does not *need* to match the file name, but it makes sense to.

Creating the New Archive Store

You next need to run archive manually to create the new archive group and corresponding Archive.pst file. The steps below accomplish this.

1   Run Archive manually using instructions on page 265 in the section Do the First Archive and Fine-Tune Your Settings. This recreates a new Archive.pst file. You'll see a new archive group appear in your folder list.

2   Outlook 2002 users should use the renaming technique on page 268 (Setting the Order in Your Folder List) to rename this archive folder group so you can place it at the bottom of your folder list again, if needed.

3   Set yourself another task to repeat this process, with a due date in the future equal to the Older Than setting.

This is all you need to do when swapping files. Your previous archive settings for all folders are retained, and your previously scheduled archive sessions will continue; this time copying old e-mail to the new empty Archive.pst file.

Backing Up Your Archive Files

Now that you have all your aged saved mail stored in your archive files, you need to add those files to your backup strategy. Take this requirement seriously. The best backup strategy is that described earlier, where your archive files are originally saved and updated to a networked file server that is part of a regular backup plan; some corporate IT departments have this available.

If you do not have that infrastructure, just use whatever local backup means you have available. If you have none, and need a suggestion, I have been impressed with the simplicity of the Maxtor One Touch external hard drive backup system; consider that if network backup is not available.

Wrapping Up AutoArchive

That completes the instructions for configuring your AutoArchive settings to best serve the system described in this book. Again, setting up AutoArchive is an optional operation just to make life easier for Outlook 2002 users who are having trouble keeping their personal folders files at a safe size. Once you lose a batch of mail due to a corrupted file, you will learn to appreciate this utility. And even Outlook 2003 users will find some uses.

Everything AutoArchive does you can do manually if you wish. However, even if you do successfully clean your personal folders by hand every couple months, you will find that the AutoArchive approach, since it is automatically done more often, will allow you to keep the maximum amount of mail in your Processed Mail folder.

Note there are a variety of ways you can use AutoArchive; there are a variety of special needs around saving old mail (see www.workdaycontrol.com for some alternate approaches). The section below is another such example.

Using AutoArchive to Keep the Exchange Mailbox Small

Even in this system where the Exchange Inbox is kept nearly empty through our filing steps, you will still find your Exchange mailbox group periodically overrunning your corporate limits. Remember, even if you are using Outlook 2003, if your organization has imposed a limit on your Exchange mailbox size, you will get "Your mailbox is over its size limit" messages when the sum of mail in the folders within the Exchange mailbox gets too large. This will be due to four folders that over time will fill up: Deleted Items, Sent Mail, Tasks, and Calendar. Let's go over these one at a time and discuss maintenance strategies and how AutoArchive might help.

Emptying the Deleted Items Folder

Your Deleted Items folder, as it fills, may help drive your Exchange mailbox over its size limit. Rarely do you want to save deleted items more than a day or two. Yet I often forget to empty it. You can use AutoArchive to do that for you. To configure this, you do not want to use the default settings described earlier in this chapter because they don't apply. Rather, right-click the Deleted Items folder, choose Properties, choose the AutoArchive tab, and configure the settings to look like those shown in figure B.1.

Cleaning Out Old Sent Mail

Your Sent Mail folder, as it fills, will be the first folder to drive your Exchange mailbox over its size limit. What I do when I see the size limit warning message is this: I open the Sent Mail folder, sort descending by date, select the

Figure B.1
Settings for
Auto Archive for
Deleted Items.

bottom half of the messages, and drag them into the Saved Sent Mail folder. This works for me.

However, to avoid manual intervention altogether, you might think that you could automate this using AutoArchive. In fact, you *can* use AutoArchive to clean the Sent Mail folder automatically. The configuration can be set to delete all mail older than a certain age automatically, which works well. Or if you *save* old sent mail, the configuration can be set to copy the mail to a working saved Sent Mail folder; this however is more problematic.

If you delete old sent mail, simply use the configuration described above for Deleted Items, but using a larger Older Than setting. This is simple and straightforward.

If you wish to *save* old sent mail, there is unfortunately no easy configuration that works well in our system. Reason: for this to work, the local Sent Mail folder you copy into will have to be in an active archive folder, which limits your ability to combine it into the same folder group as your Processed Mail folder. I like to keep my Processed Mail folder and my Saved Sent Items folder together and easily reached. With AutoArchive, this is complicated to enable; so this option is not attractive to me. Rather I stick with the manual approach of periodically dragging my sent mail to the Saved Sent Items folder.

Purging Old Completed Tasks

As discussed in chapter 9, completed tasks can start to build up and impact your Exchange Server storage space.

In that chapter we discuss ways to manually purge those old completed tasks (page 230). You can also use AutoArchive to do this. Luckily, AutoArchive archives tasks based on the Completion Date, which is exactly the behavior

Figure B.2
Settings for
Auto Archive for
Tasks.

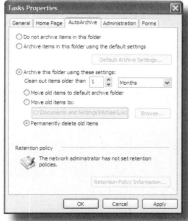

we expect. As with Deleted Items, there is no reason to save the archived tasks; we just wish to delete them.

To configure this, right-click the Tasks folder, choose Properties, choose the AutoArchive tab, and configure the settings to look like those shown in figure B.2 (previous page).

Calendar

Your Calendar is probably the least likely source of an overloaded Exchange mailbox, but it can contribute. To use AutoArchive for the Calendar, follow the instructions above for Deleted Items, using a larger Older Than setting; six months is a reasonable setting.

Appendix C
Resources

Book Website

www.workdaycontrol.com

Come here for FAQs, book updates, and training opportunities on the Total Workday Control system.

Some Useful Books

- *Getting Things Done*, by David Allen

- *Take Back Your Life: Using Outlook to Get Organized and Stay Organized*, by Sally McGhee

- *Seize the Work Day: Using the Tablet PC to Take Total Control of Your Work and Meeting Day*, by Michael Linenberger

- *First Things First*, by Stephen R. Covey, A. Roger Merrill, Rebecca R. Merrill

- *The 7 Habits of Highly Effective People*, by Stephen Covey

- *To Do... Doing... Done!*, by G. Lynne Snead & Joyce Wycoff

- *The Time Trap*, by Alec Mackenzie

- *Time Management from the Inside Out*, by Julie Morgenstern

- *Microsoft Outlook Version 2002 Inside Out*, by Jim Boyce

- *Microsoft Outlook Version 2003 Inside Out*, by Jim Boyce

- *Microsoft Outlook 2003 Bible*, by Rob Tidrow
- *Special Edition Using Microsoft Outlook 2003*, by Patricia Cardoza

Software Links

- Microsoft Office Outlook, main product page:
  http://office.microsoft.com/en-us/FX010857931033.aspx
- You can obtain a copy of Outlook in conjunction with a MSN account on Microsoft Outlook Live:
  http://join.msn.com/?page=outlook/olc&pgmarket=en-us&ST=1&xAPID=1983&DI=1402
- FranklinCovey PlanPlus for Outlook:
  http://www.franklincovey.com/planplus/outlook/index.html
- Agilix GoBinder:
  http://www.gobinder.com
- Necentric's Getting Things Done Add-In for Outlook
  http://www.davidco.com/productDetail.php?id=63&IDoption=20
- Einstein Technologies Tablet Enhancements for Outlook:
  http://www.tabletoutlook.com/
- Curosoft OutlookSync
  http://www.curosoft.com

Clip-Out Page:
The Eight Best Practices of Task and
E-Mail Management

1 Tracking all tasks in Outlook Tasks System (chapters 2- 4)

2 Using a master tasks list kept separate from your daily tasks list (chapters 2- 4)

3 Using a simple prioritization system that emphasizes must-do-today tasks (chapters 2- 4)

4 Writing only next actions on your daily list (chapters 2- 4)

5 Doing daily and weekly planning to keep your task lists up to date (chapter 5)

6 Converting e-mails to tasks (chapter 6)

7 Filing e-mails using Outlook Categories (chapter 7)

8 Delegating tasks in an effective manner (chapter 8)

Clip-Out Page:
The Total Workday Control
E-Mail Workflow

Read Each E-Mail, And...

1   **Delete:** Decide if the mail has no action and no later value and should be deleted (junk mail, useless banter, and so forth). If so delete it immediately. Don't spend much time on this. If you are uncertain, plan on keeping it and move on to the next step.

For All E-Mail You Decide Not To Delete...

2   **Act on it now**: Decide if the e-mail generates the need for an immediate action and if that action can be done quickly (completed in one minute); if so just do it now. That action might be to reply to the e-mail, forward it, make a quick call, send a new e-mail to someone else, and so on. One minute only.

3   **Mark for reply:** If the only action needed is to reply to the e-mail but it will take more than one minute to do so, flag it with an Outlook Follow Up flag (right-click on the message and choose Follow Up), and leave it in your Inbox until you can reply. (See chapter 6, page 138). If there is some other action that has to happen first, follow the next step instead.

4   **Most Important: Convert it to a task:** If an action other than a simple reply is needed but cannot be done now, create an Outlook task and copy/convert the mail to a task. Chapter 6, pages 133-135.

5   **Set follow-up task:** If your action is to make a quick reply or send a new message, after you do so, consider whether you need to set a follow-up task for that message. Chapter 6, pages 135-138.

6   **File it:** Assign Outlook Categories as appropriate or as desired, using the techniques in chapter 7. Do not spend too much time on this; if no appropriate category jumps out at you leave the e-mail uncategorized (occasionally the right step here is to create a new category). And if more than one category seems appropriate choose each of them. Consider doing this step in batches. In all cases except mail flagged for pending replies, the next step is to move the processed mail item out of the Inbox and into the Processed Mail folder. Chapter 7.

Index

D

E

e-mail
  acting on 141
  archiving 142
  Auto-categorize incoming e-mail 211–220
  By Category view 175
  By Sender view 177
  converting to Outlook tasks 37–38, 130,
     131–140
    follow-up tasks 135–138
    from e-mails with attachments 134–135
    from e-mails without attachments 133–135
  deleting 141, 142
  e-mail processing workflow 139–145. *See*
     also workflow for e-mail processing
  filing 147–188. *See also* Filing e-mail; *See*
     also category-based filing
  finding 162–165
  folders. *See* folders
  follow-up flag 138
  marking for reply 141
  Messages view 175, 175–176
  problems when out of control 127–128
  Processed Mail folder. *See* Processed Mail
     folder
  saving sent 136
  setting follow-up tasks for e-mails you send
     135–138
  views. *See* views
e-mail processing workflow 139–145
editing tasks 60
entering tasks 56–60, 88–95
Exchange Server 237–238
  advantages of 238
  Cached Exchange Mode 249–250
  determining if your outlook uses 237
  hosted Exchange accounts 238

F

file servers 242
filing e-mails 38, 147–188. *See also* category-
    based filing
  as step in workflow 141
  filing by topic is optional 148

filing e-mails, cont'd
  in multiple folders 148–150
  using categories. *See* category-based filing
  why important 147–148
finding your mail 162–165
First Things First 124, 209, 210, 275
folder list 44–45, 154
  setting the order of folders in 268–269
folders
  about using Outlook folders 43, 43–46,
     153–157, 233–252
  archive folders 236
  checking size 257–258
  compacting 268
  differences from Windows folders 235–236
  Exchange Server folders 236, 237–238
  filing in multiple 148
  four types of 235–236
  Outlook offline folders (.ost) 248–249
  personal. *See* personal folders
  problems with filing in multiple Outlook fold-
     ers 149–150
  Processed Mail folder. *See* Processed Mail
     folder
  public folders 236
  setting the order in folder list 268–269
  showing 153–157, 234–235
  three primary folders 43
  versus views 43, 44
follow-up flag 138–139
follow-up tasks 135–138, 141
foreword dating daily tasks 90–91, 113
FranklinCovey 16, 26, 29, 31, 38, 92, 95, 116,
    230, 276
FranklinCovey PlanPlus for Microsoft Outlook
    230
From column 177, 187
future due dates 90–91, 113

G

general task time 28, 108, 110, 112, 122–123,
    124, 199, 202, 203, 205, 206, 208–209
  scheduling tasks versus 208
Getting Things Done Add-In for Outlook 231

U

V

W